The Roots of
Community Organizing,
1917–1939

The Roots
of Community
Organizing,
1917–1939

Neil Betten and
Michael J. Austin

with contributions by

Robert Fisher, William E. Hershey,
Raymond A. Mohl, and Marc Lee Raphael

Temple University Press ■ *Philadelphia*

Temple University Press, Philadelphia 19122
Copyright © 1990 by Temple University. All rights reserved
Published 1990
Printed in the United States of America

Library of Congress Cataloging-in-Publication Data

Betten, Neil.
    The roots of community organizing, 1917–1939 / Neil Betten and
Michael J. Austin with contributions by Robert Fisher . . . [et al.].
        p.   cm.
    Bibliography: p.
    Includes index.
    ISBN 0-87722-662-8 (alk. paper)
    1. Community organization—United States—History—20th
century.   2. Social service—United States—20th century.   3. Social
action—United States—History—20th century.   I. Austin, Michael
J.   II. Fisher, Robert, 1947–   .   III. Title.
HN65.B47   1990   89-32536
361.2'5'097309042—dc20   CIP

Contents

v

Preface

ALL HISTORICAL research projects have a history of their own. It is important here to acknowledge the intellectual origins of this research effort as well as the numerous individuals who assisted the authors in reaching the completion of an eighteen-year effort.

The story begins in the mid-1960s at the University of California, Berkeley, where the second author was completing graduate studies in social work under the guidance of Professor Ralph Kramer. As a student of community organizing at the School of Social Welfare, he discovered that some of the critical historical events that shaped the emergence of community organizing as a method for empowering people to address a local concern were not evaluated as part of a documented history. It was clear that the 1917–1939 period represented an important phase in the emergence of community organizing. This period followed upon the Settlement House Era (1880–1910) in which the casework method was developed, culminating in 1918 with Mary Richmond's *Social Diagnosis*.

Continuation of graduate studies in the doctoral program at the University of Pittsburgh's School of Social Work made it possible for him to explore further the history of community organizing under the guidance of Professor Meyer Schwartz, who had developed the 1962 definition of community organization practice for the National Association of Social Workers. The period of graduate study provided the spark that ultimately led to the development of this book.

In early 1971, when both of the authors were on the faculty of Florida State University, an auspicious meeting occurred. This meeting was arranged by two valued colleagues, who deserve the title "midwives" for facilitating the birth of this historical effort. They are Professor Maurie Vance of the History Department and Pat Vance of the School of Social Work at Florida State University. This husband and wife team recognized early the potential for matchmaking in bringing together the first author, who is a historian specializing in urban and labor history, and the second author, who is a social work researcher specializing in community organization and administration. The partnership emerged after the mutual discovery of shared interests in identifying the historical features of grass roots organizing and community planning.

As the outline of this book emerged, it became clear that the numerous themes reflecting some of the roots of community organizing would need to be addressed by colleagues with specialized interests and expertise. These colleagues were invaluable to us and their work is reflected in various chapters throughout this volume. We wish to express our sincere appreciation to Professor Marc Raphael, Department of History at Ohio State; Professor Robert Fisher, Department of History at the University of Houston; Professor Raymond Mohl, Department of History at Florida Atlantic University; and Mr. William Hershey, Director, Lutheran Social Services of Washington. We also wish to thank our many manuscript typists for their patience and assistance in producing the final manuscript.

Michael J. Austin, Dean   Neil Betten, Chair
School of Social Work   Department of History
University of Pennsylvania   Florida State University
Philadelphia, Pennsylvania   Tallahassee, Florida

January 1990

PART I

Identifying the Roots

1

The Roots of Community Organizing: An Introduction

Michael J. Austin and Neil Betten

COMMUNITY organizers who fail to learn from one another are bound to repeat the mistakes of their predecessors. Students of community organizing, whether on college campuses or in the ghettos and barrios of this country, have repeatedly "re-invented the wheel" in their respective organizing efforts. During World War I sociologists and adult educators first identified community organizing as a specific field. It was not until the 1940s, however, that colleges and universities began to train professional community organizers.[1]

Community organizing in city neighborhoods, such as the urban political organizing in the late nineteenth and early twentieth centuries, the organizing of immigrant communities by the International Institutes beginning in 1910, and the rise and fall of the Cincinnati Unit Experiment from 1917 to 1919, begins our historical analysis of significant community organizing experiences.

Each of these developments in community organizing had historical antecedents. The attempts at neighborhood block organizing in the Cincinnati Unit Experiment, for example, can be traced historically to the settlement house movement, which peaked after the turn of the century and represented the clearest beginnings of conscious community organizing related to the reform movement's response to industrialization, immigration, and urbanization surfacing dramatically at the end of the 1800s. The Cincinnati Unit Experiment, officially begun on January 1, 1917, was based on a citizens' council of neighborhood residents, an occupational council of professionals who earned their livelihood in the area, and a general council combining elements of both. Their professed goal was "restoring the advantages of village life to city people."[2] While the Cincinnati Unit Experiment was an important historical event, its short life and aftermath provide for multiple interpretations in the process of identifying the early roots of community organizing.

The events of the 1920s expanded the purview of community organizing beyond local neighborhood organizing and social action to include the emerging social planning perspective that identified fund raising to support social agencies as the new arena for organizing. The results of this expansion can be seen in the emergence of social agency federations, such as the United Fund, and what historian Roy Lubove refers to as "the Bureaucratic Imperative."[3] Business supported federation efforts because fewer multiple solicitations, more economical distribution and collection of funds, and widening the base of financial support into the middle and working classes cost less time and money.

While the social planning dimension of community organizing provided a new organizing arena consistent with the corporate rationality of the 1920s, most historical accounts fail to take into consideration the emergence of rural community organizing and labor organizing during this period. Community organizing became an increasingly professional activity in the 1920s following the founding of schools of philanthropy, later to become graduate schools of social work. The social survey became the major social planning tool for community organizing. Both the increasing number of welfare professionals and the volunteers on boards of charitable institutions wanted to fill in the gaps of welfare service and to detect both problems and future needs more effectively through overall organizational efficiency.[4] The first efforts to organize social agencies into councils of social agencies for unified fund raising and social planning occurred in Milwaukee and Pittsburgh in 1909. By 1926, there were councils of social agencies in Chicago, Boston, St. Louis, Los

Angeles, Detroit, Cincinnati, Columbus, and New York.[5] The issues and constraints of community organizing through social planning are clearly noted by Lubove.

> Federation employed the rhetoric of the early community organization movement, but its intensive concern with the machinery and financing of social welfare diverted attention from cooperative democracy and the creative group life of the ordinary citizen to problems of agency administration and service. It substituted the bureaucratic goal of efficiency through expert leadership for what had been a quest for democratic self-determination through joint efforts of citizen and specialist. Community organization had barely emerged as a cause before it had become a function absorbed into the administrative structure of social work.[6]

The social planning emphasis found in the historical analysis of the 1920s fails to describe the continuation, sometimes sub rosa, of community organizing activities including picketing, sit-ins, strikes, and block voting of ethnic cultures, as well as the self-help groups including immigrants and wage earners attempting to cope with urban life. Working-class elements organized burial societies, rudimentary disability and life insurance programs, and loan funds. Some of these services became major health and social service institutions.[7]

The role of local community organizing as well as labor organizing became more prominent again after the 1920s with the arrival of the Great Depression of the 1930s. While the 1920s period of "normalcy" provided an ideal time for the discoveries of Freud to influence the helping professions of psychology, psychiatry, and social work, and the insights of Taylor regarding efficiency in management to influence the community organization aspects of financing and coordinating voluntary social agencies, such preoccupations had further drawn attention away from the reform activities of the early 1900s. As Clarke Chambers pointed out, "The role of direct agitation was often left largely to voluntary reform associations, to politicians, to labor leaders. . . . Social workers were more often found now working in and through government, on the staffs of numerous commissions, committees, bureaus, and agencies, than as voices crying in the wilderness."[8]

Despite the de-emphasis on social reform in the post–World War I period, there was a growing recognition that community organizing required more than commitment. It required both knowledge and skill. The surfacing of community organizing manuals during this period, as well as the emergence of city planning as a tool for anticipating and charting urban growth, provides preliminary evidence of the intellectual activity in the planning sphere.

The community organizing manuals generally stressed the approach of study, diagnosis, and treatment in which community problems were approached by the organizer from this conceptual perspective. This approach was in direct response to the industrialization of cities and the resulting goal of reconstructing the small community in both the chaotic metropolis and the isolated rural environment. A similar approach to organizing can be seen in city planning. This included making projections of the future, forming objectives, designing the strategy to achieve the goals, and then implementing the plan.[9]

While the city planners of the 1920s and 1930s were generally more problem focused, the social planners of the same period were more process focused and philosophically influenced by Dewey's concepts of democratic participation in community decision making. The authors of the community organizing manuals were concerned about the relationship between the organizer and the citizen. They understood that a tension necessarily arose between professional direction and public control by volunteers.[10]

The emphasis on the process of community organizing also included the early efforts to develop specific technologies. The most important tool was the social survey, which was useful to both the grass roots organizer and the agency social planner. It was a tool developed to identify significant social trends and developments affecting the health and welfare of all people in a community.

It is interesting to note, however, that agreement was not reached until 1939 regarding the ingredients for the formal training of community organizers. This understanding is outlined in a report by Robert P. Lane, delivered at the 1939 National Conference of Social Work. It included such varying definitions of community organization as "mobilizing resources to meet need," "initiating social services," "coordinating the efforts of the welfare agencies," and "building a welfare program." Implied in these definitions were the techniques of fact finding, program evaluation, standard setting, facilitating intergroup relations, public relations, and lobbying. The report recommended that the goal of community organization was to "bring about and maintain a progressively more effective adjustment between social welfare resources and social welfare needs."[11]

Much of the attention of community organization literature in the 1920s and 1930s focused upon the emerging social planning functions of community organizing through federated agency financing and coordination. Historical analysis of this period requires a more balanced view of community organizing, especially those activities and techniques developed at the local community and factory levels. Studies of community organizing techniques used by both rural agricultural organizers and urban labor organizers are needed to complement the more systematic attention received by the predominantly urban social planning activities that are treated in the literature of the period.

A Framework for Analysis

A framework for the historical analysis of community organizing can be adapted from the three models of community organization developed by Jack Rothman with John E. Tropman.[12] Definitions of community organizing have been debated in the literature on adult education, social work, community development, and sociology for the past fifty years. Without chronicling all the trends inherent in the definitional dilemma, a scheme describing several types of community organizing has been selected. The scheme identifies three major trends in community organizing activities: locality development, social planning, and social action (see Table 1). The description of these approaches serves as a background for the historical analysis of people, places, and events that served as antecedents to contemporary community organizing. Current practices can be traced to the early unsophisticated experiments in organizing workers, farmers, immigrants, clients, agencies, and communities.

The locality development approach to community organizing emphasizes process goals in which people with common concerns or common living situations are organized in order to help themselves and develop a capacity for further community action and integration. This approach builds upon community relationships to carry out problem-solving activities (e.g., building a school or recrea-

TABLE 1
Three Models of Community Organization Practice
According to Selected Practice Variables

	Model A (Locality Development)	Model B (Social Planning)	Model C (Social Action)
1. Goal categories of community action	Self-help; community capacity and integration (process goals)	Problem solving with regard to substantive community problems (task goals)	Shifting of power relationships and resources; basic institutional change (task or process goals)
2. Assumptions concerning community structure and problem conditions	Community eclipsed, anomie; lack of relationships and democratic problem-solving capacities: static traditional community	Substantive social problems: mental and physical health, housing, recreation	Disadvantaged populations, social injustice, deprivation, inequity
3. Basic change strategy	Broad cross section of people involved in determining and solving their own problems	Fact gathering about problems and decisions on the most rational course of action	Crystallization of issues and organization of people to take action against enemy targets
4. Characteristic change tactics and techniques	Consensus: communication among community groups and interests; group discussion	Consensus or conflict	Conflict or contest: confrontation, direct action, negotiation
5. Salient practioner roles	Enabler-catalyst, coordinator; teacher of problem-solving skills and ethical values	Fact gatherer and analyst, program implementer, facilitator	Activist advocate: agitator, broker, negotiator, partisan
6. Medium of change	Manipulation of small task-oriented groups	Manipulation of formal organizations and of data	Manipulation of mass organizations and political processes
7. Orientation toward power structure(s)	Members of power structure as collaborators in a common venture	Power structure as employers and sponsors	Power structure as external target of action: oppressors to be coerced or overturned
8. Boundary definition of the community client system or constituency	Total geographic community	Total community or community segment (including "functional" community)	Community segment

TABLE 1
(Continued)

	Model A (Locality Development)	Model B (Social Planning)	Model C (Social Action)
9. Assumptions regarding interests of community subparts	Common interests or reconcilable differences	Interests reconcilable or in conflict	Conflicting interests which are not easily reconcilable: scarce resources
10. Conception of the client population or constituency	Citizens	Consumers	Victims
11. Conception of client role	Participants in an interactional problem-solving process	Consumers or recipients	Employers, constituents, members

Source: Reproduced by permission of the publisher, F. E. Peacock Publishers, Inc., Itasca, Ill., from Jack Rothman with John E. Tropman, "Models of Community Organization and Macro Practice Perspectives: Their Mixing and Phasing," in *Strategies of Community Organization, Fourth Edition,* ed. Fred M. Cox, John L. Erlich, Jack Rothman, and John E. Tropman, © F. E. Peacock Publishers, Inc., 1987, pp. 24–25.

tion center). Locality development seeks community organizing to counter the static and traditional nature of a community as well as to overcome the people's sense of alienation (e.g., "It can't be done"). The people are viewed as a constituency of citizens, not as clients or victims, and are engaged as participants with one another as problem solvers.

The basic strategy for change in this approach to community organizing is the involvement of a broad cross-section of people as a way of determining the nature of their common problems and the logical solutions. The tactics that follow from such a strategy include the slow and meticulous process of building consensus by developing communication patterns among community groups through meetings and discussion. The role of the community organizer in this context is primarily that of an enabler, who helps a group of people to solve common problems by teaching them concrete organizing skills (e.g., conducting meetings, taking minutes) and the ethical values that are required for building consensus (e.g., respect for divergent views, tolerance for cultural difference). The primary mechanism used by the community organizer is the small task-oriented group.

The locality development approach also includes certain orientations to power, size of community, and the public interest. The orientation to the power structure of a community is collaborative: Key community leaders are seen as collaborators in a common venture. The boundaries of the community include all citizens who identify themselves as part of a geographic locality. It is assumed that community organizing will build upon common interests or at least reconcilable differences. The origins of this approach to community organizing can be found in the urban and rural areas of America.

The social planning approach to community organizing differs from locality development in that it focuses on task-oriented goals rather than process-oriented goals. Thus the social planning approach seeks community action through problem solving in the area of substantive community concerns (e.g., lack of adoption services, poorly coordinated delinquency services). The substantive problems include all areas of social concern from physical and mental health to housing and recreation.

The basic strategy of the social planning approach is fact gathering about a particular social problem in order to develop a decision-making situation for the most rational course of action. The primary tactics include both consensus building and conflict resolution. In some situations, conflict is generated in order to break an impasse in the decision-making process. The community organizer utilizing the social planning approach is primarily a fact gatherer, problem and program analyst, program implementer, and facilitator of the planning process in which other people are making the decisions. In this case, the people are primarily consumers of whatever results from the planning process. The community organizer's medium for change is primarily the manipulation of other formal organizations or agencies as well as the manipulation of data for the purpose of stimulating community action.

In the social planning approach, the power structure is seen as both the sponsor of change as well as the employer of such community organizers. The boundaries of activity can be as broad as the geographic community (e.g., city, county, state) or as specific as a functional community (e.g., where only the problems of the developmentally disabled at all ages are addressed in a given locale). With this social planning approach, it is assumed that all interests are either reconcilable or in conflict needing reconciliation. The roots of the social planning approach to community organizing can be found in the social planning councils, federations, and urban planning agencies of the 1920s.

Rothman's third approach to community organizing is called social action, and can be either task or process oriented. The ultimate goal for social action is basic institutional change and has, therefore, been viewed as the most radical of the three community organizing approaches. Change is seen as taking place in a conscious shifting of power relationships and resources. This approach to organizing focuses on the empowerment of disadvantaged populations who suffer from deprivation, injustice, and inequity.

The basic strategy utilized in the social action approach is the crystallization of issues and the direct organizing of people affected by the problems in order to take action against an adversary. The tactics used in this form of organizing include both conflict and contest in an effort to generate direct confrontation and ultimately negotiation. The community organizer serves as an advocate in a highly partisan activist role. Organizers utilized skills in agitating and negotiating in order to serve as brokers between their constituencies and their adversaries. The constituency is viewed as a victim requiring organization into some form of membership group. The primary medium of change for the community organizer is the building of mass organizations and political processes (e.g., media campaigns, lobbying campaigns, picketing campaigns).

The orientation toward the power structure in the social action approach is one of distance in which the power structure is seen as the external target. The power structure is viewed as the oppressor to be coerced or overturned. The boundary of social action is defined by the segment of the community that perceives itself as oppressed. Social action strategies are based on the assumption that factions exist in all communities and therefore competing or conflicting interests (oppressed vs. oppressors) require social action in order to reach reconciliation. However, the existence of scarce resources and the realization that "we're all in this together" necessitate a realistic assessment of the public interest.

The knowledge and skills of community organizing grew out of the practical experiences of organizers in the rural and urban areas of this country. What is found in textbooks today had its origins in the day-to-day, trial-and-error experiences of community organizers in the 1920s and 1930s.

Tracing the Taproots of Community Organizing

The roots of community organizing at the local community level can be traced to the settlement house workers in the cities and the agricultural extension agents in farm areas. In tracing the significant "taproots" of the locality development approach, we search the "ruins" of the Cincinnati Unit Experiment through the reports and personal papers of its major architect, Wilber C. Phillips. In the same vein, we explore the settlement house approach to organizing immigrant communities, with special reference to the International Institutes of the YWCA. In doing so, we identify some of the early efforts to develop community-controlled institutions while at the same time encouraging cultural pluralism. To complete the picture in locality development, we analyze the organizing techniques of agricultural extension agents and their role in stimulating rural community action.

Although the social planning approach of the 1920s has received considerable attention through the literature on agency federation and fund raising, little attention has been directed to the organizing techniques described in what we have called the "organizing manuals" of Steiner, McClenahan, Hart, Pettit, and Lindeman. In similar fashion, little attention has been focused upon the emergence of two professional orientations during this period, namely physical planning as practiced by city planners and social survey research as practiced by social planners. We trace the "taproots" of the current social planning approach to community organizing by analyzing the emerging community-planning technology of the 1920s and 1930s. Included in this analysis are the fund raising skills best demonstrated in the American Jewish community.

Our third avenue for historical analysis includes the social action approach to community organizing, with special reference to organizing the working class. We examine three distinct approaches to social action organizing: urban political machines, the conflict-based organizing style of Saul Alinsky and his relationship to organized labor, and an example of religious-based community organizing—the Catholic Worker Movement.

The ethnic-based urban political machines, which fully emerged during the 1870s to confront upper-class Protestant control of city government, themselves eventually dominated urban politics and became establishments of sorts by the 1930s. Most of the urban political bosses ironically opposed another 1930s urban working-class movement—the rise of the Congress of Industrial Organizations, the CIO. We discuss CIO organizing techniques and their influence on Saul Alinsky's pioneer organizing at the close of the Great Depression. We also examine a very unusual institution, the Catholic Worker Movement, another aspect of organizing during the Great Depression.

In viewing the community organizing role of religious groups during the 1930s, we could have concentrated on Father Charles Coughlin's right-wing activism, which had more immediate influence than the Catholic Worker Movement, or we could have examined more mainstream Catholic action organizations, but we believe that the Catholic Worker Movement had very significant long-term influence in Roman Catholic social action circles. We could have also examined various Protestant religious or political organizing. It could even be argued that the Ku Klux Klan was a variation of Protestant extremism and, no doubt, an analysis of Klan organizing techniques would be interesting. Another fruitful and related approach would be an examination of the organizing aspects of the Women's Christian Temperance Union. With the establishment of Prohibition in the 1920s, many WCTU organizers found new employment as experienced organizers for the Ku Klux Klan. Obviously, there are many different approaches one could look at, including the powerful role of the Black church in organizing urban and rural constituencies. The Communist party carried out successful social action organizing in the 1920s, and more so in the 1930s. One could also examine the organizing techniques of such groups as the Black Legion in Michigan, the Silver Shirts, the Khaki Shirts, and the various American "shirts" that attempted to emulate Italian Fascist and German Nazi movements during that troubled decade.

The roots of community organizing spread far and deep. While this book includes some roots that encompass a time period from the last years of the nineteenth century to the end of the 1930s, the primary focus is the period from 1917 to 1939, when professional community organizing associated with the social work field was emerging. We have ended the study in 1939 when the report by Robert T. Lane (known as the Lane Report) established what came to be considered standardized educational requirements for the field of community organizing. In a sense, during the last years of the 1930s, community organizing as a subspecialty of professional social work became established and was symbolized by the Lane Report. Yet at the same time, in 1939, Saul Alinsky laid the groundwork in his Back of the Yards experiment for the future conflict-based social action organizing that became so significant during the 1960s. Because of the outbreak of World War II in Europe and the subsequent participation of the United States, the continuing development of many aspects of community organizing was delayed until the 1960s. International conflict diverted society's interests away from community problems and toward thwarting the advance of Nazi Germany and its allies. Since significant community organizing was not to reemerge until well after World War II, we use 1939 as the benchmark year to end this volume. We believe that the years after World War II, particularly 1960–1980, constitute the modern period of community organizing.

There is clearly a dualism in this work. On the one hand, our study provides insight into the background of professional community organizing stemming from various social agencies. We see the community center movement, the agricultural extension service, social planning and physical planning, federated philanthropy, and the International Institute as roots of social agency based community organizing. On the other hand, there is the other vast area of organizing formulated by people who did not think of themselves primarily as community organizers but did, in fact, organize communities. And thus we include in our work the activities of the socialists involved with the Cincinnati Unit Experiment, the political organizing of machine politicians, and the many-faceted organizing roles of the Catholic Worker Movement. Then there was Saul Alinsky. His techniques reflected the combative CIO and not the traditional social agency approach, but he was consciously a community organizer and, in effect, his followers established a social agency, in the form of the Industrial Areas Foundation.

Despite the dualism in our work, the organizers who were defining the field of community organizing in the 1920s by their deeds and words had considerable confidence in their abilities to specify the parameters of an emerging field. The following chapters illustrate the contributions of these pioneering community organizers.

2

The Intellectual Origins of Community Organizing

Michael J. Austin and Neil Betten

During the last twenty years, historians have increased their efforts to examine the history of social work. The history of community organizing, however, still needs greater exploration. The community organizing aspects of the most famous settlement houses have been studied, as have attempts to consolidate private fund raising. However, there are a number of important texts that have been largely unexamined by modern students of community organization practice. In the 1920s community organizers produced a series of significant works based on their experiences. Thus, during that period, which many historians dismiss as politically reactionary and inhospitable to reforms in general, community organization theorists began to formulate the intellectual foundations of their field.

One of the first significant efforts at organizing communities for social welfare purposes began in 1869 in England when the Charity Organization Society was formed to coordinate the efforts of all private charitable organizations that provided assistance to the poor.

Source: Adapted from Michael J. Austin and Neil Betten, "Intellectual Origins of Community Organizing, 1920–1939," *Social Service Review* 51, no. 1 (March 1977): 155–70. Used by permission of the publisher, The University of Chicago Press. © 1977 by The University of Chicago. All rights reserved.

There were many examples of such community organizing in the United States during the late nineteenth and early twentieth centuries, such as the establishment in Chicago in 1893 of the Bureau of Associated Charities and associated charities in Pittsburgh (1908), Milwaukee (1909), St. Louis (1911), Cleveland (1913), and Cincinnati (1913). World War I gave impetus to the movement, and small cities and even rural areas copied these early efforts at community cooperation. The new community organizations engaged in cooperative planning to deal with various social problems. They sometimes created new social agencies or reformed old ones. Out of such early efforts at coordinating assistance to the poor, community welfare planning councils and social survey techniques developed.

In response to the earlier successes of associated charities, community fund raising organizations, which traditionally competed with one another, united their efforts to form financial federations. They strove to collect more funds with less effort. Large donors applauded the trend since it freed them from multiple fund raising campaigns, each soliciting for its own organization. Thus emerged the concept of the community chest. The Cleveland Federation, formed in 1913, is considered to have been the first modern American community chest. By 1929 there were 330 community chests, which raised $71,500,000.[1] Community chests not only broadened the base of support for private charities, but also provided coordinated community welfare machinery for solicitation, educated the community concerning social forces (thus attempting to secure additional support from newly enlightened contributors), held conferences to standardize and coordinate welfare activities on a national level, developed surveys of community welfare needs, and led in the development of new fact-finding techniques, standardization of records, and improved bookkeeping and accounting techniques. As historian Roy Lubove pointed out, community chests grew into a "public relations arm" of private professional social work, convincing ordinary people to support community service as a "fundamental civic obligation."[2] The community chests, nonetheless, remained essentially coordinating bodies, which sought to uphold the interests of both the contributors and the social agencies. The social planning activities of community organizers concerned with financing, coordinating, and managing voluntary agencies, as well as organizing by settlement house workers, influenced the community organizing practitioners and theorists of the 1920s.[3] It was not until 1939 that a consensus emerged concerning the need to define community organization practice and to train social workers in such a specialty. The Lane Report of 1939 marked this first formal agreement among agency executives, practitioners, and teachers.[4] In order to trace the ideological and intellectual evolution of community organization to 1939, it is necessary to examine the work of practitioners and students of community organizing that began to publish theoretical works and practical manuals in the 1920s, establishing common principles and methods of action. Prominent among these practitioners were Joseph K. Hart, Eduard C. Lindeman, Bessie A. McClenahan, Walter W. Pettit, and Jesse F. Steiner.[5]

The orientations of the several practitioners differ somewhat from one another, but there are also similarities. Pettit sought to preserve the small community against the threat of urbanization.[6] Similarly, Lindeman strongly emphasized the importance of small compact local groups where people assume responsibilities and guide their own destinies. In *The Community*, he described community organization partly as "a conscious effort on the part of a community to control its affairs democratically, and to secure the highest services from its specialists, organizations, agencies and institutions by means of recognized interrelations."[7] McClenahan and Steiner emphasized community planning. They envisioned a "study-diagnosis-treatment scheme" taking into account the individuality of each community. They realized that communities were "not actually the cohesive, unified solidarity which they professed to be ideally."[8] Steiner sought to apply the concept of community to city neighborhoods and to large natural areas or regions such as the county. Hart, trained as a professional caseworker, emphasized personal adjustment and democratic participation.

Jesse F. Steiner

Jesse F. Steiner, educator and organizer, stressed training community workers as students of social science. He believed that organizers must be familiar with the nature of social attitudes, methods of social analysis, the problems of social control, and the complexity of social problems. Social reformers, he argued, may focus on one idea but the community organizer must seek many ideas to solve community problems.

Steiner approached community organizing from a sociological perspective. He carefully reviewed community theory, which included the analysis of the community as a social unit and physical structure, understood community organization and solidarity in relation to social change, and examined case studies of both rural and urban communities. In addition, he recognized that organizers should view social problems on a community-wide basis. They needed plans for improvement based on each community's resources and their own knowledge of its social problems. He suggested, therefore, that community chest organizers should analyze community needs, compile statistics, and sponsor programs to interest people in welfare projects. In this way, by determining the extent of the problems and stimulating community responsibility, they contributed substantially to united community action.[9]

Steiner identified four approaches to community organizing. The first was a reaction against the predominant mode of community organizing in the 1920s, in which several specialized agencies concentrated on one particular community issue. This served to enhance, according to Steiner, "the prestige and influence of the specialized agency instead of calling attention to the wider problems of the entire community."[10] Steiner referred to this assessment as his theory of individualism. His recognition of this trend led, in part, to increased interest in bringing agencies together within a council of social agencies and in the federation of fund-raising activities in many communities.

Steiner also identified an approach to community organizing undertaken by some national organizations: "community organization through supervision." Such organizations as the National Conference of Charities and Correction (the forerunner of the National Conference on Social Welfare) and the American Country Life Association exercised indirect, conservative influence over local associations. In contrast, the National Red Cross played a direct role in supervising the community organizing activities of its local chapters.

The approaches of "individualism" (organizing around one major problem resulting in specialized organizations—for example, delinquency, mental health, child welfare) and "supervisory" community organizing by national organizations led to increased interest in the federative type of community organizing. The need to coordinate services could be met without tampering with local autonomy. Independent agencies coordinated activities within a "confederation" that kept participating agencies moving together in the same direction. The popularity of federating had spread from fund-raising organizations and federations of social agencies spread to churches, women's clubs, labor unions, and educational agencies. There was also an equally strong identification with the concept of community and as a result, social centers became community centers, federations of social agencies became community councils, social surveys became community studies, and federated fund-raising organizations became community chests.

In Steiner's fourth approach to community organization, his "theory of amalgamation," he pointed out that separate agencies sometimes united into a single organization and centralized control.[11] While this trend found support among large charity donors, it seldom succeeded because social agency executives that would lose considerable control resisted and, instead, favored federation. In contrast, the experiences of public agencies indicated more potential for amalgamation, as seen in the so-called Iowa Plan.[12]

Steiner believed that community organization should mesh with the social process and not merely serve as an administrative device.[13] He viewed the council of social agencies as a device for working with existing agencies and institutions. In the same fashion, local neighborhood associations worked with the existing agencies and institutions and emphasized direct participation of all the people in the neighborhood. Community organizing was conceived as a process of social change representing conscious social planning to bring order out of chaos and better social adjustment. Steiner believed that the interlocking causes of social problems required the close coordination of social agencies and programs.

Bessie A. McClenahan

Unlike Steiner, some analysts concentrated on the practical aspects of organizing. They wrote detailed training manuals illustrating how a hired organizer enters a strange community. For example, McClenahan, writing mostly in the early 1920s, outlined an entire process for integrating the organizer into the community. She urged the organizer to investigate the community prior to arrival, to arrange advance publicity, to set up preliminary discussions with the board of the agency in order to learn about prior activities, to meet the existing staff, to make a windshield survey of the community by riding around, and to contact staff of other agencies and political leaders. McClenahan was quite specific about initially establishing a favorable relationship between the community organizer and the agency board of directors. She suggested that the organizer and board first meet informally at a private home. She urged organizers to be vague when answering questions until they understood the board members' organizational goals and the state of the community. When on firm ground, organizers should request the board's help in securing community support and in carrying out a complete study of the community. McClenahan did not want to leave anything to chance. She even suggested the nature of the news releases announcing the organizer's arrival. "Care should be taken that no hasty or premature statement is made concerning the future activities of the organization," McClenahan warned.[14] She directed the organizer to report on each part of his or her territory and on the community as a whole, and to map out what he or she considered the best plan of organization and activities. She even commented on the daily work the organizer should undertake.

McClenahan's practical guides to community organizing were based on the study-diagnosis-treatment model basic to both social casework and medical practice. Studying the community, diagnosing its problems, and formulating plans to treat or resolve these problems became the conceptual framework for the early community organizer. As when studying a family, the organizer must investigate the spirit, temper, and point of view held by various sectors of the community. McClenahan urged that, in order to create a strong community spirit and to foster genuine cooperation for a common aim, the community itself must recognize its needs and attempt solutions to its problems. She believed the community organizer should aid and direct, but not control, this process.

McClenahan stressed that an organizer's success depended upon his or her relationship with board members representing vital links to the community. She saw the board as the policymaking body and the organizer as the implementer of the board's designs for the future. In order to function effectively, the board must truly and democratically represent the whole community, but especially the business interests. Having business support would help the organizer meet "key people" and would provide insights as he or she organized sectors of the community where board members had considerable influence.

She also suggested using a number of specific techniques. The organizing plan should reflect local institutional needs but should not replace existing agencies, since doing so would not only duplicate effort but would probably make enemies of those whose jurisdictions were invaded. She suggested that the organizer begin with an uncomplicated project, "to gain confidence" and "demonstrate success." She pointed out that the organizer should not attempt to do all the work, but should instead delegate the jobs and the responsibility and recruit existing clubs and agencies for particular tasks. Likewise, the organizer should make full use of the local press, not only to inform but also to increase the organization's influence and have it "established in the minds of the people." [15]

Walter W. Pettit

The publication of case histories reinforced McClenahan's principles. The Community Organization Department of the New York School of Social Work produced the first community case studies, and in 1928, Walter Pettit, department chairman, published his *Case Studies in Community Organization*. Pettit designed these studies, which had considerable value to community organizers, to supplement the two key works of the period written by Steiner and Lindeman.

The case studies alerted students of community organizing to practical organizing problems, such as the role of the organizer as a leader. There was always a tension between the leadership role assumed by lay citizens in an organizing effort and the leadership role of the organizer, who could work either "up front" or "behind the scenes."

Pettit also stressed the importance of itemizing community problems and engaging in community self-studies. This "scientific" or more orderly approach served as a basis for analyzing the strengths and weaknesses of the community organizing process by clarifying problems and establishing priorities. This approach was also seen as a way to understand the causes of neighborhood conflict.

These case studies also identified parallels between the casework process of study-diagnosis-treatment and community organization practice. Emphasis was placed on the organizer's ability to work with others, to establish relationships, and to study, diagnose, and treat the community. Like McClenahan, Pettit encouraged the organizer to strive for early concrete successes in order to build a constituency.

Pettit also stressed the importance of organizational tools required in community organizing, including skills in public relations, in conducting meetings, and in coordinating agency programs. Pettit, again like McClenahan, recognized the importance of the relationship between an organizer and his or her board of directors. The way in which board members were elected and the board's power to determine policy and sanction programs became sensitive issues requiring the organizer to maneuver skillfully in and around members of the community power structure who served on local agency boards.

Eduard Lindeman

Relations between the agency board and the organizer also held considerable interest for Eduard Lindeman, one of the giants in the field of social work. Influenced by the respect he had gained for the independent farmer during his rural organizing days and by the organizational aspects of the YMCA movement, Lindeman became sensitive to the strain between the specialized skills of the organizer and the lay person. He felt the conflict would be minimized if the organizer realized that his or her job primarily involved training individuals, groups, and communities to solve their own problems. Lindeman also believed that organizing should encourage the general public to solve community problems and ultimately to promote positive long-range social goals. His goals, which reflected traditional American values, included economic security, efficient government, effective public health agencies and an efficient medical dispersal system, constructive leisure facilities, free education, freedom of expression, local community-based democratic organizations, religious or spiritual instruction, and "a system of morality supported by the organized community."[16]

Having established general community organizing goals, Lindeman believed that the major conflicts would arise over the means to reach these objectives. The volunteer, the "citizen participant" through whom the organizer cultivates the community's "vital interest groups," would moderate conflict. He also stressed that the "discussion method" would help to resolve conflicts by illustrating the legitimate and diverse ways of achieving accepted goals. Because conflicts over means would nevertheless erupt, the organizer must possess a keen sensitivity to the emotional needs of individuals and reinforce their loyalty to their own organization or agency. As a result, the community organizer would help others solve their community problems through various agencies.

Lindeman's contribution to community organizing lies in such practical approaches. He repeatedly pointed out that the community organizer must understand the needs of the community.[17] He emphasized investigating the facts and seeking group or agency coordination. His community organizing principles are best summarized in his major work, *The Community: An Introduction to the Study of Community Leadership and Organization*, published in 1921. He divided the process into a number of steps.

Step 1. Consciousness of need: Some person either within or without the community expresses the need, which is later represented by a definite project.

Step 2. Spreading the consciousness of need: A leader, within some institution or group in the community, convinces his or her group, or a portion of the group, of the reality of the need.

Step 3. Projection of consciousness of need upon the leadership of the community: The consciousness of need becomes more general.

Step 4. Emotional impulse to meet the need quickly: Some influential assistance is enlisted, in the attempt to arrive at a quick means of meeting the need.

Step 5. Presentation of other solutions: Other means of meeting the need are presented.

Step 6. Conflict of solutions: Various groups lend their support to one or the other of the various solutions presented.

Step 7. Investigation: It appears to be increasingly customary to pause at this point, and to investigate the project with expert assistance. (This step, however, is usually omitted and the following one takes its place.)

Step 8. Open discussion of issues: A public mass meeting or gathering of some sort is held at which the project is presented, and the groups with the most influence attempt to secure adoption of their plans.

Step 9. Integration of solutions: The various solutions presented are tested, with an effort to retain something from each in the practicable solution that is now emerging.

Step 10. Compromise on basis of tentative progress: Certain groups relinquish certain elements of their plans in order to avoid complete defeat, and the solution that results is a compromise with certain reservations. The means selected for meeting the need are not satisfactory to all groups, but are regarded as tentatively progressive.[18]

As a student of the community, Lindeman viewed the "social sciences as an audit of social activities by a participant observer." With the data he or she collected, the organizer became increasingly concerned with forming social policy and with its translation into social action.[19]

Like Steiner and McClenahan, Lindeman was also a social philosopher deeply concerned about our ability to engage in democratic community decision making. He linked his religious convictions to the integrity of the community. Although Lindeman was influenced by Reinhold Niebuhr's work on *The Contribution of Religion to Social Work*,[20] it was another proponent of community organization, Joseph Kinmont Hart, who articulated more clearly the philosophical question of "why organize a community."[21]

Joseph K. Hart

Hart studied the process of democratic deliberation and emphasized the community council's role of providing and implementing
programs. He believed that council members, who should be "scientists in their fields," should meet regularly for general discussion. "Its
decisions should represent not politics and intrigue but deliberation
and sincere belief." [22]

Hart began his analysis of community life by describing its "un-
satisfying character." He found it fragmentary, overly individualistic,
and composed of overdeveloped, unwieldy institutions. "Our communities," he wrote, "fail to rise to the levels of even our practical
ideals. They also show the great areas of utterly unwarranted individual, group, and community suffering through the perpetuation
of maladjustment of all sorts. . . . Community ills must be cured by
community remedies, even though those remedies should be so radical as to go to the very root of community life and organization." [23]

In seeking human betterment to correct physical, psychological,
and social defects, Hart repeatedly reminded his readers of the sanc-
tity of the individual. "This task of community organization involves
the development of a social order inclusive enough, rich enough,
varied enough, stimulating enough to reach every normal human
being, to transform all our common social institutions into instru-
ments of service, and to compete with all lesser elements for the
loyalty and support of the individual. The individual must be 'on the
inside.'" [24]

From Hart's perspective, the organizer educated the community
to stimulate individual responsibility for the common good. This
approach involved the development of "community deliberation";
representatives from all segments of the community would work out
common problems. He warned, however, against overselling community organization. "Community organization does not demand
that nothing shall be done unless everything can be done; it merely
demands that whatever is done, however small and incidental, shall
be done in the view of the whole problem." [25]

Hart, and others, believed that both war and increasing urbanization and industralization destroyed traditional community insti-

tutions. Society needed to make adjustments and form new institutions including forms of community organization to coordinate "all the community resources for the solving of community problems."[26] Community resources included all social agencies, public and private, urban and rural, as well as all latent talents of the citizenry. Both Hart and Lindeman perceived that the most important community goal was "democratic forms of organization, or community-wide organization through which the entire community might express its thought and see that its will is done."[27] This "community-as-a-whole" concept of organizing was a recurring theme among the students of community organizing. Lindeman even hoped for eventual worldwide organization.[28] Hart recognized that all social problems must be viewed and solved in relation to the life of the community as a whole and that problems should be regarded as the tasks of the community.[29]

The 1920s

Community organizers saw the community as being composed of a large number of private and public social welfare agencies all vying with one another for funds and power and all having different boards of directors and aims. Although they recognized that people differed in their ideas, the community organizers considered these differences reconcilable. Throughout the 1920s, therefore, organizers functioned as applied community analysts, emphasizing the need for interaction and cooperation among community groups. At the end of the decade, Steiner wrote, "Society is made up of elements more or less antagonistic to each other, which must through a process of accommodation develop a working arrangement that will resolve the conflicts and make consistent progress possible."[30]

How was community collaboration and cooperation to be achieved? Lindeman's approach involved stating "alternatives clearly and then moving away from an either-or solution."[31] The basic principles for community organization, however, lay in the concept of the leader as an "enabler" or teacher of the citizens, whom he viewed as active, informed participants in a democratic process of problem recognition and solution. Lindeman urged that the community organizer, rather than "doing" for the community, must encourage citizens to do for themselves.[32] And McClenahan added: "To accomplish the task of creating strong community spirit and of fostering genuine cooperation for a common aim, the community itself must see its needs and work out the solution of its problems. The community secretary or organizer should aid and direct, but not control."[33]

During the 1920s and 1930s, Hart, Pettit, and others worked out and recorded the specific tasks of the democratic leader or organizer. Hart wanted to promote individual responsibility through community education.[34] Steiner stressed well-trained, well-equipped, and well-financed leadership operating by professional standards. "The community worker must be first of all characterized by breadth of knowledge of social forces and relations and have capacity for constructive leadership."[35] Pettit considered it the duty of the organizer to further the development of associations in order to strengthen the community and help it solve its problems. In his five case studies, he describes tactics used by organizers to develop strong community spirit.[36] McClenahan, too, considered it the task of the organizer to make the community aware of its problems and "to develop such a sense of responsibility for improvement that all people and organized groups will join working forces to solve their common problems."[37]

Thus, the leading proponents of community organizing emphasized education as the vehicle to develop community awareness and understanding in order to promote widespread community participation in problem solving. They argued that the community must stress both the duties and rights of members. And the "intelligent community" is the proper place for such determinations.[38] The democratic organizer would release hidden resources in each individual and in each group. "Labor, capital, all the professions, all races and religions, the inarticulate masses and the eloquent few—all have indispensable contributions to make toward a realistic democratic program of community-wide planning and service."[39] Community organizers recognized that the average citizen saw social defects, but in order to improve social conditions, the people must be made aware not only of problems but of their implications and of the best ways to solve them. Customs and traditions were no longer sufficient.

Community organizing in rural areas was also promoted. Public attention traditionally focused on urban problems, but Steiner tried to establish an understanding of city-county interrelationships in order to provide a basis for an adequate and comprehensive social service system. He realized that city and rural areas were merging because of the automobile (which the middle class could afford during the 1920s), the labor-saving machinery, and rural electrification, which brought industry out of the city.[40] McClenahan also hoped that rural problems would be solved through cooperation and the "appropriation of federal and state funds for the creation of bureaus devoted to the stimulation of interest in agriculture, the improvement of farming and rural conditions, and the extension of expert service to the local rural communities."[41]

In the 1920s, major community organizing theorists, working from a social work perspective, codified existing practice, refined community organizing techniques based on their experience, and examined some of the theoretical implications of organizational practice. They studied, and often took part in, some of the organizing ventures of the settlement house era and the federation era.

The 1930s

It was only during the Great Depression of the 1930s that community organizing received some official recognition. In the years following the stock market crash of 1929, federations raised considerable funds for social services. By 1933, however, it became evident that only government could cope with the relief and social service needs of the economically crippled nation. Government, in part, recognized community organization methods by including the marshalling of community support, fact finding, public education, and the coordination of public and private agencies within the public welfare structure. The Social Security Act of 1935 produced significant directions for community organization practice. The act required social and community planning in order for states to receive funds. It was probably the first time that the term "community organization" appeared in a federal statute: "developing state services for the encouragement and assistance of adequate methods of community child welfare organization."[42]

By 1939, the knowledge and skill required for effective community organizing had developed sufficiently to warrant recognition and study by the National Conference of Social Work. The examination of community organization practice centered around its activities of mobilizing resources, initiating social services, coordinating welfare agencies, building welfare programs, fact finding, and setting standards.[43]

The 1939 Lane Report legitimated community organization practice within social work education. The report reflected the following agreements: (1) the term "community organization" refers to both a process and a field (e.g., the practice of medicine); (2) the process of organizing a community or some parts of it is carried on outside as well as inside the general area of social work; (3) within social work, the community organization process is carried on by some organizations as a primary function (e.g., council of social agencies) and by others as a secondary function (e.g., family service agency); (4) the community organization process exists on local, state, and national levels and also between such levels; and (5) those organizations whose primary function is the practice of community organization do not as a rule offer help directly to clients.[44]

In addition to these objectives, the report also emphasized the importance of following community organizing practices: (1) using fact finding for social planning and action; (2) initiating, developing, and modifying social welfare programs and services; (3) setting standards; (4) improving and facilitating interrelationships by promoting coordination between organizations, groups, and individuals concerned with social welfare programs and methods; and (5) developing public support of and participation in social welfare activities. As Schwartz observed, the Lane Report, as a result of its exploratory nature, implicitly and explicitly raised questions that were to preoccupy members of the social work profession for the next two decades.[45]

Conclusion

Rudimentary community organizing had been engaged in during the reform fervor at the turn of the century. Activities of settlement houses and charity organizations displayed the advantages inherent in cooperative endeavors. The organizing of war chests during World War I furthered the movement for community coordination and planning, and the Cincinnati Social Unit experiment promoted the concepts of individual responsibility and democratic participation. The twenties witnessed expansion of these ideas and attempts by early formulators to conceptualize and professionalize them by setting up principles and methods to guide community organizing efforts to improve social welfare and determine unmet needs.

Interest in community organization practice surfaced dramatically in the 1920s with the emergence of federated agency financing and the need for cooperation and the integration of services. As Norton observes, "Except for a few communities the social work armies all over this great land are organized in guerilla bands only."[46] Community organizers attempted to unify these bands into an effective force in an era thought to be totally lacking in sociopolitical innovation. In the 1920s community organization theorists provided many of the tools used by New Deal reformers, as documented by Clarke Chambers.[47]

The economic crisis of the 1930s legitimated community organizing, and its advocates, like Lindeman, became highly optimistic about the future of the field. Lindeman, in 1937, identified many new directions for community organizing, including social planning.[48] In addition, the federal government recognized the importance of community organizing and used organizing tools to implement and monitor government programs.

The roots of community organization practice in the 1980s and 1990s can be traced to the intellectual contributions of the key practitioners of the 1920s and 1930s. The education of future community organizers ought to include the ideas and experiences of the early conceptualizers of community organizing.

PART II

Locality Development

3

The Cincinnati Unit Experiment, 1917–1920

Neil Betten and Michael J. Austin

 DEMOCRATIC self-help has long been idealized as a powerful force for U.S. communities that want to address social problems. This ideal is still in evidence today as individual communities struggle with problems of housing, health, employment, and environmental degradation. Attempts to achieve the ideal have a long and notable history in the United States, but limited achievement has always been the rule as citizens have encountered the inevitable problems of conflicting interests, political ambition, and lack of resources. These barriers to community self-help have prompted reformers to concentrate during the past forty years on national programs and policies regarding housing, medical care, employment, and environmental improvement. But our historical use of local self-help programs provides evidence of the potential effectiveness of such programs, tempered by proof of their shortcomings. Much can be learned from the experience of the Cincinnati Social Unit, which had a brief but vigorous existence

Source: Adapted from Neil Betten and Michael J. Austin, "The Unwanted Helping Hand," *Environment* 19, no. 1 (January–February 1977): 13–22. Reprinted with the permission of Helen Dwight Reid Educational Foundation. Published by Heldref Publications, 4000 Albemarle St., N.W., Washington, D.C. 20016. Copyright © 1977.

nearly eighty years ago. The basic lesson is that idealism alone is not powerful enough to sustain such programs.

Overall, the Cincinnati Social Unit served as a salient historical example of the impossibility of achieving a technical solution to social problems without achieving a simultaneous political solution. In the early twentieth century, Cincinnati was a city highly influenced by urban reformers. As in similar cities, the urban reformers, calling themselves progressives, attacked the party system and patronage politics, sought structural changes in city administrations, preferred less local government to more, stated that the public interest should prevail over private interests, advocated the use of experts to achieve greater efficiency, and cloaked it all in democratic rhetoric.[1]

It was in this milieu, between 1918 and late 1920, that two moderate socialists, Wilber and Elsie LaGrange Phillips, established a community-based democratic self-help system in Cincinnati. The Cincinnati Social Unit attempted to organize one twelve-thousand-person neighborhood[2] in order to give its people partial control over their immediate social and economic life and to provide a way for residents themselves to deal with social problems, particularly public health problems. Although the Social Unit had shortcomings, which will be examined later, on the whole it was successful in achieving its goals—a democratic community organization in which the residents solved many of their own problems. The vast majority of observers of that time and later support this conclusion. In addition to favorable comments from local charitable, housing, vocational, and health groups, there were laudatory reports in newspapers around the country. The *Christian Herald* called the unit a "Christianizing Force." John Loodgood of Johns Hopkins University stated in the *Trenton* (New Jersey) *Times* that "the Social Unit experiment . . . has given promise of progress among the masses that is astounding." The *Detroit News* found the unit aim "the wholly laudable one of fighting the bane of modern city existence—loneliness." The *Dayton Journal* described the unit as engaged in "a campaign of neighborliness."[3]

Articles in periodicals, both academic and popular, likewise evaluated the unit favorably. Seba Eldridge, in *Social Forces*, found that "all competent observers of the experiment agree that it demonstrated the soundness of the principles upon which it was based," and concluded that "efficient service under democratic citizenship organization is quite practical." A contemporary journalistic article calculated that "an astonishing amount of relief [is] given at a cost comparatively lower than private organizations spend for approximate results." S. Gale Lowrie, in *National Muncipal Review*, found that those "who have examined the experiment . . . are usually carried away in considering the accomplishments in the awakening of community consciousness."[4]

Grassroots Organizing

The Cincinnati Social Unit actually was an outgrowth of the National Social Unit formed in 1916 to subsidize the social unit concept and to publicize it through municipal reform and civic organizations. The National Social Unit was chaired by Mrs. Charles Tiffany, and its backers included prominent and wealthy progressives such as Mrs. J. Borden Harriman, Mrs. William Lowell Putnam, Margaret Woodrow Wilson, John Jay Edson (president of the U.S. Chamber of Commerce), Felix Adler, Herbert Croly, Mrs. Thomas Lemont, and Mrs. Daniel Guggenheim.[5]

The National Social Unit announced that it would finance a local social unit in the city best suited for the project. For whatever reason—perhaps the idealism common in America when the unit was being considered for adoption or the financial savings that the unit would achieve in terms of local welfare costs—several cities offered to adopt the social unit plan. The national group selected Cincinnati, a city with definite problems and needs but one that seemed to reflect the reform sentiments of the period.

A citywide referendum indicated that the Mohawk-Brighton district of Cincinnati supported the project more heavily than did other sections, and it was generally believed that this area was a typical urban community that would provide a realistic test for the unit experiment. This mixed residential and commercial area had both working-class and middle-class residents; the population consisted of both immigrant and native-born persons. Because of these considerations, the Mohawk-Brighton section was selected for the site of the new social unit experiment. Cincinnati's civic organizations almost unanimously supported adoption of the experiment, and the unit was publicized and explained locally in several ways. Articles appeared daily in the city's newspapers, circulars were distributed to school children, and talks were given to numerous local organizations.

Every one of the Mohawk-Brighton district's thirty-one blocks, averaging about four hundred people each, had its own Council of Neighbors. Each one of these thirty-one block councils elected a representative to an overall Citizens' Council, which spoke for the residents of the entire neighborhood. The Citizens' Council determined the social unit policy. In addition to this residential-based system, each major occupational group in the neighborhood had a separate council to protect its own interests. Representatives of each occupational group met together as an Occupational Council to provide guidance and technical advice to the policymaking Citizens' Council. The Occupational Council and the Citizens' Council sometimes met together as a General Council, particularly when overall budget questions arose. An executive office, officially lacking in any decision-making authority, was established to administer the entire operation. Wilber and Elsie Phillips, as coexecutives, administered the unit.

How did this system work in reality? In what ways was the neighborhood approach to democratic decision making a success or a failure, and why? The unit's developers, the Phillipses, conceived of their plan as a way of expanding democracy. Through organizing communities on a neighborhood basis, they hoped to redirect decisions concerning practical social needs away from the politicians and professional social agencies to the people such decisions directly affected. One of the first National Social Unit publications described the organization's purpose as organizing "people of a limited district democratically so that they can get a clear idea of what their common needs are and what they think ought to be done about them." But the Phillipses argued that the social unit, which would benefit the whole city, needed virtually universal support. As Wilber Phillips put it in a later book defending the unit, "Unanimity of desire is the heart of the matter." It "required the cooperation of every community group to render it fully effective," the *Literary Digest* correctly explained in interpreting the founders' intentions.[6]

The Block Workers

If many groups indeed supported the program, it was the individual block workers who became the nerve center of the organization. The block worker, almost always a housewife, carried out the unit's assignment in addition to the strenuous full-time household work common at this time. The unit paid each block worker a small salary for eight hours' work a week. This was something of an innovation, since the predecessor to the modern social worker, the untrained "friendly visitor," usually came as a volunteer from the leisure class. The block worker in Mohawk-Brighton first called on every family in his or her area, explained the purposes of the social unit, and later frequently reiterated its objectives as the organization undertook new neighborhood functions. Because of such consistent contact, the block worker became aware of neighborhood and individual family problems and helped in seeking out solutions.[7]

Block workers took several social surveys and a census of the health needs of the area. They attended unit classes in order to learn about the organization and to study social service methods. Unit physicians and nurses provided the block workers with detailed health instructions so that they understood the overall health program and could explain it to their constituents. In this way, block workers were educators and interpreters, interpreting unit programs to the people and relaying the people's desires and needs to the unit administration.

Block workers did more than educate. They registered births, arranged for immediate nursing and medical assistance, and reported contagious diseases, illegal child labor, and juvenile delinquency.[8] As a *Survey* article put it, "They learn through serving to know when a need exists and how and where to turn for help." They took on the responsibility of finding jobs for those unemployed in their area and acted as liaisons with the unit's professional social workers and medical staff. One widower even asked his block worker if the unit could find him a wife.[9]

Generally, the Mohawk-Brighton residents wholeheartedly accepted the block workers. "There was just one family out of one hundred and six on my block," reported one block worker, "that I couldn't make understand the unit." Another added, "My people ask me everything—how to save money, what to do about this and that in the house, and how to manage Johnnie." An indication of the block workers' acceptance can perhaps be found in the results of a neighborhood unit election held several months after the program began. Wilber Phillips proudly reported, "They were all, 100 percent of them, returned to office."[10]

By providing classes and lectures, the unit leadership hoped to instill in the block workers an attitude of professional responsibility and a sense of community spirit; this was easier than it might first appear. Through years of associating with their neighbors, block workers empathized with the families and their problems. Wilber Phillips reported that "the block workers leaned over backwards in making sure that each new step taken was in accord with the feelings and desires of those they served." Block workers often found themselves in delicate situations involving confidential information, but, as one worker said, "We block workers take a pride in never telling what we find out. We don't even tell our husbands."[11]

Citizens' Council

As explained above, the block workers made up the Citizens' Council, which provided direction for the social unit. The Citizens' Council determined which community-wide problems should be addressed and submitted recommendations to the unit's Occupational Council, but the Citizen's Council retained veto power over programs advocated by other unit groups.[12]

Input from other unit groups came through the Occupational Council, which consisted of community representatives from seven specific employment groups, primarily professional. Represented on the Occupational Council were the community's teachers, social workers, physicians, businessmen, nurses, dentists, and trade unionists. The Occupational Council provided technical advice and established plans to deal with specific problems that the Citizens' Council believed needed attention.

The Phillipses and the unit sponsors placed heavy emphasis on the role of these "experts" in solving problems. To a large extent, this attitude promoted the use of specialized expertise, again reflecting the progressive ideas of the period, particularly when combined with an espousal of democracy. "The uniqueness in the Cincinnati experiment," as the social unit's neighborhood *Bulletin* observed, "lies in the fact that the people themselves have organized for self-help [and] have at their disposal expert advice from technically trained groups." The *Literary Digest* put it succinctly. "It aims at popular control, yet makes use of the highest skill available." The Occupational Council received its technical advice on a specific issue from the particular occupational group that would, in turn, be responsible for the program dealing with that issue. This arrangement gave the occupational groups a high degree of autonomy in making decisions concerning their own areas of involvement. The committee of five persons that represented the nurses, for example, decided that unit nurses would take a generalized approach. Thus, a unit visiting nurse did not specialize, but rather might be involved in cases dealing with a variety of health problems ranging from malnutrition to tuberculosis. Visiting nurses, a very common sight in immigrant areas during these years, usually specialized in one disease or another; but since the unit nurses worked a small geographical area and cooperated with the block workers, the nurses' unit chose to innovate and emulated the wide-ranging interest of the general practitioner. Physicians, likewise, exercised autonomy and self-determination. A committee of nine persons, representing the twenty-six medical doctors living or practicing in Mohawk-Brighton, appointed a rotating group at a central health station to examine residents. However, the unit paid the physicians a fee for each patient examined, not a salary as in the case of the nurses.[13]

The Social Workers' Council included representatives of all agencies active in the district, in addition to the social unit's own staff of social workers. The group held weekly meetings resulting in interagency cooperation. Block workers, along with unit nurses, served to transmit appropriate cases to the social workers. The block worker took an active advisory role in the decisions and plans worked out by the social workers, however. Although all occupational groups worked together on the Occupational Council, the other occupational groups never became as active as those of the physicians, nurses, and social workers; the dentists and teachers had just begun programs when the social unit came under the political attack that resulted in its demise.[14]

Although the system of councils seemed complex, it produced an orderly operation. Block workers studied the people's needs, represented popular attitudes, and decided broad policy. They transmitted their recommendations to the Occupational Council, which formulated programs to meet these needs. Wilber and Elsie Phillips coordinated daily tasks to achieve program objectives. In the short time of its existence, the unit functioned effectively.

Health Needs as Top Priority

The unit achieved its most significant success in preventive medicine and public health. For several reasons, the organization's leadership chose to begin the experiment with an emphasis on medicine. The Phillipses had operated a successful health-oriented municipal child-welfare commission in Milwaukee. In view of their Milwaukee experience, they believed that a medical program, especially one concentrating on infants, would receive strong community and political support.

The unit health program began with an infant medical service provided by visiting nurses and examinations by physicians at the unit health center. Other health services included a "loan closet" for the sick, which provided such items as sheets, pillow cases, towels, and hot-water bags. The unit also made visiting housekeepers available when families needed additional help during illnesses. In addition, the dental occupational group examined children's teeth, distributed pamphlets on care of teeth, and held dental hygiene classes.

Classes on infant care and nutrition supplemented individualized attention in the infant medical service program. Soon, prenatal care was introduced. General bedside nursing, a health service for preschool children, nursing supervision of tuberculosis patients, and, eventually, medical examination of school children and adults followed. In the summer of 1918, the *Bulletin* found that health-station physicians had examined 1,000 preschool children—"not 100 percent, but it is a very good showing." It clearly was a good showing, since the block workers' survey found 1,170 children under age six in the district.[15]

The unit, however, did not provide complete medical care. The physicians at the unit's medical center merely examined patients, who subsequently utilized family doctors for medical treatment. If financial support for health care or hospitalization was necessary, the block worker secured aid through the Social Workers' Council. Visiting nurses, however, as unit employees, provided full professional services, including making calls on all those known to be ill and visiting every infant in the district in order to advise on feeding and general care.[16]

The influenza epidemic of 1918 (the "Swine Flu") illustrated the unit's successful preventive medicine program, its cohesive relationship of the various services, and its ability to respond quickly to a crisis. The flu had spread to much of the country, but had not yet been reported in Cincinnati. The unit's head nurse, reacting to an apparently abnormal number of colds, conferred with the executive of the medical council, who immediately wrote up simple instructions suggesting ways to deal with the flu, stressing rest and advising residents to report flu symptoms immediately. On the same day, the unit printed this recommendation in a leaflet, with the approval of the councils of physicians, nurses, and social workers. By late afternoon, thousands of leaflets were in the hands of the block workers, who also received instructions for a verbal explanation of the material. By 6:00 P.M., Phillips could later report, "the leaflets were in every home in the district, and every family had had a word of advice, in person, from their own carefully instructed social agent."[17]

Community Reactions

"I had experience with influenza," wrote one Mohawk-Brighton resident. "The whole family . . . were all sick. If it weren't for the social unit nurse . . . we would all not be here today." A volunteer who helped the nurses and did emergency housekeeping during the epidemic described her experience. "There were six sick in one family, and if we had not gone in to help them, some of them would have died." Another Mohawk-Brighton resident writing to the *Bulletin* praised the unit staff, who "nursed both myself and husband through our sickness, when it was utterly impossible to obtain anyone else to even come near us." Finally, *Harper's Weekly* quoted one plain-speaking resident. "If it had not been for the unit, my entire family would now be in the cemetery."[18] Influenza, much more dangerous in the early twentieth century than it is today, resulted in a death rate of 2.8 persons per 1,000 in Mohawk-Brighton compared to a reported rate of 4.1 per 1,000 in Cincinnati as a whole and 5.1 per 1,000 in the remaining three wards of which the unit was a part. The unit success received national attention both in the *New Republic* and in the *New York Times*.

The Mohawk-Brighton responses to the unit's work during the epidemic were echoed in the evaluation of the general health scheme. "The health services . . . were of an exceptionally high standard," reported a scholar writing for *Social Forces*, adding that the "understanding of health problems on the part of the neighborhood was almost unprecedented, and health conditions were improved in an almost remarkable manner." S. Gale Lowrie, in the *National Municipal Review*, wrote of the national health organizations, "Their almost universal endorsement speaks high praise" of the unit. "The statistics of the health services," argued Jesse F. Steiner, a leading scholar in the social work field, "seem to offer conclusive evidence as to the effectiveness of the social unit plan in arousing public interest in health measures," while physician Haven Emerson found "practical unanimity in the opinion of physicians of the district that the medical needs of the district have been better met than before." The residents of Mohawk-Brighton, as in their response to the flu care, voiced laudatory opinions of the unit's medical care in general. "There are those who would not know what a blessing a nurse is, especially as the nursing is done through the social unit," wrote one recipient of health care. Another typically added, "We certainly appreciate what the social unit has done for us, and I don't know what I'd do without their help."[19]

Preventive medicine remained the Cincinnati Social Unit's foremost accomplishment, particularly since a political attack prematurely ended the project, as will be explained later. The unit, nevertheless, had other activities. For example, it published the *Social Unit Bulletin* every two weeks. The newspaper contained unit information, letters to the editor, editorials, a "Neighborhood News" section announcing such events as marriages, parties, changes in address, and get-well notices, and a variety of articles. The block councils and the occupational groups each selected a representative to the board of editors of the *Bulletin*. The unit distributed the newspaper free of charge until January 1920, when it instituted a twenty-five-cent yearly subscription rate as a way of helping the unit meet what had by then become a difficult financial situation. Articles were written by block workers or by Occupational Council members. All block workers were, in a sense, reporters, since they had the responsibility of securing news items from their blocks. The *Bulletin* also encouraged an overall neighborhood participation in its publishing venture: "*What are your ideas?* This is your organization. The General Council is created to carry out your will. *What do you want it to do in this matter?*" asked the newspaper. Wilber Phillips, who liked to think of the unit as a series of little villages with a sense of community, saw the *Bulletin* as a small-town newspaper serving the neighborhood. He reminisced that in his hometown, "a dog couldn't break its leg without getting into the paper. Now, in the center of this city of 400,000, we borrowed another leaf from the village life." Phillips was not satisfied, however, to preside inactively over the *Bulletin's* activities. As coexecutive of the General Council, he had veto power over *Bulletin* content; the executive officer of the Occupational Council served as the first managing editor. Later, Roe Eastman, a professional journalist, did much of the editing.[20]

In addition to publishing the *Bulletin*, the unit sponsored block parties, community sings, picnics, baby shows, a dramatic club, a community chorus, women's classes in gymnastics and swimming, a class in cabinetmaking for men, nutrition classes, war gardens, Americanization classes, and a liberty bond drive. It worked with family problems, began to tackle juvenile crime, sought jobs for residents, and informally handled a multitude of small problems.[21]

The considerable success of the Mohawk-Brighton Social Unit was balanced by the program's small budget, the excessive time spent by the Phillipses in promoting expansion of the program to other cities while neglecting Cincinnati, and the need to defend the unit against attack by local politicians. Moreover, social conditions in the Mohawk-Brighton district and the adjacent areas of the city impeded the success of the unit.

The unit required close cooperation of people with different backgrounds, yet Cincinnati had a tradition of ethnic hostility, serious racial conflict, and antagonistic religious rivalry. Although the unit began with a public health thrust, social workers reported that Cincinnati's immigrants, who made up a significant portion of the Mohawk-Brighton population, were suspicious of physicians and impossible to hospitalize. The unit needed financial support from local sources, but Cincinnati was facing serious economic problems. Prohibition destroyed the locally profitable liquor industry, while the automobile eclipsed the city's once-proud carriage trade. Many other local industries were in trouble, and the city had to borrow money to meet current expenses. Thus, it was difficult to find local financial support.[22]

Then there was the political assault on the unit. In March 1919, Cincinnati Mayor John Galvin pictured the unit as "anti-American, fostering unrest and discontent among the working classes." Galvin based his remarks on a personal letter that the recently deceased J. H. Landis, city health commissioner and chairman of the unit's Physicians' Council, had written to Wilber Phillips, in which Landis called the unit "socialistic to a dangerous extent. . . . I do not hesitate in saying that I consider it a step toward Bolshevism." The letter was made public, and the hysterically antiradical Cincinnati *Times-Star* followed with another Galvin salvo. He accused the Phillipses of being "radically socialistic in their ideas and tendencies," and he argued that they were "building up within this city a separate and distinct government. . . . It leads to . . . revolution and the Soviet form of government."[23]

In making such charges, the mayor emulated national political figures engaged in an oppressive antiradical "red scare" campaign. Moreover, the nationwide antiradical hysteria quickly became associated with anti-immigrant feeling. Cincinnati, with an especially large German-American population, felt that it had to prove its American loyalty during World War I. The city was thus reluctant to counterattack too forcefully the "anti-red" attack on the social unit, since that attack was cloaked in the era's superpatriotism. The mayor was, therefore, on safe political ground.

Social unit spokespersons immediately rose to the defense, however. The *Bulletin* printed replies from Wilber Phillips and followed with arguments outlining the unit record. National publications added their support. The *New Republic* suggested that the mayor did not have the slightest understanding of socialism. This periodical enjoyed quoting Galvin's statement, made just three days after his social unit attack: "I am strongly opposed to labor unions in the Police and Fire Department as I would be to any form of Bolshevist government." In defense against the socialism charge, the *Bulletin* correctly pointed out that "at no time . . . had partisanship entered into its [the unit's] discussion." It added, "The social unit is above party." The independent Helen S. Trounstine Foundation investigated the socialism question. Its report, authored by William J. Norton, secretary of the Detroit Patriotic Fund, declared, "There has been no use made of the organization for the promotion of socialism or any other political or economic theory." Fred G. Butler, director of Americanization of the Department of the Interior, endorsed the unit as "a step away from Bolshevism" and as an effective means of combating "lawless agitation." Even a hostile report of the Council of Social Agencies stated that the unit was not designed for "the spread of radical socialistic propaganda." [24]

The mayor backed down. Speaking before the Women's City Club committee investigating the unit, Galvin stated that he had attacked the unit as a private citizen, not as mayor, and had been unaware that he would be widely quoted. He admitted that he had based his statements on other people's charges and lacked evidence to support his "personal point of view." But the mayor's attack blazed an easily followed path for institutions and groups that considered the unit a threat and used the radicalism charge as the vehicle for their own purposes. [25]

Although the unit had its greatest success in the health services, the medical profession became its opponent. In fact, the attitude of physicians posed problems for the unit from the very beginning.

That the city's Academy of Medicine supported the program at all came as a surprise and was the result of clever political maneuvering. The unit's wealthy national sponsors secured medical endorsements from physicians known throughout the country. Then Wilber Phillips argued before academy members that the unit's program would retain the fee system and prevent health insurance, which the academy strongly opposed. The academy, therefore, endorsed the unit—but only as a laboratory or test of preventive medicine. Before the unit began operation, opposition to the overall concept surfaced in the West End Medical Society, the local physicians' organization for Mohawk-Brighton and the surrounding area. Wilber Phillips dismissed this as the work of "an old disgruntled doctor." But investigative reporters from *Harper's* viewed the West End Medical conflict differently. "Certain members fervently believed that even a free diagnostic service would reduce the income of every local physician." [26]

As the unit health service went into operation, the physicians active in the unit were difficult to please. They insisted that the unit remain a diagnostic service only, and they refused, at first, to give even "feeding prescriptions" for malnourished infants. Wilber Phillips eventually persuaded the participating physicians to moderate their position, but physician resistance increased as the unit engaged in the additional health services.

Medical Opposition

The medical profession was easily persuaded that the unit represented a serious threat to private, fee-for-service practice, particularly after Mayor Galvin sounded the cry of "Bolshevism." Among the measures suggested as potential future services in the unit's minute books were proposals to take over grade-school medical inspection, to provide each student with two complete medical examinations a year, to work toward regular periodic examinations of all adults in the community at least once yearly, and to extend maternity service to include attendance at deliveries in addition to postnatal care. The philanthropic Council of Social Agencies (to be distinguished from the unit's own Social Workers' Council mentioned above) questioned the extent of the unit's health-care plan for the entire community. "Would not such a plan amount to socialization of medicine and . . . alter radically the economic organization of medical service?" The West End Medical Society apparently thought so; it condemned the unit once the unit came under political fire.[27]

To make matters worse, the Visiting Nurses' Association also attacked the unit. The unit had, after all, ended the fee system for visiting nurses and simply hired them for a salary. Wilber Phillips believed that the "openly hostile attitude" of association members had a simple explanation: "We were doing better work than they were." He correctly pointed out that the "far greater efficiency of the unit had greatly increased the actual purchasing power of every dollar spent for nursing in Mohawk-Brighton." When a spokesperson for the National Organization for Public Health Nursing agreed that the unit "is one of the most significant ventures in public health nursing in America" and stated that she knew "of no place where so intensive a piece of public health nursing is being done," the Cincinnati Visiting Nurses' Association paid little attention. It is interesting, however, that the unit was supported by the Cincinnati Graduate Nurses' Association, whose salaried members worked in hospitals rather than in the community as did members of the Visiting Nurses' Association.[28]

The unit was condemned not only by medical and nursing organizations but also by prominent businessmen's organizations. Both the Federation of Improvement Clubs and the Kiwanis Club officially criticized the organization, as did the influential Sands Business Men's Club. The concern of the businessmen was reflected in hostile questions asked by members of a Council of Social Agencies investigating committee. The committee was concerned that the Cincinnati Social Unit could potentially become involved in activities such as "cooperative buying and selling of certain commodities." The committee asked if the unit plan would not "tend inevitably to the consideration of other social problems, including problems of milk supply, housing, wages, unemployment, and the like." A trade union leader on the unit's Occupational Council responded that unit workers realized that many social problems stemmed from low wages, long hours, and child labor and that the organization would soon seek to reform industry. Phillips himself wondered, "Did democracy in occupational groups among the professions hint at the possibility of democracy in industry?"

In addition to business interests, city agencies—either responding to the mayor's cue or reacting against the unit's ambitious designs in their own areas of jurisdiction—jumped into the fray. Simultaneously, large contributors threatened to curtail donations to the local Council of Social Agencies if it continued to support the unit financially, and the council therefore ended its subsidy.[29]

The social unit attempted to deal with these problems. To illustrate the unit's support in the district, it held a referendum. Out of 4,154 persons who took part, 4,034 voted for the unit and 120 voted against it. In reaction to cuts in funding, the community organization tried to operate by reducing services, such as the number of visits by block workers and the number of hours the clinic remained open. The unit adopted the slogan "A penny a day for 100 days" in an attempt to raise medical program funds within Mohawk-Brighton. Large poor families found it difficult to make this contribution, so the unit suggested that families that had "no children, or only one or two . . . [financially] adopt a child from another family where there [were] five or six." The campaign did not raise enough money to keep the unit alive, and national funds dwindled.[30]

At the end of 1919, the Phillipses resigned as unit executives, and Courtenay Dinwiddie succeeded them. He kept the unit in operation at an increasingly reduced level for almost a year. On October 27, 1920, the Cincinnati Social Unit officially went out of existence.[31]

The Political Problem

The unit's success can partly be explained by the immediate rewards that resulted from participation. The block workers, who, observers agree, carried out their roles effectively, were paid both in cash and in job satisfaction. When the unit lowered block workers' incomes, it officially encouraged them to reduce their commitments. The visiting nurse service proved effective; the unit paid nurses at regular rates. The physicians participated and were paid for each examination, as mentioned before, but they probably viewed themselves primarily as guardians of their own prior long-range interests.

None of the other occupational groups, with the exception of the one representing the social workers, successfully pursued their programs beyond the planning stages. It seems more than coincidental that those groups that did the least for the unit were those that also went unpaid.

The unit had the support of thousands of Mohawk-Brighton residents; the residents participated in the health programs and voted for the unit. Their enthusiasm was understandable, since they received immediate benefits at minimal cost. In providing a nurse, caring for a family, or examining an infant, the unit provided a needed service, while the cost to the resident consisted of answers to occasional health questionnaires.

Why, then, did this experiment fail? Why was the opposition so easily victorious? After all, the unit avoided patronage politics, reduced the scope of government, supported the interests of Mohawk-Brighton residents, relied on experts to achieve greater efficiency, and utilized democratic principles and rhetoric.

Ironically, a major problem of the unit involved its democratic nature. Many of the urban progressives only talked of democracy, but the Phillipses really believed in it. This constituted a threat to some business and professional interests, since a democratically run organization might choose to replace local commercial services with cooperatives or other alternative systems; the situation also seemed threatening to the politicians.

The mayor erred when he called the unit a Bolshevik conspiracy, but he correctly pointed out that unit officials were establishing a government within a government. The Phillipses assumed that good will and a reasonable program would be sufficient for success, and they did not prepare for the inevitable emergence of opposition to the unit. When hostile forces did appear, Wilber Phillips offered long, conciliatory, reasonable arguments rather than striving to solidify grass roots support.

Using the Power Structure

The Phillipses not only neglected to build a political power base, but they also failed to organize institutional support in the community effectively. In particular, the unit leaders neglected the church organizations. This was an especially significant omission, since urban immigrants centered their social and family life in the churches. The German Americans of Mohawk-Brighton were particularly highly organized. In addition to the churches, there were German unions, mutual-aid societies, charity organizations, and cultural societies. Historian Zane Miller found that, in 1915, Cincinnati had 114 German organizations, and Mohawk-Brighton was the center of the German-American settlement. Yet the unit completely neglected any realistic involvement with organizationally active German Americans. Phillips did include high-level institutional leaders such as the Catholic bishop and the superintendent of schools in advisory capacities, but he erroneously assumed that they truly represented the people for whom they officially spoke. In reality, the bishop did not reflect the true interests and attitudes of the ethnic parish, and the superintendent of schools did not represent the teachers. Finally, those prominent and wealthy progressives who had given the unit a free hand somehow found their purses much more difficult to open when Bolshevism was charged, even though the charge was false.[32]

In short, when attacked, the unit was caught by surprise; it had to depend on its own resources, it lacked strong local allies, and it was cut off from sources of funds. Its local support could not meet the challenge or make up the deficiency, and the unit could not survive.

Any organization designed to improve the lot of a specific group of people—the poor, the middle class, or a large ethnic group—invites conflict. When a significant percentage of people in a given area is involved, opposition will surface because other interests will be detrimentally affected. The idealistic Phillipses believed the progressive rhetoric of the day. They needed to use power relationships, not ignore them. If the organizational intent is to create significant change, community organizing must be a political venture in the broadest sense of the term. The Cincinnati Social Unit program evolved in the opposite direction—from political ideology to an experiment in social service methods. "It ceased to be a workshop of the political scientist and became that of the social workers," the *National Municipal Review* correctly pointed out. In neglecting power relationships, the unit courted certain failure.[33] The tragedy is that the social unit concept worked well and could have continued to make significant contributions to the welfare of citizens in Cincinnati and elsewhere. The experiment did leave a legacy of practical experience that should be heeded today by those interested in community-based programs in social and environmental affairs.

4

The International Institutes: Their Philosophy and Role in Community Organizing

Raymond A. Mohl and Neil Betten

I N T H E 1960s the possibility of using community organizing techniques to change society received attention from both social workers and social reformers. As a result, several academic studies of community organizing appeared, some using a historical approach. Academicians have repeatedly examined Saul Alinsky's Back of the Yards organizing, which often serves as a point of departure. Community organizing, however, as social work historians are well aware, clearly preceded Alinsky, and has often been managed differently from his neighborhood orientation.

One alternative type of community organizing was carried out in early twentieth-century America by the almost sixty International Institutes orginally affiliated with the Young Women's Christian Association. Immigrant service and community agencies with unique purposes and programs, International Institutes were established in most of the heavily ethnic cities. The first Institute was organized in New York City in 1910 under YWCA sponsorship. The moving force behind the new YWCA experiment was Edith Terry Bremer, a young social welfare and settlement worker. Hired by the national board of the YWCA in 1909 to direct the agency's work with immigrant women and girls, Bremer pushed for the establishment of a social service, educational, and community center in Greenwich Village, one of New York's heavily populated immigrant districts. Promoted aggressively by Bremer, the Institute idea of work with immigrant women soon spread to other cities. By the mid-1920s, some fifty-five International Institutes had been organized by local YWCAs in such cities as Boston, Providence, Baltimore, Buffalo, Detroit, Pittsburgh, Cleveland, Philadelphia, Brooklyn, St. Louis, Milwaukee, San Antonio, Los Angeles, San Francisco, and a host of other cities. Bremer headed the agency's work from 1910 to 1954, providing a consistent and unified approach to work with immigrant communities.[1]

As the leading spokesperson for the entire International Institute movement, Bremer defined the agency as "an association of local institutes, councils, centers, and leagues for foreign-born people." The Institute movement as a whole was viewed as a federation of locally autonomous units, each with its own special character but with all adhering to the institutional umbrella and the philosophical principles established by the national agency. The International Institutes defined their organizing target as the immigrant communities of an entire city. The organizing of the foreign-born, Edith Bremer suggested, "must be carried out on a city-wide basis . . . since the group is bound by nationality and language, not neighborhood." While concentrating on nationalities, the International Institutes achieved many of their immediate social goals, gave up considerable control of local agencies to the immigrant communities themselves, and pioneered the concept of cultural pluralism.[2]

The local Institutes were funded from their own as well as YWCA sources. From 1910 until the early 1930s the Institutes remained part of the YWCA's Department of Immigration and Foreign Communities. The economic squeeze of the depression decade resulted in competition for funds within such agencies as the YWCA, and many Institute directors and boards believed their institutions could do better financially if independent of the parent organization. In addition, many Institute leaders differed with the YWCA on how to approach immigrant communities. The difference was not philosophical but tactical. The YWCA directed its mission to women and girls, while to many Institute workers it seemed more reasonable to deal with immigrant communities and families as a whole. This difference in focus, as well as differing financial interests, resulted in the withdrawal of local Institutes from the parent YWCA.[3]

In September 1934, several recently seceded local Institutes federated in the National Institute of Immigrant Welfare and opened a central office in New York City. The relationship between the YWCA and the new Institute remained amicable. The YWCA turned over to the new national organization its community files, nationality resource files, folk life collection, and general immigrant data. The Bureau of Immigrants and the Foreign Born of the National Board of the YWCA went out of existence, and the national Institute took over the Bureau's facilities and functions at the immigrant stations of Ellis Island and San Francisco. By January 1936, the new national Institute had eighteen local units. In 1943 the agency changed its name to the American Federation of International Institutes.[4]

The change from YWCA affiliation to independent agency did not alter the pioneering philosophy of the International Institute. At a time when Americanization meant conformity, forced assimilation, and loss of traditions, national Institute head Bremer advocated an unusual concept—what today is called cultural pluralism. The Institute found its most important task in helping various ethnic groups maintain their cultural identity and keep a positive self-image. Each immigrant, Bremer stated, "is possessed of a cultural identity which is important to him and of significance to others. It is with the recognition of this that true private social work begins." Likewise, an Institute report described the key Institute function as helping the immigrant "to carry over and keep his attachment to the arts of his people." Bremer realized that the sense of nationality constituted a most important factor in the self-concept of immigrants in any new country. "This should not only be respected, but used as a basis for group and community interests." She thus saw cultural continuity as worthwhile in a practical sense. "There is no richer material for cultural growth than that which can be saved for the foreigner out of his own inheritance." Her pluralistic commitment even reached into the sensitive area of religion. While assimilationists subtly (and often overtly) attacked the religious background of immigrants, Bremer saw the need "to have restored the broken religious affiliations." She argued that "American Protestant ways should not be thrust upon the young women of other Christian churches. We believe their own ways are best for them."[5]

Thus the national Institute advocated, and local institutes undertook, the organizing of nationality associations to preserve ethnic identity and serve immigrant interests; opened facilities for diverse nationality, family, and religious events; and sponsored programs stressing immigrant values and abilities.

The international folk festivals emerged as a popular way to preserve and reinforce immigrant arts and cultural heritage. By 1935 the national Institute could report that forty-five communities held festivals that year. It was in St. Paul, Minnesota, that the Institute began its festivals, and that city remained in the vanguard of festival achievement.[6]

At the usual three-day festivals in St. Paul, representatives of ethnic communities danced and sang in native costume, displayed their arts, and provided ethnic foods at nominal prices. All participants, numbering about six thousand by 1942, worked as unpaid volunteers, including Institute employees. Immigrant participants, however, did most of the work. "This was truly a people festival; that is, it belongs to the people who were creating it for their pleasure and for the values it held for them," said St. Paul Institute festival founder Alice Sickels.[7]

The festivals had several purposes. They were intended to illustrate to Americans the strength and beauty in ethnic diversity and teach immigrant groups to accept each other. "All of them, old and new Americans alike," Institute founder Sickels stated, "need first of all an opportunity to know one another, and in order to get acquainted, people must do something together." A committee of the foreign-born designed and built old-world streets for their festivals, recreated the dances and songs often lost in migration, rented the necessary building, printed programs, and planned entertainment programs for over thirty thousand people. This brought together numerous ethnic groups that ordinarily had little to do with each other.[8]

The festivals implicitly argued, and vividly illustrated, the worth of immigrant culture and the desirability of its preservation, providing self-esteem to ethnic communities. It was through the festivals then, that the Institute attempted to preserve immigrant culture. Before the St. Paul festivals were initiated, local ethnic groups had never performed their dances and songs outside ethnic halls or the Institute building. Indeed, many people had forgotten the old dance steps; the costumes had sometimes worn out or been lost during the migration period. The Institute's goal of culture preservation was expressed in the 1934 program: "It is their hope that the cultural gifts of the immigrant may be preserved at least in part in their adopted country." According to a leader of the St. Paul Polish community, "the International Institute had given the Polish people in St. Paul back their culture." He explained that they had always been on the defensive under German, Russian, or Austrian control and that "even in America they were expected to forget Poland. But the festival of nations awakened the interest of the second generation in their own background." A Croatian woman added: "We Croatians never used to dance the old dances in our halls. We were ashamed of them. . . . Now our children dance with us, and we wear our old country costumes."[9]

Of course, the festivals did not emerge suddenly as a full-blown success. The St. Paul program began modestly, organized primarily by immigrant women from the eighteen nationalities that made up the St. Paul Institute's advisory council. The first festival was held in 1932 in a small YWCA auditorium. As many as thirty-five hundred people attended and fifteen nationalities took part. A year later, at an outdoor site, five thousand attended with twenty nationalities involved. From there it quickly grew to twenty-eight foreign nationality groups, including, in 1934, American Indians. Two years later, the village square and shops representing thirty countries were added. They became a major feature of subsequent festivals. By the end of the decade local Blacks became part of the program. In 1942, approximately six thousand participants took part and thirty-two thousand people attended the three-day event. St. Paul considered the international festival a major city attraction.[10]

Through festivals and other similar commitments, International Institute workers encouraged consciousness and pride in the immigrant heritage, fostered interethnic cooperation and understanding, and emphasized the ethnic contribution to American life. They urged newcomers to retain their native language and customs while simultaneously learning American ways. The Institute movement as a whole attempted "to restore a normal way of life for transplanted people."[11]

In Boston, Philadelphia, and San Francisco, International Institute workers sought to adhere closely to the pluralistic ideals laid down by Edith Terry Bremer. In Boston, for instance, Institute director Marion Blackwell fully agreed with Bremer's thinking on maintaining ethnic pluralism. In a 1938 letter to the Armenian newspaper *Hairenik*, Blackwell wrote, "I believe it is disastrous to sever old-country traditions and ties, and I do not believe in the melting pot idea which would make all people in America of one kind." Similarly, Annie Clo Watson, director of the San Francisco Institute from 1932 until the 1950s, asserted, "We do not want the people who come from older countries to become Americanized"; rather, Watson contended, "our purpose is . . . to help them feel at home in the American community while keeping their own customs." Consequently, through group and community work, Institute workers aimed to preserve and pass on the old-country traditions and tongues, thus fostering ethnic pluralism and cultural diversity.[12]

The community organizing and group work of the Boston International Institute reveals the variety of pluralist programming. The South Boston Armenian Women's Club, for example, had classes not only in American history but in Armenian history. Similarly, an Italian girls' club met weekly at the Institute to study Italian history, language, and literature. The Institute's Greek worker helped organize an Orthodox Young People's Christian Association, which studied Greek language and history and put on plays and concerts. The South End Greek Mothers' Club met at the Institute monthly to read and discuss Greek literature. A Syrian Girls' Club met at the

Institute to study Arabic, and a Syrian Mothers' Club met for lectures in Arabic and to sing Arabic songs. Ukrainians, Russians, Germans, and Swedes gathered at the Institute for folk dancing and folk singing, Finns for Finnish musical activities, Russians for Russian language classes, and Poles for the study of Polish history and culture. Russian and Czech groups sponsored lectures on the history of their respective homelands. And in the mid-1930s, the Boston Institute conducted a series of weekly radio broadcasts celebrating the musical accomplishments of Poles, Swedes, Finns, Russians, Greeks, Chinese, and other ethnic groups. In all these ways, the Boston International Institute encouraged communal efforts in support of pluralism and ethnic identity.[13]

In Philadelphia, the International Institute was engaged in a similar kind of community effort. As in Boston, most of the Institute's cultural programs were carried out through group work with numerous affiliated clubs. A Polish Students' Club, for instance, had classes in the Polish language and put on Polish plays in the community. An Armenian Girls' Club, organized to study Armenian literature, made it a point "to carry on all their meetings in Armenian so that they may have practice in the language of their parents." The Young German Circle was interested in rescuing old traditions and in the revival of old German folk songs, folk dances, folk costumes, and art, while another German society pursued "German gymnastics." Several Italian organizations studied Italian art, music, and literature, and groups of Finns, Russians, Swedes, and Ukrainians engaged in similar efforts. Some forty-three cultural and ethnic community groups met regularly at the Philadelphia International Institute during 1933—a typical year—and total attendance exceeded eighteen thousand.[14]

A similar pattern prevailed in the San Francisco International Institute. This social agency sponsored a variety of group and cultural activities, working with such diverse groups as Armenian, Polish, German, Mexican, and Swedish folk-dance clubs, an Italian Choral Club, a Russian Literary Society, a Mexican Singing Society, Russian, Greek, and Danish orchestras, a Japanese Girls' Club that studied Japanese literature, a Filipino Mothers' Club that put on plays in the Filipino community, and (in 1933) fourteen separate Chinese cultural groups and clubs. In all of these community and group activities, the International Institute strongly emphasized old-country musical, dramatic, artistic, dancing, and handicraft traditions.[15]

Immigrant cultures were similarly highlighted by the big folk festivals sponsored by most International Institutes throughout the 1920s and 1930s. Most Institutes also put on a variety of international banquets, handicraft exhibits, harvest balls, Christmas festivals, and similar events that built a spirit of pluralism, cooperation, and community among the newcomers. Programs of this kind at the Philadelphia Institute, for instance, included "folk story nights" at which Institute clubs used music, drama, and puppetry to illustrate nationality legends and folk tales; "internationality dinners," which featured immigrant songs and dances as well as foods; and Christmas parties and festivals portraying Christmas in many lands. Illustrating the cultural variety of such events, the program of an international Christmas party at the San Francisco Institute in 1930 consisted of "Russian kindergarten children, Chinese girls singing Christmas carols, Russian soloists, Greek group dancing, Swedish Christmas songs and dances, English carolers and finally the singing in unison of 'Holy Night' by the various nationalities, each in his own native tongue."[16]

All these events had a broad educational impact on the immigrant communities. They built bridges of understanding between the old and the new, between children and parents, and between newcomers and old-stock Americans. They contributed to ethnic, cultural, and language maintenance. Immigrants regained a measure of pride in their heritage. The second generation came to appreciate and respect the native customs and traditions of their parents. The essential message of the International Institutes was that diversity rather than conformity, cooperation rather than conflict, was the essence of American democracy. Clearly, these Institute cultural activities were extraordinary efforts at community organization and education.

While they promoted ethnic pluralism through community organization, the International Institutes also sought to explain immigrant traditions and cultures to native-born Americans. "Half of the problem," Edith Bremer wrote, "is the education of Americans as to who these foreign born are and what their groups have done for civilization and for this country." These were especially significant objectives during the post–World War I years when nativism, the "Great Red Scare," and the movement for immigrant restriction added impetus to the demand for rapid assimilation. When Bremer wrote in the early 1920s, "We do not believe in the superiority or the dominance of any race. . . . We believe in the worthiness of each race of people," she confronted numerous national trends such as the rise of the Ku Klux Klan, the culmination of Jim Crow legislation, a nationwide nativist movement, the effort to end immigration (supported by the "liberals" of the day), and the widespread belief that Blacks, Mexicans, and eastern and southern Europeans were racially inferior to Americans of western European background. Her ideas, although common today, were scorned by a wide range of political factions during the 1920s.[17]

Within the context of this cultural pluralism, the International Institutes both provided national services and directed and trained local people for community work in various American cities. The national Institute also continued the services that the YWCA Bureau had started. The Institute sent bulletins, reports, and government releases to local agencies and Institute affiliates throughout the country. The first annual report issued by the new national Institute in 1935 pointed out that "local officials have been kept in constant touch with important legislative issues on immigrant matters being considered in Congress." Actually, more than fifty cooperating agencies received Institute materials in 1935. The Institute provided lectures for various kinds of organizations, explaining concepts inherent in the agency's pluralistic approach. In 1935 the national Institute staff also lectured to WPA recreational leaders, to other national groups (forty separate addresses), and gave ten additional lectures on naturalization laws and naturalization proceedings. In addition, the Institute office helped students from numerous universities conduct research on immigrant life and problems. The national agency serviced two hundred requests for folk art and folk festivals in 1935.[18]

At immigrant entry stations, the Institute provided counseling in many "problem" areas. These included separation of families in the process of immigrating into the country, deportations that the Institute considered unwise and illegal, denial of entry upon return to the United States after many years of American residence, deportation of foreign-born people for receiving care in a hospital supported by public funds, arrival in the United States with incomplete or inaccurate documents, forcible payment of high bonds to secure admission of visiting foreign relatives, and detentions of ill immigrants for many weeks at immigrant-station infirmaries. Institute workers each year counseled and processed thousands at these centers and continued contact and aid when the immigrants arrived at their local destinations. Thus, work on the national level overflowed into resident communities.[19]

"The story of the development of 'private' social work for the immigrants and for the foreign communities is the story for the immigrants themselves." So wrote Edith Bremer in describing International Institute work. This description had particular significance on the local level where the Institute trained the foreign-born to provide for themselves the various services needed in the immigrant community. Local International Institute affiliates had similar approaches but often had to respond to different kinds of crises. In addition, a high degree of autonomy resulted in greater efficiency in meeting unique needs of different populations, which faced concerns that were more similar than different. Thus the Institutes, for the most part, carried out parallel activities.[20]

When a new immigrant family arrived in a city, an Institute nationality worker dedicated to help "in the immediate social adjustment" became one of its first visitors. The local Institutes carried out continuous home visiting and social casework in the foreign communities, but only, as an Institute report stated, "on grounds understandable and acceptable to foreign communities themselves."[21]

If the immigrant had to fulfill any additional government bureaucratic requirements, the Institutes stood ready to help and to mediate between the newcomer and the government. If the immigrant needed services from other social agencies, the Institute helped translate and interpret these needs. International Institutes, Bremer explained, "cannot escape from serving to a certain extent as social mediators between the foreign-thinking worker and the unconsciously American-minded agencies."[22]

In order to interpret fully the problems of individuals within communities of the foreign-born and to realize what was acceptable to these communities, Institute workers had to have a real understanding of the foreign-born. This was attempted in two ways. First, the Institutes staffed their agencies to make full use of foreign-born talents. International Institute personnel typically consisted of two elements: American "secretaries" (i.e., administrators) with professional social work training, and nationality community secretaries having, as an Institute document explained, "the tools of language and of intimate knowledge of the arts, the religion, the code of morality, the social concepts of family life, of community conduct, of law and government." Thus, the Institutes had personnel "who understood the culture of their people because they had lived its life."[23]

Institute nationality secretaries received in-service casework training, had language tools for direct communication with their immigrant community, were a familiar figure to that community (lessening inhibitions in dealing with the agency), and most important, had a thorough understanding of the old country. Bremer believed, "The American with an acquired insight and an acquired tongue cannot substitute for a bona-fide representative of another country who has come to love America."[24]

The Institutes' staffs used research as a second method of understanding foreign-born communities. They usually took a periodic census of the foreign-born, compiled background studies of life and culture in the countries of their origin, and studied the history and development of the various ethnic groups in the United States and in the local community. They tried to understand the overall culture of the foreign community, and they recognized the considerable role nationality had as a social force. By studying and accepting the old- and new-world situation, the Institutes could better confront what Bremer described as "the effect upon family life and . . . the incessant conflict between the folk-ways of the old-world habitant and folk-ways of the new American environment." And in truly understanding the situation, the Institute could interpret it and become an authoritative resource on immigrant life to the Americans of that community.[25]

Institute leaders realized that individuals, especially immigrants, exist in groups and that the most effective effort would result from group work. "We believed," an Institute report noted, "that the nationality sense is naturally a dominant factor for any foreigner during early years of life in the new society." And it added that "nationality sense" should be "used as a basis for group and community interests." Institute spokespersons, both locally and nationally, realized the hold of the immigrant community over its individual members. These communities of "co-nationals exercise a powerful influence. Upon questions of propriety, loyalty, behavior, it exercises what must be recognized as public opinion, as social pressure," Bremer pointed out. She argued that "the nationality community is our working unit" since "work for the individual is inseparable from the interest in and cultivation of the nationality community that circumscribes her life." Because International Institute spokespersons understood the European homelands, they believed "community based work also responded best to the immigrant heritage." The small group organization appeared to be the best substitute for the old-country town, society, or village sociability. "The art lies in discovering the common interest."[26]

So the Institute arranged groups "to bring persons together, out of their homes for friendly interchange on some basis of common interests." They came to the Institutes for classes, parties, to plan festivals, to discuss and engage in politics, or whatever the community needed to carry out. To secure the support of the nationality community and its leaders, to develop ethnic self-expression, to form nationality organizations, and to work together, the International Institute considered it "necessary to promote community organization." With the groups formed and participating in a familiar and comfortable environment, among friends who "they know appreciate their people," the member groups began to work together. The Institutes stressed objectives in which the whole of a nationality community could take an interest, as well as those that different nationalities could enjoyably share.[27]

Although involved in the International Institutes' local activities, community organizations of the foreign-born determined their own

directions. Once organized, they needed very little support from Institute personnel. The Institutes often initiated and fostered such organizations until they achieved "self-maintenance." Once the groups
functioned effectively, they assumed much of the work and control
not only of their own groups, but also of the International Institutes.

Whether the Institutes communicated with people with different languages and cultures, or operated citizenship classes, or organized singing groups, or established informal educational activities,
or served as interpreters between the European parents and the
American child (each having different ideas of social conduct), they
carried out their functions with considerable direction from the immigrant communities themselves. An International Institute publication listed one of its major goals as having "immigrants participate
in the work of International Institutes . . . to share in councils on its
policies and its programs and in responsibility for its support and
maintenance." Often the immigrant involvement went even further
than these ambitious objectives.[28]

The Institutes expected their constituency eventually to take over
and participate in the management of the Institute themselves. Immigrant leaders soon became the majority on local boards and assumed
key roles on major operating committees. As nationality secretaries
rose in the administrative hierarchy, and as second-generation social
workers joined Institute staffs, the Institutes became even more representative of the nationality groups. The Institutes, which began as
an elite American Protestant concern to help immigrants, evolved
into agencies directed and in part controlled by the ethnic communities themselves.[29]

How did this arrangement and extensive immigrant involvement
in, and even direction of, Institute activities work out in specific situations? An examination of the International Institute of Gary, Indiana, will make concrete the typical pattern of Institute activity carried out in many other urban immigrant centers. Under the direction
of Agnes B. Ewart, and later of Maude Cooley Polk, Gary's Institute
began in 1919 in the basement of a branch library. Four nationality
workers made up the staff—one each for Gary's Polish, Czechoslo-
vakian, Bulgarian, and Italian communities. All the workers spoke
several languages and handled other ethnic groups as well as their

own. By the mid-twenties, an expanded staff included Mexican, Serbian, and Greek nationality workers. These workers attempted to serve immigrant needs, preserve ethnic identity, and "international-ize" the community by promoting mutual understanding and respect among ethnic groups and between natives and newcomers.[30]

Although American settlement house leaders had advanced such ideas in earlier years, language difficulties, immigrant opposition, and insufficient understanding of ethnic traditions had frustrated all but a few immigrant-oriented settlement house programs. Gary's In-stitute staff recognized their objectives and the use of immigrant so-cial workers as new and unusual. "Existing social workers had never approached the problem from our angle," Bulgarian nationality worker Luba Tzvetanova wrote in her monthly report for September 1919. "Their basis has been plain charity, very often with utter lack of sympathetic understanding for the party concerned." The Insti-tute worker hoped to be "a friend in every day life first, and then a friend in need."[31]

During the twenties, Gary's International Institute channeled considerable energies into individual service and casework. Contacts with church and community leaders in ethnic neighborhoods served to introduce nationality workers to immigrant families. During the Institute's first decade, nationality workers handled as many as five and six hundred individual cases each month. Most of these dealt with legal problems or paper work involved in immigration and citi-zenship. Typical cases were recorded in the monthly report for Sep-tember 1920: Institute workers helped prepare necessary affidavits to bring workers' families to the United States; aided families in getting "their kinsfolk off from Ellis Island"; visited a Chicago jail to assist a Bulgarian woman sentenced to deportation; secured payment for a woman in Lithuania on property owned in the United States by her dead husband; helped several immigrants settle affairs in America so they could return to Europe. In addition, they visited people in hos-pitals; directed those in need to physicians and free medical clinics; found employment for men and women; got college scholarships for boys and girls (mainly at American International College in Spring-field, Massachusetts); assisted with income tax difficulties; located relatives in Europe; made applications for passports, citizenship, and soldiers' compensation; interceded with immigration authorities on behalf of immigrants; wrote and translated letters in many languages; even secured a divorce for an immigrant woman whose husband loved "good times," which "he carried in a bottle in one of his big coat pockets." Serving the varied needs of immigrants with diligence and respect, the International Institute soon made itself an indispensable community agency.[32]

In addition to doing individual casework, the Institute promoted ethnic-group activities that sometimes helped immigrants adjust to life in the United States. For instance, nationality workers organized English classes, mainly for foreign-born women and girls at first. Such classes were established at the Institute and in immigrant homes for Italians, Russians, Poles, Greeks, Mexicans, Romanians, and others. Polish and Greek women were reported to be the most ambitious and eager English students. Institute workers attributed the reluctance of others to opposition from husbands. The Institute's annual report for 1922 recorded one husband's feeling about education for his wife: "She old, she no learn nothing, she hard head." Despite such attitudes, English classes for women continued into the 1930s. Essay contests on such topics as "My Life in America," "My Experiences at Ellis Island," and "What I Think about Immigration" generated enthusiasm for English classes, as did the five-dollar prizes awarded to winners. By the mid-twenties, the Institute sponsored classes for men as well. The U.S. Steel Corporation and its several Gary subsidiaries helped finance Institute classes for workers. During the depression, when the Gary public schools discontinued free adult English classes, the Institute expanded its educational program. Later, New Deal programs provided the Institute with FERA and WPA instructors. While the International Institute resisted full-blown Americanization, it saw only advantages in teaching immigrants the language skills needed to adjust to life in the industrial city.[33]

Although the Gary Institute considered English an important tool for survival in a new environment, it regarded preservation of the immigrant heritage as equally important. Thus, building ethnic consciousness through group activities became one of the organization's most significant tasks. The Institute opened its facilities to existing immigrant clubs, mutual aid societies, and social organizations, while nationality workers helped organize new ethnic associations throughout the city. Gary affiliates of such national ethnic organizations as the Polish National Alliance, the Sons of Italy, and the Croatian Catholic Union worked with the Institute. Other Institute-based organizations sprouted locally and included the Czechoslovak Liberty Club, the Polish Mechanics Society, the Free Poland Society, the Russian-Slavonic Mutual Aid Society, the Lithuanian Political Club, the League of Italian Families, the Serbian Society, the Albanian Society, the Mexican Sociedad Protectora, and the Hidalgo Society. Some emphasized a particular avocation or served women and children: the Serbian Dramatic Club, the Russian Independent Musical and Dramatic Club, the Mexican Knitting Club, the Polish Women's Club, the Mexican Women's Club, the Assyrian Women's Society, the Polish Children's Club, and the Sokol Gymnastic Union. In 1924, seventy-two different groups used Gary Institute facilities for 472 meetings, with a total attendance of 14,582. Immigrant groups and families also used Institute rooms for weddings, receptions, christenings, dancing, card parties, holiday celebrations, and Christmas parties. The Institute encouraged such group activities as a means of maintaining ethnic ties and immigrant culture.[34]

If the Institute served as a gathering place for Gary's immigrants, nationality workers also kept in close touch with happenings in ethnic neighborhoods. They attended immigrant churches, met with community leaders to discuss common problems, and worked closely with schools and teachers. During a two-month period in 1919, in addition to all their other activities, nationality workers attended the dedication of the Greek church and a Russian cemetery; made contacts with Russian, Serbian, and Croatian priests; attended services at a Serbian church and temple Israel; visited classes at several schools; went to a Croatian glee club rehearsal, a Russian dance, a Russian concert, an Italian Columbus Day celebration, and five Greek, Mexican, and Bulgarian coffee houses; and accepted invitations to parties given by Russians and Bulgarians. Group work within the immigrant neighborhoods made other Institute programs successful.[35]

To build ethnic pride and to cushion cultural shock, every International Institute emphasized cultural programs based on immigrant traditions. From the outset, the Institutes rejected prevailing demands for complete assimilation and conformity. Through concerts, dances, festivals, plays, and exhibits, Institute nationality workers sought to preserve and enhance the immigrant heritage while simultaneously broadening American culture. An undated memorandum from the National Board of the YWCA presented Institute assumptions:

> America has an opportunity no other country has ever had—the opportunity of assimilating the old traditions of many lands into a new tradition of her own. The International Institute, because of its geographical situation in the heart of the foreign section of our great industrial towns, is afforded a uniquely favorable chance for developing this new tradition based on the festivals and songs, the art and handicraft, the folklore and customs of other races.

Accepting the need for Institutes to deal realistically with the social and economic problems of immigrants, the memo further urged nationality workers to be alive to possibilities for "capturing the beauty of earlier civilizations in order to preserve it for future generations in America." For newcomers, involvement in immigrant community activities and programs would build pride in one's heritage and provide a "wholesome outlet" for "excess energy" previously expended "in the stifling dance hall, the movie theater, or on the street corners of the crowded cities." Special emphasis was placed on working with immigrant children, who too often "scornfully cast aside the colorful language and symbolic customs of their forefathers" and "all too rapidly assimilated the movie, jazz and the gutter speech of the modern American city."[36]

Nationality workers at the Gary Institute accepted the principles of the YWCA memo and enthusiastically promoted immigrant cultural programs. Each year the Institute sponsored festivals, "harvest pageants," Christmas plays, concerts, folk singing, folk dancing, exhibits of arts and handicrafts, international banquets and dinners, and special affairs on immigrant holidays. Occasionally, immigrant clubs held lectures on the art, literature, and history of native countries. Institute-sponsored foreign-language classes for American-born children of immigrants sought to maintain ethnic languages.[37] The National Board of the YWCA in New York continuously distributed books, pamphlets, handbooks, bibliographies, and mimeographed materials to aid the cultural activities of local nationality workers.[38] Beyond building immigrant pride and self-respect, such group programs, because they often involved many different nationalities in a single project, helped promote interethnic understanding. Institute workers considered the establishment of mutual respect among nationality groups to be one of their most important objectives. Thus, they brought immigrant women together for "international" luncheons and teas and helped organize an International Girls' Club. Numerous other Institute activities had the same goal, as when a Hungarian Gypsy Orchestra provided music for an Italian Club affair or when the Polish Girls' Club made costumed dolls for Mexican children as a Christmas project. A "hard times dance" in 1921 included people from eight different nationalities. Such Institute programs eased adjustment to industrial America for immigrants from rural villages, while simultaneously helping them resist total orthodoxy and Americanization.[39]

The Gary Institute also tried to temper nativist bigotry by familiarizing Americans with immigrant traditions and contributions. The task was far from easy in the intolerant twenties. In her annual report for 1921, executive director Maude Polk wrote, "We often feel that our biggest job is in educating American-born Americans in knowing and appreciating the foreign-born American." The Institute invited the public to most of its festivals and exhibits, while local newspapers publicized Institute activities. In addition, nationality workers spoke on Institute work at meetings of the PTA and other Gary organizations. When hostility to Mexicans intensified with soaring immigration from south of the Rio Grande in the 1920s, the Institute engaged in a "constant effort to break down prejudice against Mexicans through talks before various groups." The goal of establishing mutual understanding and respect between natives and newcomers made the International Institute an important force for progress and social welfare in the Steel City.[40]

The Institute worked for progress and reform in other areas as well. It developed a recreational program, for example, designed especially to take advantage of the rapidly diminishing natural beauties of the area. By 1919 U.S. Steel had appropriated for industrial use twelve unbroken miles of Lake Michigan beachfront, effectively preventing Gary residents from using the lake for recreational purposes. Yielding to pressures during the 1919 steel strike, the company donated 116 acres to the city for a lake-shore park. But because it was located about six or eight miles from the center of town, few workers used its facilities. Indeed, in 1920 Institute workers reported numerous immigrants who had lived and worked in Gary for as long as twelve years and had never seen Lake Michigan. The Institute established a summer camp on the beach at Miller, then a small village east of Gary. Immigrant clubs and supervised groups of boys and girls used the camp for beach parties, picnics, swimming, and overnight outings.[41]

In addition to family casework, educational programs, and group activities, nationality workers became involved in a multiplicity of community affairs during the Institute's first decade. They encouraged "Big Sister" work to prevent female delinquency. They promoted public health with baby clinics, hygiene courses for immigrant women, and posters listing good health habits. They raised funds for numerous social welfare projects (on one occasion collecting money to purchase cribs for an Ellis Island nursery). They circulated petitions in 1923 calling for introduction of the city manager plan in Gary. In 1925 nationality workers cooperated with settlement houses and other social agencies in a study of housing in the Black ghetto on the "unlovely south side of Gary." In one of its most ambitious projects, the Institute in 1929 made a detailed social survey of Gary's immigrant communities. Focusing on Greeks, Poles, and Mexicans, nationality workers interviewed neighborhood leaders and residents on their European backgrounds and American experiences, compiling the information in a detailed report for the National Board of the YWCA (other Institutes throughout the country made simultaneous surveys of immigrant communities). Throughout the twenties, the International Institute combined social welfare goals with social reform fervor.[42]

The Great Depression of the 1930s brought observable changes of emphasis to some Institute programs. The Institute continued its cultural activities and ethnic group work. However, with massive unemployment in the steel mills in the early thirties, the Institute took on some of the characteristics of a welfare agency as well. The Institute's report for December 1932 poignantly described the immigrants' plight, "Men who have not yet brought their families to this country can neither bring them nor send money for their support; lack of proper food and medical attention has resulted in serious health problems; homes which were only partially paid for are being lost; clothing is wearing out and cannot be replaced; gas, electricity and water have been shut off." Many transient workers, men thrown out of jobs elsewhere, flocked to Gary in search of employment, compounding welfare needs.[43]

The Institute saw its main task as giving a "psychological lift" to those suffering "the long strain of discouragement and diminishing resources." But, recognizing that "moral support is quite indigestible on an empty stomach," the Institute also provided some relief. It distributed milk and second-hand clothing to the immigrant poor. Rummage sales, dances, and other affairs raised small sums for relief. During winter months, the Institute secured permits for dependent families to cut firewood on Gary Land Company property. The Institute distributed candles to those whose electricity had been shut off for nonpayment of bills. On behalf of immigrants, Institute workers interceded with local relief officials, who too often discriminated against the foreign-born. As the New Deal programs began in 1933, the Institute arranged jobs for young men in the Civilian Conservation Corps, and later secured work for unemployed laborers on public projects. In addition, it helped provide free transportation for Mexicans and Europeans who wanted to return to their native lands.[44]

As the depression deepened, nativist hysteria mounted. Voluntary departure soon became forced expulsion. Newspapers and articles in national periodicals demanded deportation of aliens to reduce relief rolls or widen job opportunities for American workers. Gary's relief agencies frequently denied aid to men with foreign or "communistic" ideas. Immigrants who had never become American citizens were especially vulnerable to the new intolerance of the thirties. High naturalization fees prevented many unemployed aliens from becoming citizens during the depression. Much of the Institute's work in the thirties dealt with naturalization problems. The

Institute helped people who had entered the United States under false names, who had lost entry papers, who could furnish no proof of residence prior to 1906 (when the United States government began registering immigrants), or who could not remember the date of their arrival or the name of the ship that brought them. With typical ingenuity, Institute workers solved the difficulties of a man who "left Europe when it was time to dig potatoes and landed in New York on a rainy Saturday." Special citizenship classes, even radio programs, speeded the naturalization process for aliens who might otherwise have been deported. As the Institute noted in its report for December 1932, "We have had to be on guard constantly to see that the foreign people secured the justice and fair treatment which they deserved. . . . This is especially true of the Mexicans."[45]

The experience of the Gary Mexican community reflected the resurgence of intolerance in the United States during the trying depression years. Economic pressure caused 90 percent unemployment in the steel mills and heavy demands on local welfare agencies. A local American Legion post first promoted the idea of "repatriation." Many Mexican immigrants had retained Mexican citizenship; indeed, many had been imported illegally by labor recruiters from railroad and steel companies, making naturalization all but impossible. Mexicans thus had few defenses against involuntary deportation. To speed the removal process, public officials denied relief to needy Mexican families and the steel mills refused to rehire Mexican workers without citizenship papers. In the early thirties, as many as fifteen hundred Gary Mexicans were returned to Mexico by truck and train under intolerable conditions, while another eighteen hundred were sent back from East Chicago, a nearby community with a similarly large Mexican population. Local welfare officials and native Americans viewed the repatriation movement as "an example of constructive relief," but International Institute workers soon saw it for what it really was—a new expression of nativist bigotry and racism. The Institute sought to protect Mexican interests as much as possible, aiding in the citizenship process and seeking relief and jobs for those discriminated against by public welfare agencies and steel mills.[46]

Institute support of Gary's troubled Mexican community typified the organization's efforts over two decades after its founding in 1919.

Throughout the twenties and the thirties, nationality workers fought against open intolerance and nativism. They developed programs to give newcomers the tools they needed to adjust to life in urban America, but they simultaneously countered insistent demands for rapid assimilation. Most important, the Institute encouraged immigrants to retain their traditions, languages, and customs, to be proud of their backgrounds. At a time when most Americans denigrated immigrants and condemned their different ways and "un-American" habits, Institute cultural programs helped the foreign-born maintain a sense of worth and importance. Like similar agencies in more than sixty American cities, Gary's International Institute eased the transition from the old world village to the new world metropolis. The Institute, rather than assimilating immigrants, helped them retain their old culture. Rather than Americanizing them the Institute helped immigrants adjust to the urban and industrial environment of twentieth-century America. Like few other organizations during the decades of intolerance and depression, the Institutes affirmed the values of a democratic, pluralistic society.

The International Institutes organized ethnic communities so that they could more effectively organize themselves. The Institutes provided research and guidance enabling nationality groups to rediscover themselves and proudly accept their heritage as a positive element in a pluralistic society. The Institutes also supported and defended their constituencies in confronting bureaucratic problems and political hostilities of the host society. In this way the Institutes also became focal points around which the ethnic communities could organize to counter bias and to achieve either individual or multiethnic goals.

5

Grass Roots Organizing in the Community Center Movement, 1907–1930

Robert Fisher

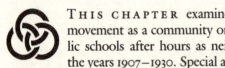 THIS CHAPTER examines the community center movement as a community organizing effort to use public schools after hours as neighborhood centers during the years 1907–1930. Special attention is given, in the earlier years, to the pioneering local efforts in Rochester, New York, and to the People's Institute in New York City; for the later years, case studies from a number of cities and surveys of the national movement form the data. Four basic questions are addressed: What did organizers assume were the community problem conditions? What were the stated goals of community organizers? What were their strategies? How did they structure the organization? The results suggest that this early community organization effort experienced four different, if overlapping, types of practice, which I call Community Development (1907–1914), Professional Planning (1915–

Source: Adapted from Robert Fisher, "From Grass-Roots Organizing to Community Service: Community Organization Practice in the Community Center Movement, 1907–1930," in *Community Organization for Urban Social Change: A Historical Perspective*, Robert Fisher and Peter Romanofsky, eds. (Westport, Conn.: Greenwood Press, Inc., 1981), pp. 33–58. Copyright © 1981 by Robert Fisher and Peter Romanofsky. Reprinted with permission.

1917), Community Mobilization (1918–1919), and Community Service (1920–1930). The sequence of practice in the community center movement went from efforts to get residents involved in grass roots community development to programs designed by organizers to deliver services to neighborhood residents.

Community Development, 1907–1914

The roots of the community center movement lie deep in the urban social reform movements of the 1890s and early 1900s. The first centers were founded by social settlement workers, public-recreation advocates, and civic reformers. Settlement workers such as Mary Simkhovitch and Mary Follett saw in community centers the essence of the settlement idea: using the neighborhood as an organizational unit for counteracting urban problems.[1] Recreation proponents viewed community centers as a logical extension of their efforts to expand the use of public schools beyond traditional academic functions.[2] Similarly, multifaceted urban reform organizations such as the People's Institute in New York City sought, in public-school community centers, appropriate and inexpensive sites for organizing neighborhood social and civic clubs.[3]

Edward Ward, who initiated the first social centers in Rochester, New York, in 1907, aptly expressed many of the underlying assumptions of problem conditions in his work *The Social Center*. Ward believed that neighborhood-based, democratic, "home-like" civic clubs could counteract the lack of effective and intelligent urban government and the disconnecting qualities of urban life.[4] Five years later, the People's Institute, a multifaceted reform organization, established the first social center in New York City in response to what its leaders perceived as the pressing problems of contemporary urban society: the prevalence of class segregation with its potential for dramatic class conflict; the large numbers of unassimilated, impoverished immigrants; and the rapid growth of "harmful" commercial leisure-time recreations, such as burlesque, pool halls, bars, and motion pictures.[5]

The stated goal of community centers in this initial phase was to assist community self-expression. Rothman and others would refer to this as a "process goal." A process goal seeks to foster collaboration, cooperation, and participation in self-help neighborhood projects. This differs from a task goal, which seeks to complete a concrete task or solve a community problem that is predetermined by community organizers.[6] The espousal of process goals is evident in a pamphlet written by Clinton Childs, the community organizer of the first social center in Manhattan.

> A community clubhouse and Acropolis in one; this is the Social Center.
>
> A community organized about some center for its own political and social welfare and expression; to peer into its own mind and life, to discover its own social needs and then to meet them, whether they concern the political field, the field of health, or recreation, of education, or of industry; such community organization is necessary if democratic society is to succeed and endure. There must be an [*sic*] unifying social bond of feeling, tradition, experience, belief and knowledge, a common meeting ground, spiritually and concretely speaking. But there must also be a community expression through activity, self-government and self-support.[7]

While organizers continued to voice process goals throughout this period, they never adopted the neutral role Childs suggests. Organizers hoped to guide as much as to stimulate community development. Moreover, process goals reflected more than the organizer's preference for a truly democratic community program. Being outsiders, organizers needed resident involvement to develop the new community institution and they sought to legitimize their work by emphasizing neighborhood self-help and citizen participation.[8]

The organization of each center followed a relatively similar pattern. First, a voluntary reform group secured limited funds and permission from local officials to use a public school as a test site. Next, a trained organizer was sent into the designated community to develop support for the social-center idea and to arrange for use of the school by clubs, organizations, and individuals. The organizer would help form a "neighborhood group" composed of local representatives appointed by the clubs that met at the center and "of prominent residents of the district who manifested an active interest in the project." The group would be under the direction of a "community secretary"—usually the initial outside organizer—who would plan, govern, and administer center activities with the assistance of the neighborhood group.[9]

Programs varied from city to city and from center to center. In Rochester, the school served as the site of a number of activities, but organizers there placed emphasis on "the importance of the school as a public forum where citizens of the neighborhood could discuss civic questions with absolute freedom."[10] In New York City, the People's Institute envisioned a wide-ranging program that included civic clubs, neighborhood information bureaus, literary clubs, ethnic pageants and festivals, motion pictures, amateur concerts, dramatic presentations, and athletic programs held in the school playground or gymnasium. As in Rochester, civic forums were established for the discussion of "subjects related to the everyday life of the People" and of "matters of intimate importance to the neighborhood," such as labor struggles and socialism.[11] But generally, activities at centers did not encourage fundamental social change or social action. This was partly the product of the organizers' limited goals and partly the result of using a public facility as the organizing site. Where center programs hinted at social action, as in Ward's effort in Rochester to develop centers into neighborhood-based reform groups, local officials cut appropriations and tightened supervision. Accordingly, the approach adopted was what sociologists label a "consensus strategy"—a reformist, socially approved method that does not threaten existing power relationships.

The organizational structure of these early efforts was designed, at least in theory, to promote process goals and to develop programs that would reflect the self-expression of the neighborhood. Centers were to be funded by neighborhood residents with a minimum of public assistance, and democratically governed "from the bottom up" through the neighborhood group. At first, public support, not self-support, was the goal of organizers. In Rochester, Ward's initial center was begun with a five-thousand-dollar allocation by the City Council to be expended by the Board of Education. But, with the victory at the polls some three years later of a faction opposed to "socialistic centers," appropriations were drastically cut.[12] Because of such political problems and because of the penchant of New York City progressives for fiscal austerity when considering public, social programs, the People's Institute advocated privately initiated and supported centers. Such centers combined dues from local residents and donations from upper-class-financed groups like the Institute with a limited allocation from the Board of Education to cover rent and maintenance of the building.[13]

The extent of resident participation in leadership of the centers is uncertain. Many contemporary commentators active in the movement trumpeted centers as self-governing and applauded the amount of resident participation in center decision making. But the lack of any concrete evidence of citizen participation in the neighborhood groups, and the comments of more detached observers, suggest strongly that organizing from the bottom up remained, at best, an unfulfilled ideal. Governance structure more closely resembled what Sherry Arnstein calls "partnership"—an organizational structure where professionals and citizens work together for community improvement.[14] But partnership was never very equal. Citizen participation was limited primarily to membership in the clubs and participation in center activities. While club and organization leaders may have participated in the neighborhood group, all concerned seemed willing to leave planning at the centers to the professional organizers who initiated the centers.

Community center organizers were strong proponents of the neighborhood ideal and of decentralization. They felt their goal of promoting solidarity between potentially conflicting groups in the metropolis could be achieved most simply at the neighborhood level. And the public school was the natural site for establishing community organizations in each neighborhood. Community centers, accordingly, were administratively and physically decentralized; that is, each center administered its own programs, and all activities were based in a local public school and oriented to the surrounding neighbors.[15]

By 1915, social centers had attracted considerable attention. Charles Evans Hughes, then governor of New York, told center organizers in 1910: "I am more interested in what you are doing than anything else in the world. You are witnessing the foundations of Democracy." The 1912 national campaign platforms of the Democrats, Republicans, and Progressives all endorsed the social center movement. At the local level, many centers prospered; by 1915, the center initiated at PS 63 in Manhattan became independent of direct financial ties with the People's Institute, achieving to a noteworthy, if limited, degree the goal of self-support and self-government.[16]

Professional Planning, 1915–1917

A few developments around and after 1915 point to an emerging second stage in the community center movement. The change in community organization practice is most apparent with the formation in 1916 of the National Community Center Association (NCCA) and with the multifaceted efforts of the People's Institute in the Gramercy district of Manhattan. But all centers initiated after 1915 were affected.[17]

Ideological assumptions regarding community problems shifted subtly. Fear of class conflict and concern with the "leisure-time problem" and the stratified, poorly integrated urban society remained. But organizers were now more concerned with the lack of coordinated social programs and services in neighborhoods, the lack of professional organizations to direct and develop community efforts, and the need to expand community programs beyond the public school in order to plan effectively for the entire community.

Goals shifted accordingly. Organizers now emphasized the need to coordinate social service resources, improve communication between existing services and potential consumers, and train professional community workers.[18] Task goals became more important than process objectives. Concern with community planning and professionalization superseded the earlier objective of neighborhood self-expression. Process goals were not suddenly dropped, nor was the emphasis on integrating neighborhood residents into community institutions forgotten. Community participation remained an ideal. But service delivery and professional coordination of activities took precedence over self-help goals in the years 1915–1917. This is illustrated in a description of the Community Clearing House, an effort designed by the People's Institute to support community center activities in the Gramercy neighborhood.

> Through this "neighborhood gateway to all the city's resources of helpfulness" any man, woman, or child, rich or poor, American or alien, can be placed in immediate touch with the service which he needs. He can

discuss his trouble, register his complaints at the effective point, and enlist himself as a nonpaid civil servant, helping his nearby or remote
neighbors.[19]

Types of programs at community centers continued relatively un-
changed. Forums and club meetings, for instance, continued to provide necessary recreational services for neighborhood residents. Additional programs that ultimately preoccupied organizers, however,
best exemplify the change in practice to professional planning. The
People's Institute, for example, organized a community center in 1915
at PS 40 as but one aspect of a larger project—a model neighborhood in the Gramercy district of Manhattan. The neighborhood
plan included coordinating existing social service programs, establishing the Training School for Community Workers and the Community Clearing House, conducting an investigation by health-care
professionals into neighborhood health conditions and facilities, as
well as running the community center.[20] Furthermore, in 1916, the
Institute and representatives of other organizations founded the National Community Center Association, a professional group of community organizers and social workers. The association sought to improve the practice of community work and provide direction and
unity to decentralized local efforts. But it also reflects clearly the new
types of professional-oriented activities that occupied the interests
and energies of leaders in the movement.[21]

Changes in organizational structure mirrored the rising professional concerns of organizers. The new emphasis at the centers
called for expert and scientific management of community centers.
As John Collier, a leader of the People's Institute organizing efforts,
declared, "Democracy needs science, and the community movement aims to put science—which means experts—into the people's
hands."[22] In practice, however, professionals were supervisors, not
advisors. When neighborhood groups were initiated at new centers,
professionals and persons prominent in reform efforts, not neighborhood residents, were appointed to fill the positions. New programs, such as the Training School, Clearing House, and NCCA,
were service oriented and were administered and governed completely by professionals. Mary Simkhovitch, a prominent leader of
the social settlement movement, saw the trend clearly. In 1917, at the

annual meeting of the NCCA, she admonished the audience by noting that only social workers, not center participants, were attending
the conference.[23]

Increased administrative centralization was also evident in both
the newly developed community centers and the effort to develop a
national professional association. In the Gramercy district, People's
Institute representatives played an increasingly large role in the
direction of center activities. This was partly attributable to the
broader goals and widespread programs in Gramercy; community
planning for the entire neighborhood demanded centralized control of all aspects of the plan. The development of the NCCA also
reflects the increased centralization. While the association was not
intended to supersede the local autonomy of neighborhood centers, the NCCA was initiated by community organizers who saw a
need to coordinate and unify neighborhood efforts at the national
level. While most community organizers during this period idealized the neighborhood as the natural organizational unit, they were
not parochial localists. Rather, they felt that coordination at the
national level and increased central direction of local efforts were
critical to the success of both the national movement and the local
centers.[24]

The third trend in organizational structure was the growing conflict between advocates of privately initiated and funded community
centers and those who demanded that these activities be controlled
by the public, that is, local government. The NCCA conference of
1916 pivoted on this single issue. Edward Ward, the speaker for the
public-support side, attacked the voluntary, self-support advocates,
who were led by John Collier of the People's Institute. Influenced by
the appeal of Margaret Wilson, the President's daughter, for public
support, the conference endorsed Ward's position.[25] But Collier was
not completely averse to or unfamiliar with the trend toward public
control of centers. In 1915, the New York City Board of Education
established a position of director of community centers. Most community organizers, Collier included, felt that more public supervision of community centers was necessary in view of the rapidly increasing number of centers throughout the city. But despite the
decision in favor of public support at the NCCA conference and the
expanding role of local governments, centers in New York City re-

mained largely the product of voluntary organizations working under the limited supervision and with the permission of city authorities. Public officials were simply not very interested in community centers at this point.[26]

By 1917, community centers, no longer referred to as social centers, existed throughout the nation.[27] But community organization practice in the centers was distinctly different from the earliest efforts of Ward and Childs. In this second stage, the lack of effective service delivery and community planning replaced community solidarity as the central problem condition; task goals superseded process objectives; consensus strategies persisted, but with less focus on grass roots organizing and political education; and organizational structure grew more centralized, professional, and bureaucratic. Why did these changes occur? According to the People's Institute, the initial experiment in community development was a success, and, by 1915, it was necessary for the Institute, as an innovator in the newly emerging field of community work, to move on to larger-scale projects such as the efforts in the Gramercy neighborhood and the formation of the NCCA. To some degree, this analysis is valid. As noted before, the social center begun by the Institute at PS 63 achieved limited self-support by 1915. Funding from the Institute was no longer necessary to maintain the center; the center was now paying for half of its costs, and the other half was paid for by the Board of Education. Assuming that their initial goals had been completed, Institute professionals sought to expand their program. As Zald and Denton note in their examination of YMCAs, this broadening of goals over time is fairly common.[28]

But with the practice of professional planning, goals and programs were not simply broadened. The more professional and task-goal orientation was the result not only of completing prior goals, as the Institute would have asserted, but of the organizers' seeking to implement changes more compatible with their actual goals and abilities.[29] Community development practice shifted to professional planning largely because the initial effort of organizers could not or did not seek to attract citizen participation at the level of decision making. Organizers thus had to shift their goals from developing self-help programs to creating professionally led, service-oriented programs. They shifted from seeking to work *with* to working *for* the neighborhood residents. Organizers undoubtedly sought to expand their programs and increase their effectiveness by adopting the more professional practice. But the shift of practice to professional planning was effected primarily by the lack of commitment to fulfilling the "from-the-bottom-up" goal of community development.[30]

Community Mobilization, 1918–1919

The entry of the United States into World War I introduced external factors into the community center movement that sealed certain trends begun in 1915 and altered the direction of others. In late 1917, the Federal Council of National Defense and local subsidiaries at the state and city levels organized a bureaucratic, centralized program to "nationalize neighborhoods" in support of domestic mobilization efforts. The community center movement enthusiastically supported this program, viewing it as official endorsement of the community center idea of organizing citizens and coordinating activities in cities at the neighborhood level.[31]

Obviously, the war altered basic assumptions of problem conditions. Neighborhood issues were de-emphasized as the more pressing national problem of war mobilization was made paramount. According to organizers, society was still too stratified, immigrants remained unassimilated and unrepresented, harmful commercial amusements continued to prosper, and community efforts lacked coordination. But the primary problem was the threat of Germany and the need to mobilize domestic resources against this enemy and in support of the U.S. war victory.

As the problem and the end became simpler and clearer than in prior years, goals became more focused. The mobilization effort demanded a type of community organization practice more dynamic and directed than simply community development or professional planning. Process goals became important again as the war mobilization sought to unite citizens and get them involved. But while organizers devoted much energy to getting residents active at the neighborhood level, the objective was not essentially one of process. Organizers did not encourage neighborhood determination of how or whether residents would support the war. Such activity would have been viewed as subversive. Rather, as before, but even more so now, process goals were designed to serve predetermined task goals. The task of center organizers was to coordinate local agencies and citizens in support of programs developed by the national, state, and city councils of defense.[32]

Programs were altered accordingly: Recreation became less important; forums were watched more closely for subversive activities; patriotic propaganda dominated motion-picture, civic-club, and social-club activities. Moreover, community centers became the sites for coordinating war-related activities such as Americanization, Red Cross relief, Liberty Loan drives, soldiers' aid work, and community thrift, food austerity, and nutrition programs.[33] Such programs again reflected the consensus strategy of community organizers—to unite all citizens in the "war to save democracy." But during the war period, the style of conflict tactics was introduced. Unlike a consensus strategy, which assumes a mutuality of interest in society, a conflict or confrontation strategy uses such tactics as protest and agitation to heighten the conflict between antagonistic and contending forces. During the war, an enemy target was the focus of activities, and organizers used extensive agitation and propaganda tactics to mobilize residents against the threat. This conflict style, however, is certainly different from the conflict strategy used by the Communist party in the 1930s or by Saul Alinsky in the 1940s, for example. For the community center movement, the enemy was not only outside the community, it was also beyond the borders of the nation; the goals were social stability and unity at home, not a restructuring of power and resources in the local community; and the programs were not only socially acceptable to, but initiated by, the Federal government. The war period thus offers a unique use by the government of conflict style in the service of consensus goals.

Organizational structure reflected the vast changes stimulated by the war and the Council of National Defense. Administrative and political centralization was formalized. National, state, and city councils of defense provided personnel, direction, and supervision of neighborhood community center activities. One participant at the

National Conference of Social Work in 1919 hoped, for example, that the "new community organization" of the war period would centralize and strengthen organizations, "swinging them in a solid front in one attack after another upon the pressing and urgent needs of the hour."[34]

Likewise, the move to public supervision of centers was accomplished during the war. In New York City, the Mayor's Council of Defense coordinated community programs on a citywide basis, and city officials were appointed to serve on neighborhood groups.[35] Self-support was still encouraged, but public funding achieved wider acceptance, and government control increased dramatically. During the war, thirteen states passed laws providing for the financing of community center activities by public taxation.[36]

The trend toward increased professional control of center activities was also furthered during the war. At PS 40 in the Gramercy district, twenty-eight professional representatives from public and private war-related agencies were appointed to the center's decision-making body. Community councils, the governing bodies at centers during the war, consisted of members appointed from above "and ratification by any more generally representative local body was said to be largely nominal."[37]

Centers prospered in a sense during the war years. Many commentators noted that the goals of developing "community action," "cooperative collectivism," and a concern for "mutual welfare" were facilitated at the local level by the demands and programs of the war.[38] Furthermore, the number of activities multiplied, and funds increased. The extent of coordination between agencies and recipients was unprecedented.[39] Community centers expanded throughout the nation. In 1919, one survey estimated, community centers were operating in more than 107 cities, not to mention the vast number of centers in communities with populations under five thousand people.[40] The whole "community movement" achieved widespread recognition and prestige during the war, recalled Jesse Steiner, the author of the first major study of community organization. While the word "community" was used infrequently prior to 1917, during the war it became a "magic talisman of value in dealing with social problems." As the power of government grew, Steiner added, "the local community took on a new significance for a democratic people unaccustomed to the inevitable centralization of the war period."[41]

Organizing practice had changed quickly and noticeably since 1917. Entry into the war altered assumptions of problem conditions and goals; strategy remained reformist, but the demands of mobilizing citizens to support the war encouraged a conflict-style approach; and, continuing and accelerating trends since 1907, organizational structure became highly centralized, professional, and bureaucratic. But whereas earlier shifts in practice were the result largely of internal developments, the shift from professional planning to community mobilization reflected the effect of a national, supralocal event.

Community Service, 1920–1930

The end of the war ushered in a new stage in organizing practice. Despite the hopes and efforts of reformers, postwar social reconstruction never became a national priority. The Council of National Defense bureaucracy was quickly dismantled, and voluntary organizations returned to more private and charitable activities. In 1920, the People's Institute, faced with declining funds and new leaders with little interest in social reform, withdrew completely from community organization work.[42] Nevertheless, the community center movement continued to expand; the number of cities operating centers more than doubled, from 107 in 1919 to 240 in 1924. Throughout the 1920s, community centers remained a significant element of community organization work from coast to coast. But the practice of community organization continued to change.

After the war, organizers viewed "urban disorganization" as the central problem condition. Urban disorganization was a catchall term for the negative social products of urban-industrial growth.[43] Among those problems noted most often were rapid social and geographic mobility, unassimilated immigrants, the superficiality of personal contacts, the decline in importance of neighborhood-based activities, the breakdown of community solidarity, and the growth of "crowd behavior."[44]

This "tangled web of modern urban life" required the "conscious organization of social forces," Eleanor Glueck asserted in her 1924 study of school centers.[45] As in the initial stage of community development, organizers in this period encouraged process goals to counteract urban stratification. In reaction against wartime experiences, organizers wanted to de-emphasize the service-oriented, bureaucratic trends of professional planning and community mobilization. Echoing the earlier sentiments of Clinton Childs, center organizers said that the function of centers "was not so much to hand down traditions, values, principles nor morals, but rather to form a matrix in which new values could be worked out by neighbors facing a new social situation."[46] But, as before, though certainly less so than during the war, organizers entered the community with specific goals in mind. While community work in the 1920s was labeled an "essential and continuous process," the primary goal of organizers was not to encourage self-help but actually to integrate, coordinate, and adjust groups of people "in the interest of efficiency and unity of action."[47]

Program offerings in the 1920s differed markedly from those of the war years: School community centers became synonymous in the public's mind with athletic programs, and activities related to social and political issues were few and far between.[48] In New York and other cities, two types of centers developed after the war: government "official centers" and private "permit centers." Official centers concentrated on athletic programs and typified the movement in the 1920s and thereafter. Permit centers were open fewer evenings each week but tended to sponsor more political discussions and social clubs. Neither, however, initiated or supported local efforts to "organize the community comprehensively." While the programs of the 1920s emphasized "expressive releasing" activities more than ever before, this approach was consistent with the consensus strategies and programs of earlier years.[49]

Activists in the community center movement were, from its inception, ambivalent about organizational structure. Like most professionals, they preferred autonomy, decentralized authority structures, and limited standardization and bureaucratization. They wanted as much personal freedom as possible. But they also wanted the resources and power that came with centralized, government support of centers. Local officials were equally uncertain. They liked the power and standardization that accompanied their active participation, but preferred the cost-saving features of center self-support and self-government.[50] In the 1920s, fresh from the bureaucratic experience of World War I, local officials came to accept community centers as part of city government's responsibility to supply social and recreational services. While community organizers remained ambivalent, local officials implemented a highly centralized and bureaucratic structure run by professionals who were appointed by city politicians. Meaningful grass roots participation was nonexistent.

As local governments expanded their control and support of centers, the role of private groups declined. Private groups wholly administered only 7 percent of all centers in cities. Public funds supported all activities at 44 percent of urban community centers, while 89 percent were financed at least partially by tax revenues. In New York City, while the number of permit centers exceeded official centers 225 to 68 in 1927 and 351 to 118 in 1930, the total aggregate attendance at the permit centers declined from 1,126,955 to 1,095,058; whereas at the official centers, there was a striking increase in attendance from 3,356,312 to 4,379,792. Official centers were better staffed and organized, but the primary reason for the large attendance was that they possessed the physical resources to offer many more activities, especially athletic programs.[51]

Many commentators found this trend distressing. They felt that the relative decline of privately controlled centers ran counter to the goals of developing cooperation and democracy at the community level. They were upset as well by the standardization and restrictions that accompanied bureaucratization. And yet, community organizers writing about these developments knew that the expanded public role was critical to maintaining centers and providing extensive recreational services in urban areas.[52]

Centralization accompanied bureaucratization. Centers were physically decentralized, but administrative and political centralization was the norm, continuing the pattern formalized by World War I. Decision making, especially at official centers, remained highly centralized as boards of education or parks and recreation departments assumed ever-greater control over community centers.[53]

Reflecting general attitudes of the decade, practitioners of community organization were skeptical and critical of earlier efforts. They ridiculed the simplistic, idealistic notions of "uplifters" prior to 1920. They sought to develop a more sophisticated, scientific approach—a more professional approach—to the practice of community organization. Community organization began to be viewed as a subdiscipline of the emerging field of social work, complete with its own extensive literature, methodology, and theoreticians such as Clarence Perry, Leroy Bowman, and Jesse Steiner.[54] In theory, organizers still sought to develop a partnership with community residents. But, as Bowman suggested, serving the complex needs of communities now superseded the question of democratic decision making. He noted that professional community workers remained open to resident participation in leadership

> if the need is felt and the leadership arises [from the community]. This is a far cry from the community religion of a few years ago when the drive was on to go out and get people into community organizations, democratic in the extreme and supposedly dominated by neighborly sentiments.[55]

What Bowman viewed as the religion of ultrademocracy was replaced, in the 1920s, by the ideal of an efficient and effective community organization led by sensitive and responsive professionals. Indigenous leadership in most types of community organizations, one "ultrademocrat" reported, was nonexistent or, at best, nominal. And the same was true for community centers. The process of formalization, especially at official centers, was accompanied by an increase in the number and role of paid professional staff. Organizers were aware of at least some of the problems inherent in both increasing professionalism and declining resident participation, but in the 1920s most accepted professional leadership as a fait accompli.[56]

In many ways, the school community center movement had come full circle by 1930. The first social centers were initiated by Ward and the People's Institute in response to the limits of school recreational centers. Recreational centers provided only recreational facilities and were governed, administered, and financed by reluctant and unpredictable local officials. Social centers were intended to develop a broader program rooted in resident participation and support. Now, altered by developments in the 1920s, centers were again largely recreational facilities administered and supported by local government bodies.[57]

Why these changes occurred in the 1920s defies simple explanation. Many of the developments reflect an oft-noted tendency of organizations to bureaucratization and formalization; in this case, both were stimulated by the war and were institutionalized in the 1920s. But there was more at work here than a natural order of organizational development. Of primary importance was the conservatism of the decade. The postwar years were generally hostile to social reform efforts. Organizers found little support, financial or otherwise, for their social change programs. Government-sponsored programs, even more than private ones, encouraged athletic, not political, activities. Community center goals, programs, and structures mirrored the "return to normalcy." The same was true in the social work profession. As Lubove notes, social work in the 1920s was characterized by the bureaucratic goals of efficiency and expert leadership. Of all social welfare practitioners, community workers were most inclined to criticize such goals. Glueck asserted, for example, that the one-dimensional, bureaucratic center of the 1920s opposed "the ideals set for it by leaders of the community organization movement." But most community workers were imbued with the new professional and more conservative values, and they were either unaware of or unwilling to challenge the departure from earlier objectives of the community center movement.[58]

Conclusion

The general sequence of community organization practice illustrated by the community center movement is as follows. Community development changed into professional planning as centers achieved legitimacy, began to broaden goals, but failed to enlist meaningful citizen participation. Professional planning developed into community mobilization as a drastic change occurred in objective conditions—namely, the entry of the United States into World War

I—and as a national bureaucratic structure was imposed on the community center movement. Community mobilization practice shifted into community service as the maintenance of centers became an accepted and expected responsibility of local government and as the climate for social reform efforts deteriorated. In sum, efforts quickly developed into professionally run social service organizations, and, except for a deviation caused by World War I, that pattern continued from 1915 through the 1920s.

The pattern underlines the essence of this type of community organization program. Organizations initiated by liberal social welfare professionals serve a primary role as interest groups on behalf of and as test cases for the official adoption of social service programs. When the value of the program is acknowledged, the social change, grass roots orientation is replaced by an almost complete preoccupation with delivering the social services. Community workers such as those who organized the first community centers may have hoped to do more in the way of community organizing, but social service delivery best suited their reformist vision and goals, consensus strategies, scanty resources and power, and professional orientation.

6

Rural Organizing and the Agricultural Extension Service

Michael J. Austin and Neil Betten

D U R I N G World War I and in the 1920s, agriculture extension agents engaged in community organizing. County extension agents disseminated farming and homemaking advice gained from research at land-grant colleges of agriculture.[1] National political and economic pressures for increased agricultural production for the war effort involved extension agents in the promotion of improved mechanization. During the urban depression of 1929 and the early 1930s, young people remained on farms rather than face unemployment in the city, and the extension service organized clubs for the eighteen to twenty-five age group.[2] In addition, extension agents during the agricultural depression of the early 1920s helped farmers shift from an emphasis on increasing production to the development of cooperatives in order to cut costs and market products.[3] As the 1930s depression deepened, extension workers also helped to clothe and feed the rural poor.[4]

One of the significant results of community organizing was the Farm Bureau Association, which grew out of a campaign launched in 1905 by the U.S. Department of Agriculture in the Southwest against the boll weevil. As an organization it emphasized local initiative and democratic forms of control. It followed a decade of experi-

94

ments by the federal Department of Agriculture with farm demonstration work organized on a county basis resulting in the passage of the 1914 Smith-Lever Act.[5] The Smith-Lever Extension Act had the effect of consolidating federal and state extension efforts in agriculture and home economics and of placing program administration and supervision in the land-grant colleges.[6] The Farm Bureau Association, together with the State Agricultural College and the Federal Department of Agriculture, employed county agents throughout a county, which was frequently divided into ten to twelve districts. In each district, a local committee was formed with a chairperson who became a member of the Board of Directors of a county association.

During the period of the 1920s, many rural areas ended their isolation. Automobiles and radio helped to increase communications between the universities and the farmers as well as between farmers. Farmers sought out contact with city businessmen who controlled the price the farmers received for their crops.[7] Between 1910 and 1930, the number of farms decreased, acreage per farm increased, and tenants operated more farms, a preview of today's large corporate farming system.[8] Agriculture grew more specialized and farmers traveled more frequently to socialize with others who shared their specialty.

The Agricultural Extension Agent

Community organizing was rooted in such methods as those practiced by John D. Hervey, a county agent in Southeastern Ohio who introduced home demonstration specialists to groups of farm wives. Hervey's home projects were very popular. Specialists instructed select groups of women, who went back to their own towns and held meetings that spread modern knowledge of clothing construction, child care, nutrition, first aid, and nursing throughout Washington County, Ohio. Hervey held "hill meetings" where he conducted demonstrations and introduced specialists to the farmers. Many graduates of his 4-H Clubs enrolled for the four-year course in agriculture at Ohio State and several returned to the county as indigenous leaders.[9]

Seaman Knapp, an early extension innovator, developed the idea of spreading the news through independent county correspondents.[10] Ohio county agents attended regional news-writing schools held by the extension service. Within a year, a number of agents were supplying county papers with farm items. Since 1924, 4-H youngsters have been trained in county correspondence to assist the old war-horses of the county press. One county weekly in Ashtabula County, where Howard Wauth was a young county agent, was packed with farm news sent in week after week.[11]

Another example of community organizing in rural Ohio was provided by township meetings held to share the common problems of raising corn. In Black Creek township in 1922, it was decided that during the next growing season a tar barrier against chinch bugs should be erected, and a seed-corn demonstration and a contest on different methods of raising corn should be held on the ten-acre tract of the university agricultural extension service. In such meetings the "discussion method" was used to promote the development of grass roots organizers among the farmers themselves and to improve communications between extension agents and the farmers.[12]

Extension agents worked with county councils made up of representatives from each of the organized farm groups (such as dairy, fruit, cotton, tobacco, vegetable, etc.) or of each community within the county. Representatives were chosen by the people in the community to participate in extension programs. County representatives were also elected at annual town meetings.[13] Four types of local leaders emerged in conjunction with extension programs: (1) liaison officers between the extension agents and the people; (2) demonstrators, who also enlisted the active participation of others and assumed responsibility for documenting the practices that were adopted; (3) representatives of the community or township, who received from the specialist or the home demonstration agent training on special subjects and methods of presentation, which they would pass on to members of their own groups; and (4) leaders who were sufficiently competent to train others in local leadership and provide some supervision.[14]

Members of the community were involved in the process of community organizing through numerous educational programs. Extension programs provided the milieu in which people developed self-help, self-direction, and leadership. Rural people became partners with the government in the selection, financing, and direction of local extension programs.[15]

By 1925, improved transportation and communication made other developments possible. Farmers organized around technical agricultural interests such as breeders', dairymen's, and poultrymen's associations, which reflected the growing specialization in rural social life.[16] The tight-knit rural neighborhood gave way to a mobile and better-informed rural community with ties both to the soil and to the city, where social contacts with influential businessmen were developed.

Farmers' Organizations

In the 1920s, farmers experienced a growing competitiveness and differentiation in terms of farm size and specialization. Farmers wanted "more" and began, in Terpenning's words, to experience "an awareness of needs which can be supplied only through united effort."[17] It is not surprising, then, that the period 1915 to 1930 saw the formation of thousands of farm groups such as the American Farm Bureau Federation, an expansion of the Grange and the Farmers' Union,[18] and that Boys' and Girls' Clubs (4-H) sponsored by the Agricultural Extension Service also greatly increased in membership during this period.

The particular economic interest that banded specialized farmers together was also reflected on the social scene in the form of study classes on subjects ranging from music and art to auto mechanics and little theater groups. Rural social change involved increased integration of village and town communities, in which farmers experimented with more than one center of social life and more than one set of interests.[19] Galpin coined the word "rurbanism" to emphasize the village-country interdependence that was developing.[20] Increased affiliations in educational organizations such as the PTA were related directly to the increased number of farm children attending village and town schools. A considerable number of school-district consolidations took place during this period. "In one small village, the retired farmer element defeated the bond election for a new school. A

group of farmers formed a company, put up the money for an addition to the school costing $10,000 and rented it to the school board.
The eventual result was the consolidation of the five districts and the
erection of a $110,000 building.[21]

The focus of group activities in the 1920s shifted from fraternal
to civic or educational organizations, as evidenced by the rapid
growth of countywide social organizations in the form of 4-H
Clubs, Farm and Home Bureaus, libraries, health units, and social
welfare agencies.[22] This expanded social life brought villagers and
farmers together in increasingly intimate contact and led to joint
concern for the general welfare.

Yet, just as every action has an equal and opposite reaction, a
strong rural philosophy emerged in the 1920s as a reaction against
increasing influence of the cities and the loss of young farm people
to the city. There was a desire to separate the rural from the urban
influences in order to keep the boys and girls on the farm.[23] Farm
Bureau and county agents, viewed as outsiders and nonresidents in
spirit, met increased resistance. Farmers saw them as missionaries
attempting to change the rural community. Seaman Knapp, pioneer
in demonstration work, dealt with this resistance by establishing a
demonstration farm in a community he wished to reach, and then
waiting for curiosity to bring his neighbors around.

Another form of rural community organization centered in rural
Community Councils. These were first formulated in cities in con-
nection with Councils of Social Agencies and the Social Center
Movement, yet had an independent development in rural communities. In 1909 in West Newbury, Massachusetts, the first Federation
for Rural Progress began with representatives of leading organizations and agencies of the town plus the church, school, and two
Granges. Their purpose was the establishment of a comprehensive
community program. Committees were appointed on farm production, farm business, conservation, boys' and girls' interests, and
community life. The Community Council served as a link between
organizations and helped to coordinate the projects of different
organizations.[24]

The traditional lines of demarcation between town and country
were further broken down.[25] Church buildings, school houses, the

farmers' club or Grange buildings were utilized by rural people as centers for social activities. The majority of rural community buildings were located in towns or small cities, which served as trade and financial centers and as the locus of community leaders.

The period of 1915 to 1930 saw an increase in the number of co-operative corporations for joint buying and selling. Through cooperation, the farmer sought to secure some of the middleman's profits and reduce marketing costs.[26] Extension services also increased and growth of both associations and memberships more than doubled between 1915 and 1930. In 1933 about a third of the farmers in the United States belonged to at least one cooperative. Membership seemed to be positively correlated with farm ownership, size of farm, and amount of education. Farmers Incorporated was a typical co-operative, which purchased supplies and goods for resale to members, located in a medium-sized Virginia village where half of the five hundred farmers in the community belonged to this organization; and from 1924 to 1930 business increased about 50 percent to a total of nearly $170,000 annually.[27]

Farm Cooperatives

While the Agriculture Extension agents worked with farmers during World War I to increase production, these same agents directed their attention to a very different expressed need after the war—economics and management. The rapid decline in farm purchasing power following the war made it evident that the problems could not be met by individual effort. Extension agents therefore began to help farmers organize for group study and group action. When the great wave of enthusiasm for cooperative marketing swept the country, farmers urged that extension agents help them develop cooperative buying and selling associations. Although neither the agents themselves nor the U.S. Department of Agriculture was able to answer this demand satisfactorily, the agents were instrumental in helping farmers secure needed information.[28]

Although some of the cooperatives organized during the period failed, most of the associations were founded on a sound financial basis. In the early history of each of these organizations, extension agents helped the officers of the cooperatives build the organization, but it was the policy of extension divisions never to manage farmers' organizations or dictate their policies. Neither did the farm organizations dictate the policies of the extension divisions.[29]

Extension workers as practitioners in adult education disseminated information by word of mouth, radio, and through printed materials such as news and feature articles, pamphlets, circulars, bulletins, and reports.[30] Newspaper articles included such themes as: "New Oats Variety Outyields Old Twofold," or "How to Take a Farm Inventory," or "Farmwife Makes Springhouse 'Ice Box'; Tells How."[31]

One of the major techniques used by extension agents to reach the average farmer and his family was the demonstration. An early pioneer in extension work, Seaman Knapp, would teach farmers how to cull chickens. Farmers likewise carried out demonstrations and shared the ideas and techniques with their neighbors. Similarly, farmers were encouraged to take part in organizing groups of farmers to address local needs, speak at meetings, hold office and thereby gain experience in guiding a cooperative or promoting the social, recreational, and civic welfare of the community. Aside from the simple demonstrations, there were also demonstrations that were "result" oriented, in which recommended practices were shown to be superior to former practices. Such demonstrations were conducted by farmers, homemakers, or 4-H Club members under direct supervision of the extension agents.[32] The ultimate purpose of the demonstration process was the building and growth of rural communities.[33]

The "discussion method" was the basic communication tool of county extension agents. The simple word-of-mouth technique for promoting acceptance and credibility of new ideas was successful due to the considerable geographic distances between farms. Agents had to overcome the farmers' contempt and yet enhance the rugged individualism and self-sufficiency of farmers.[34] Many farmers believed that they were in a partnership with nature and that social programs would have little impact on business successes or failures. The resulting suspicion about cooperative enterprises and civic action arose, in part, from the process of surviving alone without the help of others.[35] The outsider from the local agricultural college had to gain acceptance in a community if advice was to be regarded with anything but contempt. Personal contact between the county extension agent and the farmer proved to be invaluable in overcoming communications barriers.

The community organizing activities of extension agents built upon the rugged independence of rural people by emphasizing a philosophy of self-help.[36] As the local, state, and federal governments became more involved in the lives of rural people, there was increasing recognition that receiving help was not charity but a citizen's right. In 1921 Lindeman noted that the Grange was the social organization that held the key to organizing rural people around agricultural and social problems. He emphasized the importance of trained community organizers who understood the specific needs of the clientele and recognized that different organizing approaches were needed with farmers than were used in the city. The rural problems related to relationships, disease, and lack of educational facilities required community organizers to be well grounded in the realities of farm life in order to communicate effectively with farmers.[37]

The agricultural extension agent possessed skills in adult education and health sciences but was less well equipped to deal with family disorganization and poverty. The Red Cross was one organization that began to address these problems. During World War I the Home Service Work of the American Red Cross was instituted for the families of enlisted men and introduced new methods and standards of social service into many rural communities. After the war, this service was extended to the civilian population. The Red Cross community service programs, during the war, had given many of the rural population a broader vision of organized community life. After the war, extension workers found themselves dealing mainly with community groups in committees and public meetings rather than with individuals. Surveys were conducted to find out the needs of rural communities and to establish the basis for new community programs. For example, one survey identified some of the problems faced by women on farms related to the problems of poverty and family health.[38] Sanderson noted that the industrial depression necessitated the organization of county relief administrations throughout the country and social welfare services gained a new position as an essential service of rural life.[39]

Organizing for Public Health

The post–World War I period also saw the expansion of organized public health programs, where counties or groups of counties adopted the model of a county health organization. Many types of clinics were established, with inoculations and medical examinations of school children along with educational programs for school children and community programs on public and personal hygiene. Results of this work were measured in lowered death rates for infants and mothers, and reduced the incidence of various types of preventable diseases.[40] During this period, there was a greater increase in county health programs in the South than in any other region, which include 80 percent of all new county organizations developed between 1927 and 1931. This was partly due to the subsidies from such agencies as the Rockefeller and other foundations, the American Red Cross, and other private or semiprivate agencies.[41]

In rural Canada, the Junior Red Cross functioned as the official vehicle for teaching health in the schools. The method used was the organization of a small club, which met once a week and whose officers were chosen from among the children themselves. Students discussed matters of personal, school, and community hygiene, and were involved in maintaining the school's sanitation, light, heat, ventilation, and so forth. There were five hundred such clubs recorded in Ontario. In addition to the junior program, senior Red Cross societies included outpost hospital work, courses on first aid and home nursing, and special institutes for farm women held monthly in private homes featuring demonstrations and discussions. Health projects included hot school lunches, labor-saving devices in the home, well-baby clinics, restrooms at trading centers, education in home hygiene, fly screens placed on homes, and better sanitary conveniences at schools, swimming holes, and bathhouses.[42]

One of the first attempts at community organizing for citizen health and welfare emerged in St. Augustine, Florida. When the city's only public health nurse moved away, the American Red Cross representative was called for help. She recorded the following: "We called the whole community into conference: the county commission, which had employed the nurse; the city commission; the King's Daughters, who had been for years furnishing relief to needy families; the Catholic Daughters of America; and others. This conference brought out the fact that all the organizations were working, in their individual and ineffective way, for the same thing."[43] They pooled interests and money toward support of a general welfare program and budgeted for a public health nurse and a welfare worker. The Red Cross was called upon to secure adequately trained personnel and to assist in establishing standards of service. The conference formed itself into a formal welfare federation, each organization represented by two delegates to compose a board of directors, and they in turn elected an executive committee to be responsible for the whole program. Inherent in this process were three community organizing principles that were implemented: (1) It takes an entire community to relieve, correct, and prevent its own ailments; (2) the community can be reached through its organized groups; and (3) group representation provides the most effective vehicle for a widespread educational program.[44] These principles only reemphasize E. L. Morgan's contention that "community organizing outside of cities will need to recognize two things: first, the county as the organizational unit; second, the community as the operating unit."[45]

The organizing of rural health projects relied heavily upon public health nurses, who had little or no training in social casework and community organization. It was generally conceded that the public health nurse should also be a trained social worker since her work brought her into contact with situations that required considerable knowledge of community forces and agencies. It was not enough that her professional skill merely enable her "to interpret the physician's orders correctly."[46]

Community organizing by extension agents also included the development of youth programs. Young people were organized to engage in activities similar to those of their elders and related to rural farming problems. The Junior Extension, also known as 4-H Club ("Heart-Head-Hand-Health") programs, was established to deal with agriculture and home economics. Members engaged in various projects such as raising a calf, growing an acre of some crop, making a dress or hat, or canning. There were also projects in health work, and a variety of community service projects camps for 4-H Club members combined educational and recreational features and proved to be very popular.[47] The 4-H Clubs were organizations of boys and girls from ten to twenty years of age, with a definite program covering the production of farm and home products and personal and social development. The emphasis of each program varied according to the interests in each county and state. The 4-H Club programs sought to avoid commercial exploitation of the children, the excessive use of prizes, and unnecessary competition between children.[48]

Rural Black Community Organizing

Agriculture extension agents as well as other community organizing efforts in the South, on the whole, neglected the Black poor. Rural Blacks thus turned to their own resources, especially their churches, to provide the focal point for community organizing. The Black church served as the center of Black community life related to self-help, educational and leadership development, and a heightening of community consciousness. The task and responsibility of the local church was clearly community-wide and provided an opportunity for the expression of religious, social, and political leadership. The Black church also served as a community center for the sick, the poor, the aged, the youth, and the family. The church was often used as a channel through which programs and fund raising could be directed and community information could be shared. In the area of public health, the church served as a community clinic and provided advocacy services seeking better sanitation and water resources.

The Black minister was the key community organizer. No person was properly introduced to the Black community unless he or she came through the minister, and no organizers from outside the community could expect success without the minister's cooperation or endorsement. The Black preachers were religious, social, and political leaders, and the Black church was the primary center for rural organizing.

The Black church served to unite the Black community in the rural south and provided services that were not accessible to Blacks in rural white communities. While Black churches predominated in the South, it is important to note the role of Black churches outside the South. For example, the Congregational church in Springfield, Massachusetts, had a large facility accessible to its members with a parish home for working girls, a free employment bureau, a women's welfare league, a night school of domestic training, a girls' and boys' club emphasizing the handicrafts, music, and athletics, and a branch church in Amherst, Massachusetts.[49]

Conclusion

In the early days of state and local agricultural extension operations, agents tended only to disseminate information to farmers. Extension agents came to the conclusion that their objectives were best achieved by consultation with farmers, at least in terms of procedures to be employed. Thus, extension became more democratic in determining activities and two trends in program planning emerged: providing farmers with a larger share of responsibility in determining the activities for a given year, and making available the annual Outlook Conference reports containing the judgment of economists and other social scientists regarding national and world facts and trends that might affect the local situation in the ensuing year.[50] In other words, the people concerned were given the opportunity to develop their own countywide programs.

Rural community organizing required a special knowledge of farm life and skills to help farmers attain twentieth-century farming techniques. The by-product of organizing farmers was equally important in rural America. The organizing of women into self-help groups and young people into youth groups required extension agents to draw upon their group work and adult education skills.

PART III

Social Planning

7

Social Planning and Physical Planning

Michael J. Austin and Neil Betten

U R B A N problems of the later 1920s and the unemployment of the early 1930s provided new challenges for community organizers. While settlement house workers sought to recreate the best of village life in the urban scene, community problems based upon the economic factors of the depression and severe unemployment were becoming more complicated. The demand for hard data on city problems required more sophisticated tools of analysis. Social planners and urban sociologists responded to this demand with the use of survey methods, and the physical planners responded with analytic tools for planning land use and housing development. In addition to tracing the roots of social and physical planning during the 1920s and 1930s, special emphasis will be placed on the bridges between these two professionalizing occupations and the contributions of their special technologies to community organization.

During the 1920s a small group of sociologists developed new approaches to analyzing community social problems. The writings of Park, Burgess, Thomas, Faris, and Wirth began to provide the basis for analyzing neighborhood problems in the Chicago area and became known later as the Chicago school of sociological thought.[1]

At the same time local community councils became increasingly aware that the problems of unemployment, recreation, education, and juvenile delinquency required community-wide attention rather than simply neighborhood effort. They viewed neighborhoods as mechanisms to reach the city residents and not just entities unto themselves. The Block-Aid campaigns to pool part-time chores into full-time jobs for unemployed men were examples of community organizing activities to combat the effects of the depression.[2]

Neighborhood organizations also began to pool their efforts in meeting the needs of changing neighborhoods. In Cleveland, for example, special efforts were made in the late 1920s to coordinate the community center program of the local public schools (primarily recreational activities for teenagers and adults) with the program of a local settlement house focused primarily on cultural and educational activities.[3] These efforts were designed to preserve family unity during times of great stress.

One of the most significant community organizing efforts of the early 1930s resulted, in large part, from the involvement of several University of Chicago sociologists in identifying some of the causes of increased juvenile delinquency in the Chicago area. The emergence of the Chicago Area Project for the prevention of juvenile delinquency served as another milestone in the evolution of community organization practice. It gave further recognition to the survey method as a social planning tool for community problem-solving.

The development of the Chicago Area Project was based on Clifford Shaw's studies of delinquency and Frederick Thrasher's survey of thirteen hundred gangs in Chicago.[4] Thrasher's findings placed major emphasis on the environmental causes of juvenile delinquency and his solutions included preventive services that relied heavily upon community organizing activities. He recommended better coordinated children's services, services made available to all children in high delinquency areas, creation of new agencies, and better community education programs. He cited the organization of the Cincinnati Social Unit Experiment as a model for organizing citizens for crime prevention.

By identifying a high correlation between neighborhood residence and juvenile delinquency, Shaw and others founded the Chicago Area Project in 1934 as a nonprofit corporation seeking public and private funds.[5] The Project represented an early effort to depart from the traditional middle-class social agency model of service and, as in the case of the Cincinnati Unit Experiment, involved neighborhood people themselves in studying their community problems, formulating goals and policies, and operating their own programs. Numerous citizen committees and subcommittees were organized and led by local neighborhood leaders. Although many of the activities emulated those of a YMCA or settlement house, these services were now developed for the entire neighborhood and controlled by neighborhood residents instead of middle-class professionals. In addition, local people were recruited and trained to staff the programs, relying heavily on existing social groups, churches, and clubs.

These early efforts at delinquency prevention have a striking parallel to the thrust that the theories of Ohlin and Cloward gave to the efforts of the 1960s in New York City to prevent delinquency through the Mobilization for Youth Project funded by public and private monies.[6] Their thesis also emphasized the environmental causes of delinquency and the finding that youth lacked sufficient opportunities for social advancement, rather than their inherent pathological nature. During the 1930s, staff of the Chicago Area Project attributed delinquency behavior to the rapid social change experienced by migrants from rural backgrounds as they adjusted to city life. Communal or collective action was seen as a partial solution to the problems of delinquency along with continuing research to document emerging needs. The early community organizers of the Chicago Area Project used their knowledge of ethnic group culture and local institutions to identify influential residents. The residents were organized into civic committees in order to develop youth welfare organizations among residents of delinquency areas, employ so-called indigenous workers wherever possible, and preserve the independence of the groups.[7] The organizing efforts were viewed as successful when residents demonstrated their capacity to identify and seek solutions to delinquency problems in their areas.

The emerging Chicago school of sociology in the 1920s contributed greatly to understanding environmental determinants of delinquency. In similar fashion, poor housing and poverty gained the attention of physical planners. By 1927, planners had devised comprehensive plans for 176 cities.[8] The 1920s spawned a short-lived movement to replan or create new cities. Of particular significance in city planning was the development of the playground movement and the organizing of recreation on the neighborhood level. The linkage between playground space and delinquency prevention provided one of the early opportunities for physical and social planners to recognize the environmental factors in preventing delinquency through recreational programming.

Like the playground movement, the increasing interest in decent housing also pointed up the need for both physical and social planning. As historian Allen Davis noted, during the height of the Progressive Era the settlement house investigators were obsessed with the inadequate toilet and bathing facilities and the absence of light and ventilation, and they documented the incredibly bad housing conditions with precision and sympathy.[9] These conditions continued throughout the 1920s and 1930s and, therefore, it is important to trace briefly the origins of physical planning in an effort to understand its impact on community organizing and the relationship to social planning. The severity of the depression contributed to the envisioning of broad approaches to complex social problems and "a heightened interest in planning, *per se*, that followed the bankruptcy of the laissez-faire philosophy."[10] While a common interest in housing surfaced between physical and social planners, there was no structure for dialogue or collaboration except through a few emissaries from both groups. However, both groups were to influence each other as we shall note later in a discussion of their respective planning techniques.

Physical planning arose in the United States during the reform, recreation, and conservation movements of the nineteenth century. Perceptive citizens, sometimes in conjunction with local government, sought to alleviate the blight of city slums. Frederick Law Olmstead initiated the idea of building city parks as a respite from urban squalor, civic leaders in Boston built playgrounds, proponents of settlement houses sought to elevate living conditions among the poor, and Ebenezer Howard attacked housing problems in his Garden Cities proposal.[11] "Most of these planning efforts were not aimed directly at the reduction of poverty and deprivation, but sought to use land planning, housing codes and occasionally zoning to eliminate slums and reduce densities in the tightly packed tenement neighborhoods."[12] The City Beautiful Movement at the turn of the century revived comprehensive city planning by popularizing and showing the need for it.[13] By 1917, the American Institute of Architecture announced that 233 cities were sponsoring improvement programs.[14] Two components of city planning emerged from the Movement: professional consultants and quasi-independent planning commissions. During World War I, however, planning became increasingly an official function of local governments.[15] "Local governments gradually awoke to the havoc being wrought in the suburbs, and legislation was enacted to require subdividers to make certain improvements as a condition to approval of the development. These early regulations were feeble, but they were an acknowledgement that some measure of control was necessary to protect the city for the people who live in it."[16]

Urban planning became increasingly popular during the 1920s. By 1922, 185 cities had established planning boards or commissions.[17] The completion of Mariemont, Ohio, in 1921 initiated the planned community movement. Designed by John Nolen, Mariemont emphasized single-family units. Palos Verdes Estates in Los Angeles was completed in 1923. Other planned communities soon appeared. Among them were Shaker Heights in Cleveland, the Country Club District in Kansas City, St. Francis Woods in San Francisco, Nassau Shores on Long Island, and Westwood Village in Los Angeles. In none of these communities was attention given to housing and living conditions of the poor, since they were intended for the upper income groups.[18]

The physical layout of cities dominated the thinking of community leaders during the 1920s. Hampered by small budgets, cities were reluctant to hire professional planners. As a result, most planning commissions were independent of government and membership consisted of Chambers of Commerce and well-to-do citizens. Thus, physical planning relied too heavily upon consultants, realtors, lawyers, architects, and engineers, who looked upon planning as a citizens' effort to be "sold" to recalcitrant politicians.[19] Planners that were hired considered themselves to be "designers, makers of plans, creators of the city beautiful. They were employed by the city planning commissions organized deliberately in order to set them apart from the presumably corrupting influences of city hall."[20] Reflecting the conservatism and middle- and upper-class values of commission members, planning had become stigmatized and almost purposeless by the end of the decade. Plans were made but were seldom carried out. Concerned with only five areas—streets, transportation, parks and recreation, civic appearance, and zoning—planning became stereotyped and ritualistic. Planners "were adrift in a world of mimeographed and badly written reports, a gush of technical language, public relations, and pseudo-public relations."[21] Planning in the twenties was such that land could continue to be viewed as a speculative commodity. Plans "simply imposed a few ground rules under which speculation was to be carried on." Engaging in planning allowed cities to compete economically with one another. "To have a master plan or a zoning ordinance was a badge of modernity and 'progress.'"[22]

In 1923, the Regional Planning Association of America (RPAA) was formed with the goal of discovering "the basic principles underlying good urban residential environment and, more generally, the urban structure best suited to the satisfaction of human biological and social needs."[23] RPAA, composed of architects, physical planners, and social critics of both centralization and suburbanization, sought to combine physical and social planning to provide for community needs. The origins of RPAA are traceable to the post–World War I housing shortage.[24] Members of the Association recognized that the housing problem had to be solved as a part of community planning as a whole. Lewis Mumford, influential member of the Association, incorporated the idea of regionalism into community planning. Mumford urged decentralization and regional reconstruction based on the use of electrical power to promote industry and the automobile to transport people. If the region were to be used as the central planning unit, it would involve, according to Mumford, the building up of old centers, the breaking up of congested centers, and the founding of entirely new centers to promote social life, industry, and culture.[25]

RPAA stressed the value of three components of a community planning program: the relationship between quantity and quality in housing, the amount and cost of capital, and the traditional view that government's role in housing should be limited simply to minimum-standards legislation. Yet, the RPAA wanted local governments to stimulate financial support for local housing, especially housing for low-income groups that had been largely ignored by existing lending and building institutions.[26] Work of the 1927 New York State Board of Housing, in attempting to get government aid through tax exemptions, in addition to use of high supervisory housing standards and research in housing costs and design, stands as an example of the implementation of several RPAA proposals. In 1924 and 1928, RPAA tested its ideas in the development of Sunnyside and Radburn, two projects experimenting with innovations in residential housing design. "Sunnyside demonstrated the RPAA's proposition that large-scale design and site-planning could effect certain economics and produce a superior residential environment."[27] Radburn confronted the problems presented by automobiles and leisure time. Its neighborhood design was based on Howard's "new town" theories.[28] Although RPAA was a concrete body and worked through several organized government groups, it remained more of a philosophy than a plan.[29] Most early regional planning was confined largely to metropolitan areas and counties.

Beginning with the depression and continuing throughout the 1930s, city planning underwent a period of evaluation, new direction, and broadening of focus. From a concern with alleviating one single problem emerged the goal of comprehensive planning to reform the total urban environment. The ultimate goal of city planning became more socially oriented, though plans continued to emphasize the physical environment. City planning during the thirties emphasized "that the ideal urban environment should reconcile the maximum opportunity for individual choice, in living and working and whatever else is done, with the protection of the individual from the adverse effects caused by the action of the others."[30] A large degree of responsibility for the new trend in local planning rested with the Urbanism Committee of the National Resources Committee. It recognized that the plan's success rested upon governmental policy and intervention and that physical planning has no meaning apart from social and economic factors. It was responsible for urging that local planning be made a part of governmental structure. A report of the Committee concluded, however, that "thorough understanding and acceptance of planning by the local legislative body, the chief executive, and, most of all, by the citizenry in general, would appear to be a prerequisite for such a change."[31]

Three events of 1929 forecast the new directions planning was to take during the 1930s: completion of Radburn, New Jersey, establishment of the first school of city planning at Harvard, and the publication of *Regional Plan of New York and Its Environs*. The Harvard school initiated the movement for educating and professionalizing planners in the field of planning itself rather than solely in architecture or engineering. The *Regional Plan* differed from stereotyped 1920 plans by using social science research and by breaking "new ground in its treatment of the neighborhood unit, public finance, government services, and the economic base of the city."[32] From the depression emerged a new definition of local planning. Planning became involved in coordinating, administering, and organizing the new institutional structures. It became deeply involved in the political process. Public officials and professional planners began to discuss common concerns. Planning agencies acquired a heavy load of administrative duties and a new relationship to municipal government.

The two issues stressed most heavily during the thirties were slum clearance and low-rent housing. The need for urban rehabilitation was realized and this in turn implied the need for planning. In 1933, the National Planning Board was established. Its most significant work was encouraging planning at local levels and giving technical assistance to local planning agencies.[33] In 1937 the Housing Act was passed, establishing federal-local responsibilities in public housing. From 1912 to 1931, housing had hardly been mentioned by the National Planning Conferences. After 1931, it became the major topic of discussion.[34] In 1933, Hoover's Conference on Home Building and Home Ownership issued a policy statement concerning slums: "Unless this problem can be met by private enterprise, there should be public participation, at least to the extent of the exercise of the power of eminent domain. . . . A further exercise of some form of government powers may be necessary in order to prevent these slums from resulting in serious detriment to the health and character of our citizens." [35]

During the depression federal funds were used by local and state governments for public works, highways, dams, bridges, public buildings, and relief. "Cities benefited through projects for new sewers, drainage, streets, schools, recreation centers, but there were no essential changes in the character of the city." Too many people were concerned with unemployment to consider a possible reformation of the urban framework. [36]

Rural physical planning was not neglected by the federal government either. In 1933, the National Industrial Recovery Act established the Subsistence Homesteads Division in the Department of the Interior. This Division sponsored rural housing projects for part-time industrial workers. In 1935 the Resettlement Administration directed massive soil conservation and agricultural adjustment projects. It planned four "greenbelt" towns, exploiting Ebenezer Howard's Garden City "idea of a permanent belt of agricultural land surrounding these communities." [37]

From an early emphasis entirely on the physical aspects and layout of the community, city planning, by the end of the thirties, had taken on many responsibilities traditionally handled by social planners. [38] Although the quality of planning during the 1920s and 1930s was not high according to urban standards today and failed to remedy many urban problems, it represented the foundation from which future planning developed. By the end of the thirties it was widely recognized that good planning was a good investment. Physical planners realized that knowledge of local conditions, even to the point of house-to-house canvassing, was crucial for good planning. [39]

During the 1920s and 1930s physical planners developed a set of planning techniques that are still in use today and symbolize the emergence of a new profession. The techniques of economic studies, employment studies, population studies, urban activity systems studies, urban land-use studies, and transportation studies are the primary tools of the physical planner. [40] Economic planning included studies of the density of an urban area, its production, distribution, and consumption patterns, its trends toward growth, leveling off, or decline, and forecasts of the effects of population levels on land values and requirements.[41]

The employment study provided information of concern to population studies, which in turn are used in estimating space needs for residential areas and community facilities as well as serving as a yardstick for use in scaling land requirements for industrial and commercial areas.[42] In studies of the population, three factors were investigated: (1) population *size* as a yardstick for estimates of space needs; (2) population *composition* including qualitative considerations such as age, household size, and income—data in this area aid in estimating residential space requirements; (3) population *distribution*, which points to land usage and facility location.[43]

Urban activity system studies included the behavior patterns of individuals, families, institutions, and firms, which occur in special patterns that have meaning in planning for land use.[44] In this study the planners examined the past and used observations and knowledge about basic changes in urban society to anticipate the space-related kinds of activities of persons and institutions that are likely to be dominant in the future metropolitan area.

Urban land use studies included nine types of background studies, ranging from the mapping of urban settings including vacant and used land, to surveying environmental quality and flood potential, to studying both the financial and aesthetic value of land, to an assessment of public attitudes and preferences regarding land use.[45] Related to land-use planning was transportation planning, which included studies of traffic volume and desired traffic patterns.

Perloff summarizes the evaluation of physical planning in the cities in these stages:

From (1) an early stress on planning as concerned chiefly with esthetics, planning came to be conceived also in terms of (2) the efficient functioning of the city—in both the engineering and the economic sense; then (3) as a means of controlling the uses of land as a technique for developing a sound land-use pattern; then (4) as a key element in efficient governmental procedures; later (5) as involving welfare considerations and stressing the human element; and, more recently (6) planning has come to be viewed as encompassing many socio-economic and political, as well as physical, elements that help to guide the functioning and development of the urban community.[46]

Much of the activity and technique generated by physical planners in the 1920s and 1930s was related to the general inability to quantify the problems of urban America. As the physical planners developed the tools to tackle the problems of urban blight, the social planners developed their own techniques including organizing selected people for collective action as well as alerting the whole population to social blight. The major tool for alerting the masses was the social survey.

The social survey emerged around the turn of the century as an instrument of investigative journalism. The Pittsburgh Survey of 1907 marks the beginning of massive citywide surveys of social conditions and their impact on people.[47] The inventorying of community problems reached bandwagon proportions by 1921 as the Russell Sage Foundation established a new Department of Surveys and Exhibits to provide consultation to cities throughout the country. Within the first year of operations the new Department had received requests from over one hundred cities in thirty-four states.[48] The Russell Sage foundation also established a new magazine called the *Survey* under the dynamic, muckraking editorship of Paul Kellogg, who directed the first Pittsburgh Survey.[49]

The surveys usually included long lists of recommended changes in community life but failed to define the actual survey methodology. Since standards for evaluation were rarely thought out, the surveys reflected more common sense than rigorous research. As examples of investigative reporting, the findings easily became dated and were useful only in the community for which the survey was conducted. To increase impartiality, surveys were conducted by outside consultants but it soon became apparent that the results were heavily biased by the consultants and the people that hired them. Since timing was extremely important, problems arose when survey recommendations were not followed up or priority areas were not identified by the community.[50]

The social surveys relied heavily upon the philosophy of scientific management and the efficiency orientation. Kellogg identified the basic goals of the social survey:

1. To bring a group of experts together to co-operate with local leaders in gauging the needs of one city from several perspectives.

2. To study these needs in relation to each other, to the whole area of the city, and to the civic responsibilities of democracy.

3. To consider at the same time both civic and industrial conditions, and to consider them for the most part in their bearings upon the wage-earning population.

4. To reduce conditions to terms of household experience and human life.

5. To devise graphic means for making these findings challenging, clear, and unmistakable.

6. To establish natural relations with local agencies, to project the work into the future.[51]

McClenahan suggested that the most effective survey included four basic steps: (1) gathering data, (2) outlining a community plan and program based on the interpretation of data secured, (3) conducting a publicity campaign to arouse community support, and (4) securing the adoption of the plan for community organization.[52] She also identified five types of surveys: (1) the general survey, which was usually sponsored by a local community to gain a broad view of its situation; (2) the comprehensive or interlocking survey, which concentrated on a detailed analytical study of a system or agency; (3) the unit survey, which comprised a close study of a specific neighborhood or city block with respect to an obvious problem; (4) an informal survey, which was seen as being a quick review and summation of a local situation; and (5) the continuous or permanent survey, seen as an annual review of the status of community welfare.[53]

Results of the surveys were measured by the increasing willingness of public officials to see social planning as germane to city governance. The use of public speakers, newspapers, letters, forum discussions, political pressure, and propaganda brought home the message that social problem solving requires public attention and commitment.

By the late 1920s, it became apparent that the survey method required both more rigor and more localism. Social planners began to recognize the need for a more statistical basis for social planning and directed their energies to the improvement of social accounting and thereby moved the survey process to a higher plane of quality and professionalism.[54] At the same time, it was recognized that brief visits by outside survey consultants were insufficient to map community problems thoroughly. As a result, the survey process was slowly assumed by more and more local community councils of social agencies or community chests. Ruth Hill noted that a major reason for this shift from national survey consultants to local social planners is the change from a provincial to a community point of view on the part of many influential citizens. "They are now able to look at the facts of their community life without becoming emotionally defensive."[55]

Local citizens began to recognize that they had some influence over the destiny of their communities. The results of social surveys in Denver also indicated that the social needs could be linked to the physical needs of people through playground planning. In March 1929 the Denver Plan, which stipulated that no child should live more than a quarter mile from a small playground and that complete recreational facilities be within easy access of all citizens, elicited rather widespread criticism from a number of professional planners, who regarded it as too bold. "Future generations of Denver's children will be grateful to the vision of the present planning commission, but of even greater significance is the commission's claim that the adoption of its plan has caused a number of planners elsewhere to widen the scope of their proposals."[56]

By the early 1930s the social survey had become primarily a planning tool for assessing the needs of social agencies in contrast to serving as a community-wide study. The need for a factual, statistical base for planning preoccupied most social planners. More attention was directed toward evaluating social programs in order to become more accountable for the expenditures of public and private dollars.[57]

The second Pittsburgh Survey of 1938 symbolizes the evolution of the social survey from the 1907 community-wide effort characterized by investigative journalism to the 1938 study of social services ranging from agency financing to specialized service needs in health, welfare, and recreation. This same period reflects the shift from social reform activities to social planning activities. The wider aspects of social problems were ignored in favor of more focused attention on more discrete planning issues.

The legacy of the social survey can be found in the continuing need for all communities to assess their unmet needs repeatedly through some form of community study. The surfacing of such needs was designed to promote public recognition of the need to expand services, create new services, or terminate outmoded services. The social survey technique reflected both a descriptive and statistical approach to problem identification. It also dramatized the need for broad-based citizen participation in the *process* of identifying local problems.

The social survey emerged as one of the major social planning techniques of the period. In similar fashion, the land-use survey emerged as an important tool of the physical planners. Both planners were concerned with the rational development of communities, the resolution of urban problems, and the importance of fact finding. Both types of planners were generally employed by the power structure of a community whether in public or private agencies.

Social planning between the two Pittsburgh Surveys underwent significant change. Planning to meet the social needs of people shifted from a comprehensive approach to the "inhuman manifestations of industrialization and urbanization" to a specialized approach to planning social services. In a similar fashion, physical planning emerged from a wide range of interest in the esthetic, legal, and engineering aspects of urban development to a specialized, but comprehensive, approach to land use and zoning. The professionalization of physical and social service planning continues to this day.[58]

8

Federated Philanthropy in a Jewish Community, 1904–1939

Marc Lee Raphael

CENTURIES of Jewish legal development helped to make philanthropy a collective integral part of the business community. The Jewish federations, which represent the public, corporate community in American Jewish philanthropy, have continuously generated for themselves greater and greater control over welfare, social-service, and Israel-oriented concerns. Both individuals and organizations in the private and "religious" sectors of the community have participated in providing leadership, making decisions, promoting democratic self-determination, and responding to consumer preferences by contributing time and effort to fund raising and allocations.[1] This chapter presents a study of Jewish federated philanthropic activity in Columbus, Ohio, from 1904 to 1939 and attempts to highlight those areas of Jewish communal organization that are still relevant today.

The origins of the Jewish Charities of Columbus can be traced to November 21, 1904, when Joseph Schonthal, the president of Bryden Road Temple (formerly Benai Israel) was selected to head the organization. The constituents were the Ladies' Benevolent Society, the Helping Hand Society, and the Sheltering House. Consolidation was by no means unique to Columbus; everywhere in the country cities began to combine their charities to avoid duplication of effort. The stated purposes of the Jewish Charities of Columbus were broader than those of the earlier Hebrew Relief Association; its object was not only to assist immigrant and transient Jews but to relieve distress and suffering that was the result of poverty among the local Jews. Additionally, the Jewish community hoped, by organizing its own philanthropies, to eliminate Jewish dependency on the Associated Charities of Columbus. This was indeed the result: During 1908–1909 the Associated Charities served 1,866 Protestants, 218 Roman Catholics, and only 15 Jews, and during 1914–1915, the organization helped 3,275 Protestants, 3,894 Catholics, and 16 Jews. Noting this impressive self-help effort, the Associated Charities remarked that the "policy of the [Jewish Charities] is that no Jews shall be allowed to become a tax on any other organization."[2]

In January 1909, the Jewish Charities was reorganized, and a formal federation was created—the Federated Jewish Charities (FJC). Federations, or community-wide organizations to unify and standardize the methods of relief and centralize fund raising, had been developing in Jewish communities ever since the Federation of Jewish Charities was created in Boston in 1895. The Columbus Federation combined all the agencies of local and outside Jewish relief work, and consisted of members who donated at least three dollars per annum and who elected a Board of Directors of twenty-five men and women. A group of fifteen of the directors (the "Relief Committee") met weekly and approved all cases seeking assistance, while an Executive Committee of five officers and two Directors allotted the funds to institutions outside of Columbus. These out-of-town recipients of Columbus Jewish philanthropy were the Cleveland Orphans' Asylum, Cleveland Old Folks' Home, Denver Juvenile Infants' Asylum, and Denver Juvenile Hospital for Tuberculosis Patients—institutions strongly supported by German Jewish philanthropic efforts in many midwestern communities.[3]

Of the total expenditures during the first four months of operation (January 1 to May 1, 1909), the Federation spent 50 percent of its total funds ($915 out of $1,847) on local relief and the care of transients. The Relief Committee of the Federation maintained a room in a private residence (the "Sheltering Home"), to which anyone needing food and shelter was sent. Several members of the Relief Committee had the privilege of granting and signing a card, the possession of which entitled the transient to one night's lodging and meals. A secretary, the only paid officer of the Federation, and several volunteers had charge of the local relief work.[4] One local resident reminisced about the Sheltering Home:

> For people who had nowhere to sleep overnight, eat overnight—they could go to the Salvation Army, these beggars and sleep, but they felt it was a shame to let these people go to places like that, so they opened up this organization and they would make a great big dinner, charge fifty cents a ticket, and the women would go in and do their own cooking. . . . Any Jewish person that wanted to stay overnight, have a kosher meal—I think they allowed them two days, something like that to stay there free.[5]

On certain occasions, transients emerged who were dangers to the community. Late in 1902 D. Naaman and S. Leverski, temporary residents at the Sheltering Home and speaking only Yiddish, pawned a fake gold chain for a considerable sum at Wolf Levinson's pawn shop. Before the afternoon was over, similar chains were pawned at Sam Friedlander's, Sam Levy's, Isaac Cramer's, and I. B. Jashenosky's pawn shops. Several of the pawnbrokers, after Sabbath prayers at the synagogue, realized during their conversation that they had been duped by the same con men, and writs were filed for the arrest of the criminals.[6]

The Sheltering Home, despite its usefulness, was to serve as a focal point for a philosophical difference in philanthropy between the Reform Jewish leadership of the FJC (20 to 22 members of the Board of Directors were long-standing members of the community's Reform Temple in 1916) and the immigrant community. The leaders viewed the Home as a one-night lodging place for transients approved by the FJC, while the poor Jews insisted it be available to anyone from outside Columbus who wished to lodge there. The most explicit attack on the immigrants came in 1916, when the superintendent of the FJC, Joseph Hyman, presented his annual report:

> The transient poor, an endless stream, formed about one-fifth of our applicants. . . . The great majority of transients are parasites and will remain so just as long as there are sympathetic persons who will relieve their

conscience by assisting without aim other than getting rid of the individual. The Jewish transient is . . . an increasing menace. The Achnoses
Orchim and the Shelter Home are the Schnorrers Hotel, and help perpe-
trate the evil. Just as long as it is known that there is food and shelter
awaiting him the transient will continue to travel. The remedy in most
cases is work. Should the transient refuse to work, no other aid should be
given. And there is the difficulty. After assistance is refused by the Federation there are always sympathetic individuals willing to help. It is needless
to say that this sort of aimless assistance is worthless; that it does more
harm than good.[7]

A committee was appointed by the directors to control the situation, and in his next annual report Hyman could announce, "The
imposter, the schnorrer, the magid, the tramp, the self-appointed
collector of Palestinian charities has suddenly disappeared." That
these persons disappeared is without foundation; that the FJC
ceased to serve them is certain.[8]

Nevertheless, the Associated Charities was impressed with the
Federation of Jewish Charities' organization and operation. It saw
the Federation exercising "care and precision," possessing a "pleasant
sense of efficiency and lack of waste," and providing deliberation in
all its work. In 1918 the Federation moved into the old Louis P.
Hoster residence at 555 East Rich Street when Joseph Schonthal, the
patron of Jewish philanthropy, purchased and remodeled the home.
Naming it in memory of his late wife, he gave the Hermine Schonthal Community House to the Federation. It was to serve the Jewish community for three full decades at this Rich Street location
(1918–1950).[9]

"Uncle Joe" or "Pop" Schonthal, as he was affectionately known,
retired in 1910 upon the death of his wife Hermine in order to devote
virtually all his time and money to philanthropy and social service
efforts. In addition to the Hermine Schonthal Community House
and Jewish Infants' Home of Ohio, Schonthal provided the Schonthal Camp near Magnetic Springs, a school and asylum for indigent
children in Riga, Latvia, scholarships to hundreds of students at
Ohio State University, and abundant personal attention to juveniles
appearing in court. More than his gifts of money were his gifts of
person; hundreds of Columbus Jews remember parties he hosted for
numerous children's groups, visits he made to hospitals and clubs,

and counsel he provided to groups as diverse as Big Sisters and Girl Scouts to Hebrew Free Loan Association and confirmation classes.[10]

The FJC utilized the money it could raise ($6,656 in 1916, $9,550 in 1917, $19,812 in 1919) exclusively for local Jewish needs. Relief continued to dominate the Charities' efforts (there were 906 applications for relief in 1916), for sickness, accidents, and the premature death of a breadwinner were repeated events. The main activity of the society, like that of many charity societies of the period, was handouts; very little was done about programs that would go beyond almsgiving. Although the "total income which we have for all charitable expenditures is in reality hardly sufficient for local relief alone," several organizations assisted the FJC in the relief work. Chief among these were the Hebrew Free Loan Association, the Jewish Educational Alliance, the Jewish Infants' Home of Ohio, and the Ezras Noshim.[11]

The Hebrew Free Loan Association (HFLA) offered needy immigrants quick loans without interest and provided crucial support to the FJC. Joseph Schonthal noted that the Charities "could not have survived without the HFLA." During 1916 the Association made seventy-four loans totaling $3,063, and in the following year registered forty-seven loans of $2,108; these included replacing the dead horse of a peddler, supplying a peddler with his first pack of merchandise, and providing rent money for those unable to meet their payments. Not only was no interest charged, but only small weekly repayments were required. Borrowers were overwhelmingly peddlers of fruit or junk, while the predominant reason for borrowing money was to buy merchandise for peddling. Whatever the motivation, people threw themselves into the work of fund raising for the HFLA, as they did for almost every other Jewish charity in Columbus. An endless round of fairs, picnics, theater productions, and fund raising at social gatherings resulted in the Association's budget.[12]

Founded in 1911 in a single room, the Jewish Educational Alliance, within six years, had moved to a large assembly hall with eight spacious rooms. The forerunner of the Schonthal Center and then the Jewish Center, its work was primarily with children. It offered a five-day-per-week kindergarten in the morning, sewing, library, dancing and music class in the afternoon, classes for adults, teenage clubs and study rooms at night, a Sunday school (for children whose parents were not affiliated with a synagogue or whose synagogue had no school), concerts, lectures, debates, dramatics, and much more. Its director, H. Joseph Hyman, a graduate of the University of Cincinnati and a disciple of Boris Bogen, one of the pioneers of Jewish social work, was to gain valuable experience in Columbus before assuming more difficult duties with the Joint Distribution Committee after World War I.[13]

For many years, Columbus Jewish orphans were taken care of by the Cleveland Orphans' Asylum, an institution heavily supported by the Columbus community.[14] When the Asylum decided to use its Home for Cleveland infants only, several Ohio cities initiated discussions with the hope of establishing a second home to serve Jewish orphans. By 1919 Dayton, Youngstown, Akron, Toledo, Hamilton, and Cincinnati had given Joseph Schonthal commitments of annual support, and he purchased and remodeled a building at 571 East Rich Street, which was opened in February 1920 and dedicated in April 1920 as the Jewish Infants' Home of Ohio (JIH). Governed by a State Board of Directors, a Local Board of Directors, and a local administrative board, the JIH housed twenty-eight children by early 1922.[15]

In 1900 ten orthodox Jewish women, under the leadership of Tova Goldberg (1860–1954), organized the Ezras Noshim (Helping Women).[16] Its purpose was "to relieve the distress among the sick and needy of Columbus," and by 1923 it had 350 dues-paying members who raised funds through two major annual events: a gigantic summer picnic and a winter ball. Under the guidance of Tova Goldberg, president for more than forty years, Ezras Noshim supplied Ohio Penitentiary inmates with Jewish holiday dinners for many years, assisted needy families in obtaining Passover holiday supplies, and provided generous and regular aid to needy individuals and families, the immigrants of Columbus.

> We had some women here in the city who was [*sic*] very active in those days. . . . I would call one of those women and say I got a family in. I put them in such and such a home, on such and such a street, and they would go down and see that they got living quarters and furniture that they had to have. . . . I would call Mrs. Goldberg. She was head of the Ezras Noshim, and she would take care of those people.[17]

In 1923 the Federated Jewish Charities changed its name, "in accordance with the spirit of the times," to Jewish Welfare Federation (JWF). By the early 1920s "charity" was out of favor, for the leadership of the Jewish Charities assumed that the populace would imagine only someone handing out and others receiving money, rather than the multiplicity of services, such as preventive casework, provided to the Federation's constituents.[18]

The Columbus Jewish community, by now a community of some eight thousand, gained valuable fund raising experience through support of the JWF. "Teams" were organized, with "captains" appointed by the JWF leadership, and friendly competition among "teamworkers" assured maximum collection of monies. The pattern of the campaign was based on a fourteen-million-dollar nationwide emergency "Drive" conducted in 1922 to raise funds for European Jewish communities.[19]

More than $57,000 was collected by Columbus Jewry, but the total was not nearly as significant for the future as the means utilized to reach this goal. The wealthiest members of the community were invited to a carefully planned program at the Progress Club featuring distinguished out-of-town speakers. The results were most gratifying; in one night $42,000 was pledged. The drive demonstrated how much easier it was to raise funds for international emergencies than for local needs.[20]

On June 24, 1926, pursuant to the call of Edwin J. Schanfarber, general chairman of the Campaign Committee, a new centralized philanthropic organization emerged in the Columbus Jewish community. Organized by the leading businessmen and professionals for the same reasons that financial federations emerged everywhere in America in the 1920s, the United Jewish Fund (UJF) had two goals: to collect and distribute funds for "human welfare" (needy Jews all over the world), and to "avoid duplication of effort and expense in (cultural, philanthropic, educational) fund-raising programs" within the Jewish community. A new Board of Directors, consisting of twenty-five members, was created, elected by every person who had contributed fifty dollars to the campaign.[21]

Five days later the Board made its first allocations, referring to its Finance Committee sixteen applications for funds and disbursing, over a three-year period (April 1, 1926, to March 31, 1929), $50,000 to the Jewish Orphans' Home of Cleveland, $55,000 to the Joint Distribution Committee, $30,200 to the Columbus Hebrew School, $20,000 to the United Palestine Appeal, and $10,000 to the B'nai B'rith Wider Scope Committee. By mid-December 1926 almost $30,000 had been distributed by the UJF. With its very first allocations, the UJF established a pattern that was to characterize its disbursements for fifty years: the overwhelming amount of its funds to be distributed to national and international causes rather than to local ones.[22]

Within one year, the first challenge to the UJF's control over all fund raising not of a religious nature was issued by the orthodox immigrant community, which felt that the allocations distributed to its favorite organizations were insufficient. At a March meeting in 1927 the Board of Directors reaffirmed its "objection to Jewish fund-raising . . . not through the Fund" and appointed a committee whose task would be to prevent competing fund raising. While this type of conflict was to surface periodically, the first challenge was successfully stifled.[23]

That the orthodox community might be dissatisfied with the UJF is not hard to understand. Not only were both the Board of Directors and the officers dominated by Bryden Road Temple members, but the meetings of the UJF were held at the private social club of the Reform Jewish community (Progress Club). Temple members contributed more than three dollars for every dollar given by non–Bryden Road Temple members ($185,299 compared to $55,045 from 1926 to 1929); therefore, the pet institutions of the Reform movement or established Jewish community were heavily funded from the communal treasury. It is no wonder then that the representatives of the immigrant, orthodox Jews argued continuously with the Board over allocations, demanding greater support for their favorite organizations.[24]

The UJF, from its inception, demonstrated superb fund raising skills. Effective community organizing was the foundation on which the successful campaign was to be built; leadership continuity, year-round interpretation, and community involvement were the keys. Its first campaign, April 11–18, 1926, was launched with a program at the Progress Club, and more than half of the $250,000 three-year goal was pledged by five families. Small gifts, however, were not ignored. Chairpersons were appointed for thirty-three Central Ohio counties, and intense efforts were made to locate one or more Jewish canvassers in even the smallest towns. The campaign was conducted by sending attractive printed literature to every identifiable Jewish household in the city. Thus many of the techniques to be developed later in a more sophisticated manner were already unveiled in the 1920s.[25]

At the end of the UJF's first three-year period of operation, E. J. Schanfarber already despaired of raising the funds necessary over the next three years: "A campaign cannot be successfully conducted at this time." By the end of 1929 the Board could note only that all cash reserves from the 1926–1929 campaign had been exhausted; with "the death of 'Pop' Schonthal we lost our largest giver [whose] contribution would represent six or seven percent of the total"; "there is a great deal of enthusiasm, but not much money, among the mass of smaller givers in the community" and "there seems to be a lack of interest and enthusiasm among the medium sized givers." The Board thus recommended a severely shrunken 1930 campaign of fifty to sixty thousand dollars, an amount that Schanfarber felt would be neither subscribed nor collected. His fears were quite well founded; not only was the community able to raise only forty-two thousand dollars, but there was not one contribution of more than eighteen hundred dollars. The impact of the Great Depression was clearly being felt.[26]

As a result of the depression, there was no fund raising campaign during 1931, and in the following two years only 210 and 112 persons contributed ninety-nine hundred and eight thousand dollars respectively. While the Jews of Columbus were unable during these years to care for others through the United Jewish Fund, the Jewish Welfare Federation was kept enormously busy providing relief, counseling, medical services, and shelter for members of the local Jewish community.

As the depression worsened, the JWF intensified its local relief efforts; in 1931 the Federation cared for 136 families (745 persons), provided 400 free meals to transients and free clinical services to 430, sheltered 7 aged persons, and cared for orphans at the Jewish Infants'

Home as well as transients at the Sheltering Home.[27] During 1932 the range of services became even broader: 67 families (285 persons) received relief, 59 families (271 persons) received services that enabled them "to make the proper adjustments in their affairs," 1,010 homeless men were served by the Jewish Sheltering Home, 825 persons were given dental care, and 556 individuals, with problems ranging from unemployment to desertion, were given moral and financial assistance. The Jewish Welfare Federation, which expended thirty-two thousand dollars in all of its 1932 programs, was funded almost entirely in these efforts by the Community Fund (thirty-one thousand dollars).[28]

Another indication of the demands placed upon the local community is available from depression years statistics submitted by all of the Ohio Jewish family welfare agencies to the national Council of Jewish Federations and Welfare Funds. Although the demands multiplied rapidly in all of the cities except Dayton, only Columbus and Cleveland were continuously able to increase the dollars spent on needy Jews between 1929 and 1933. By the latter year Columbus Jews were providing almost twice the relief assistance to more than three times the number of families as on the eve of the depression.[29]

Beginning with 1934, and continuing through the 1948 campaign, an increasingly larger sum was contributed to the UJF by Columbus Jews each year. The number of pledges, as well as the amounts pledged, rose steadily through the 1930s as the depression receded, increased dramatically with the outbreak of World War II, and skyrocketed on the eve of the establishment of the Jewish State.

As a result of more successful campaigns, the UJF component of the fund raising campaign could again share its largess with Jews everywhere. Allocations as early as 1934 included eight thousand dollars to the Joint Distribution Committee, twenty-seven hundred dollars to the B'nai B'rith, fifteen hundred dollars to the Jewish Orphans' Home, a thousand dollars to the American Jewish Committee, and eight hundred dollars each to the Hebrew Immigrant Aid Society and the National Jewish Hospital. With the distribution of funds in 1935 the allocation pattern shifted even further in the direction of national and overseas funding. Local organizations received only three hundred dollars (1.2 percent) of the more than twenty-four thousand dollars allocated, while needs outside of Columbus accounted for twenty-three thousand dollars (95.1 percent). The vast majority of other federation campaigns of 1935 allocated a higher percentage to local needs. Included were Akron (4.2 percent), Cincinnati (27.3 percent), Cleveland (27.3 percent) and Dayton (20.3 percent)—all, like Columbus, with separate Jewish Family Welfare agencies for relief efforts.[30]

Gone now were the allocations to small communities and other organizations in eastern Europe and Palestine supported by the immigrants, for with the depression years the twenty-five-member Board of Directors "disintegrated" and a committee of nine wealthy men—all leaders at Bryden Road Temple—made the allocations.[31]

Not until 1939 was E. J. Schanfarber, the campaign chairman and JWF president since 1926, sufficiently pressured to permit "greater participation on the part of the community in raising . . . [and] disbursing the funds." As a result, the JWF was reorganized and an enlarged Board of Directors (twenty-five) was elected. Part of this pressure was external; events in Europe on the eve of World War II almost immediately doubled the budget demands made on local Federations and welfare funds by national and international organizations, and it was impossible to meet these goals without broad communal participation. Part of the pressure was also internal: accelerating philanthropy drives within the orthodox community for the support of organizations not funded by the JWF. The results of the reorganization were impressive: Both the number of contributors and the amounts collected increased by more than 100 percent between 1938 and 1939.[32]

Three other developments occurred for the first time in 1939 and 1940 and were to be of significance in subsequent decades. First, there emerged a desire to involve others besides men in the campaign, and both a Women's Division and a Junior Division were soon to emerge; and second, there was a conscious desire, when reorganizing the UJF, not to include any of the community's six rabbis, although "each plays an important part in the molding of public opinion and has an interest in the welfare of human beings which does or should transcend that of all others" on the new Board of Directors. The explanation provided was that given congregational jealousies, to include one and not all would cause envy, and the best solution would be not to include any rabbis. This was to initiate growing tension between the rabbinate and fund raisers in the community.[33]

Finally, as a response to both the Jewish and non-Jewish press, which delighted in highlighting generous philanthropic gifts, the JWF "unanimously decided that no publicity be given to the nonsectarian or Jewish press concerning donors, amounts of contributions, or the total amount sought or raised in the campaign." While the last of these strictures was ignored, ever since 1940 the local JWF has withheld from the media the specific contributions of all individuals. While disappointing many who desired the positive publicity for themselves and the embarrassment it would bring to others, this obviously satisfied the majority of subscribers.[34]

The new Board of Directors, including now seven or eight east Europeans among its twenty-five men, quickly moved to expand the UJF allocations so as to encompass numerous small Palestinian organizations—ranging from the Palestine Orchestra Fund to the Palestine Hebrew Culture Fund—as well as the community's traditional places of support (Cleveland Jewish Orphans' Home, National Jewish Hospital, B'nai B'rith, American Jewish Committee); and although the amounts allocated to the Palestinian agencies were but tokens, the precedent had been set. With each succeeding year the JWF became less and less the exclusive club of the Bryden Road Temple Board, and a charity network more responsive to diverse groups. While communal democracy was to remain more an ideal than a reality, E. J. Schanfarber's decision in 1939–1940 to expand community participation was to have lasting import.[35]

PART IV

Social Action

9

The Urban Political Boss as Community Organizer

Neil Betten and William E. Hershey

THE WARD politicians, minor political office holders, and political bosses of post–Civil War America's rapidly developing industrial cities hardly thought of themselves as community organizers. They were, nevertheless, superb organizers of the various immigrant communities that poured into the United States especially after 1880.

Urban political organizations were of considerable variety. Most were part of the Democratic Party, but some were Republican. While some were based on the power brokerage of publicly elected officals, most were led by party leaders who rarely ran for public office. Most had many bases of organization although some were organized around political patronage alone. In dealing with the urban political machines from the 1870s to approximately the early 1930s, this chapter will provide a composite of the common features of those organizations and how the political urban leadership interacted with and organized its constituent communities.[1]

Urban political bossism, as it came to be known, was based on social factors, economic elements, political foundations, and leadership styles. The prevalence of newly arrived immigrants and the eventual children of immigrants, that is, the ethnic factor, emerged as the major element of the social foundation of machine politics. The ethnic communities became the basis for many of the political organizations. Historians, until about the mid-1960s, almost universally described the immigrants as ignorant of democratic ways and easily manipulated and exploited by the corrupt political bosses. In the past twenty-five years historians have come to see the matter quite differently. For the most part, there was a quid pro quo relationship. The political leadership provided the ethnic communities with various kinds of support, which will be discussed below, and the ethnic communities provided political leadership with votes and political workers.[2]

In the economic realm, the new immigrants who arrived in the United States from about 1880 to the early 1920s found themselves primarily working in heavy industry, sweatshop factories, dangerous mines, and in generally unskilled, low-paid jobs. They lived in the growing slum areas of industrial America in crowded housing, often without indoor plumbing, building code enforcement, proper ventilation, privacy, and acceptable environmental conditions. In good times the immigrant communities could expect fairly steady employment, but there were periodic depressions, panics, and recessions from the mid to late 1870s until the complete economic collapse of the Great Depression of the 1930s. Until the New Deal of Franklin Roosevelt, economic disruption occurred at a time when the government sponsored very few social programs. Programs that did exist usually failed during economic depressions as a result of either inadequate resources or massive corruption. Some private charities existed, of course, but recipients often found it degrading to submit to the inquisition that usually accompanied their meager assistance. In fact, these charities rarely survived serious economic declines. At a time when much of the public generally accepted the social Darwinist view that helping the poor would in the long run aid the unfit of society and ultimately cause more problems than it resolved, and the Horatio Alger myth that persuaded middle-class Americans that the road to economic wealth was open to all, it is not surprising that the American political leadership rejected programs directed to the immigrant poor.

This was also a time of rapid industrial development. In the post–Civil War years, the railroads replaced textiles as the major

American industry, and steel dwarfed railroads by the turn of the century. The country was being built on rails, steel, and cheap energy, as well as the labor of the immigrant work force. Industry drew enormous population concentrations, which meant that the cities needed to grow physically to accommodate the population. Streets needed to be paved, sewers built, garbage collected, public transportation developed, and new government facilities established to respond to the economic and social growth. In order for funds to meet the industrial and population needs, the economy had to be strong enough to provide tax revenues. The general economic expansion and often concurrent full employment resulted in a favorable environment to finance the needed urban development.

This economic basis for the political environment was closely related to the political basis. The bosses built their organizations on the ethnic vote and financed them, in large part, from the bribes and kickbacks that business interests provided. By present standards the urban bosses were clearly tainted. American society, however, seemed much more tolerant of political corruption during the years of boss-dominated cities. The most famous of the urban political bosses, William M. Tweed of New York, was highly unusual in his excesses. Most bosses operated within the limits of "acceptable graft."

These were corrupt times. On the national level, the worst political scandals were associated with the building of the railroads and with illegal exploitation of natural resources. On the state level, legislators could be bought by the business leadership of the country for a mere pittance, unless they were known as particularly honest—then it cost more. The business community itself was constantly involved in stock manipulations, watering of stock, illegal monopolistic practices, and practices that, although not technically illegal, would become illegal shortly after the latest innovations to control and stifle competition were fully understood.

For the most part, urban corruption was associated with the bosses, who were often Democrats. The corruption on the state and national levels and within the business community was associated primarily with Republicans. Neither party was free of this taint, nor was any region of the country. In the South the Reconstruction governments had their problems, although the corruption, in dollar amounts, was rather trivial in comparison with other areas of the country.

In addition to the ethnic vote and the corrupt environment of American society, the political basis for the bosses also included the political and economic support of a portion of the business interests. Those business elements that benefited from urban development, builders of housing or government buildings or developers of public transportation for example, supported the urban political bosses who worked with the business developers.

The political leadership could also depend upon the help of their own municipal workers. This aid came in the form of financial support, often a kickback of a given percentage of the salary of the municipal worker to the party coffers or in the form of "voluntary" work that the individual municipal worker willingly undertook during elections or at other times for the party in power. This was of course built on the patronage system. The political leadership appointed municipal workers to virtually all public positions. Newly elected politicians commonly fired the entire police force of a city and created an entirely new police force overnight through the patronage system. This occurred at times for police officers, firemen, and teachers, but even more commonly for the standard clerks, laborers, and bureaucrats who carried out the daily needs of city government.

The city governments themselves became major employers. The political party became the unofficial personnel department and employment service. Party loyalty was a prerequisite for employment. The ticket to a job was assured if one was the family member of a machine politician. Loyalty to the party was the key qualification for job distribution by ward captains.

The bosses were also expected to support the party from their own financial resources. They presented a model that was to be followed by all workers in the party. Theirs was the largest contribution. Although there was no formal financial assessment of workers, each person was told or knew from experience how much he or she was expected to contribute to the party. Often memos were openly sent around to all party loyalists in government positions with the accompanying message that a certain amount of money was expected for the next campaign. The level of payment for each job level was outlined.

The theme played over and over again in ward politics was loyalty; the Boss helps you and you help the Boss. Specifically, it meant discipline and the power of enforcement of the aims of the organization. Party discipline was maintained primarily through a system of rewards and punishments meted out by the boss and his deputies. The rewards came in the form of political appointments to government jobs and filling vacant positions through promotion within the organization. The hardest-working or most popular persons in the ward were favored with political preference. Key party workers and their entire families were covered by this reward system. Positions could be created to fit a particular worker's qualifications and promotions could be encouraged even when the job was covered by civil service. The important factor in building this power base was that the boss had the final say in all appointments. This centralized locus of power kept the loyal worker indebted to the boss of the party. Thus it was in the interest of municipal employees to battle with all their might to keep the party that provided their jobs in office, and to make proper donations to the party coffers in order to ensure their own income.

Finally, the political basis for the boss system rested upon the extremely effective organizational style of the political leaders. The organization ultimately depended upon the commitment of its most fundamental activists. These were the neighborhood-based unpaid party volunteers. Their role was to reach out to their constituents by understanding the problems of each individual and making their problems known to the next step in the hierarchy of the party so that they could be either resolved or ameliorated in some fashion. Party functionaries at the lowest level, often without any titles, would hope someday to be repaid for their activities by moving up in the hierarchy of the party or at least receiving some kind of political appointment, perhaps of the most mundane kind. To hold the position as court bailiff, while not a major responsibility to a professional, would seem a very considerable goal in life when the alternative was a twelve-hour day in a steel mill or a fourteen-hour day in the sweatshops of New York's lower east side. For the most part, the party workers were not motivated by an ideological commitment or by the satisfaction of doing good, but by the return they could expect to receive as a result of their years of work and loyalty.

The lowest level of party functionaries reported to those higher up. Usually they had a title such as sergeant and reported to a smaller group of party functionaries, the lieutenants, who reported to an even smaller group that were at the heart of the process, the captains. The captains collected and relayed all the significant developments in their wards, organized "get out and vote" campaigns, and served as conduits for cash and services reaching the people from the machine leadership. Captains were responsible for the welfare of the constituents, functioning like a social service agency with a basket of food and some coal when things got tough or an entree to the crowded charity hospital, or as an advocate with the police.[3] Through the appointment of ward captains, bosses were kept informed based on the captain's elaborate files of requests made by people in the district and responses given. Party workers took turns keeping the file up-to-date but the captains themselves were responsible for answering each and every request for assistance. The captains' offices in the ward were remarkably similar to welfare agencies or community centers with food banks attached. Many captains spent their entire day in service to people in the ward. Plunkitt of Tammany Hall described a typical day, which began at 5:00 A.M.: "going down to jail to put up bail for a man, assisting a family burned out during the night, lining up a job for another man, attending a funeral, buying tickets for a church supper, putting in an appearance at a bar mitzvah, and finally at 8:30 P.M., showing up with a present at a wedding."[4] All these activities included a personal touch. The captains informed the boss about what was going on in the ward and advised when a personal appearance was necessary. These personal visits from "on high" were events that were noted throughout the community. It gave to the ward a sense that the bosses personally cared about their people's wishes, feelings, and personal needs.

The captains reported to the district leaders, the key leadership element in the party structure. In some cases they were known as ward leaders and these political survivors represented a constituency of voters as well as an organization loyal to themselves. They rarely ran for elected public office, although sometimes they served as alderman or city councilmen. They mainly served as leaders of the party. It was in that role that the district leaders usually chose from among themselves the head of the local party. It was this party president or party leader that functioned as the city boss. Occasionally he might be a mayor, but it was even more likely that he would select the person running for mayor and remain behind the scenes to control the political apparatus.

Parallel to this formal structure were the ward clubs and county social organizations. These clubs were far more than social bodies, however; they provided informal settings in which persons could be screened, recruited, and finally signed up for party responsibilities. The clubs provided a kind of poor man's social hall where every person was valued on the basis of how many votes he or she controlled. In 1924, George Washington Plunkitt colorfully described this principle: "This is the way and the only way to make a lastin' success in politics, do as I did. Get a followin', if it's only one man, and then go to the district leader and say, 'I want to join the organization. I've got one man who'll follow me through thick and thin.' The leader won't laugh at your one man followin'. He'll shake your hand warmly, offer to propose you for membership in his club, take you down for a drink and ask you to call again."[5]

Thus, this organizational structure reached into the very tenement houses of the immigrant working class and up through the highest elements of party life. This was a highly centralized system based on party loyalty, rewards, productivity, and the ability to produce votes and supporters.

The leadership style of the urban political bosses was built upon this organizational structure. The bosses were consummate organizers. They selected competent lieutenants, captains, and sergeants, who in turn were expected to choose their associates. No part of the party was left without a tie to the central organization. The wards were organized by geographical units, by ethnic representation, and by potential support groups such as businessmen, laborers, and youth. Bosses expected contributions of time and financial resources to the party coffers as a grateful response for past favors. The bosses sought to organize the potential influence of business, religious, and ethnic groups. These groups were kept loyal to the bosses and the party through a series of agreements, past commitments, and promised returns.

The bosses were also the financial managers of the party. They had to be skilled in financial and human-resource development. They had to raise the funds for the candidates and they had to allocate the financial resources of the party. They were also personnel managers. They had to be able to set tasks for all party workers, develop a supervisory network ultimately answerable to themselves but one in which authority could be easily delegated.

The bosses had to be skilled negotiators. It was in the informal settings of personal meetings and brief chats at social affairs that the boss made the contracts and developed the personal agreements that guided the party. Most of the essential business of the machine was executed by bosses on a one-to-one basis and in an informal manner. The official meetings of the party to nominate the slate of candidates were merely perfunctory. The actual selection had preceded the formal action. The personal element was even considered in financial matters. People often came to the bosses for loans that were occasionally repaid, but more often not. Loyalty was loyalty and the bosses took care of their people. Administering such a complex network of both formal and informal relationships required considerable organizational skills. As consummate organizers, bosses could lead formal meetings, manage informal negotiating sessions, handle complex financial matters, keep responsible personnel working around the clock often under stressful circumstances, and at all times keep the essential mission of the party clearly in view of everyone.[6]

The leader had to serve as the intermediary and unifying element among the numerous ethnic groups within the party's constituency. Such unity often became essential in winning elections. Ultimately, the party leader had to be able to orchestrate the election and reelection of party stalwarts, and in doing so provide the patronage on which much of the political organization rested. To get reelected meant that officeholders of the party in power had to perform in such a way that the immigrant working class believed in the advantages of the party's victory. In other words, the bosses had to get things done—and they did.

Under the political bosses city government had a positive role. It actively supported the urban development at a time when the standard political outlook differed considerably. The approach of the bosses, who had to get the job done to be reelected, was not ideological, but pragmatic. The party often, by necessity, provided benefits to parts of the working class but at the same time was not antibusiness, nor was it "left" in any fashion. Quite the contrary, the bosses made a fetish out of their patriotism and probusiness perspective.

Since the machine provided a means to citizenship, the traditional political party seemed but an extension of the country's governmental apparatus. The new citizens were simultaneously assimilated into a new land and a new party. The party itself was blatantly, even joyfully, patriotic. Early Tammany Hall Fourth of July celebrations were extravagant events that overshadowed other social happenings of the day. The Declaration of Independence was read, solemn speeches were made followed by consumption of multiple cases of champagne. The Tammany organization literally wrapped itself in the American flag. "It's [the Hall] just a mass of flags. They even take down the window shades and put up flags in place of them. There are flags everywhere, except on the floors. We don't care for expense where the American flag is concerned." Political organizers found that they had a greater sense of cohesion among the persons being organized when their own organization and specific goals were seen as part of some larger and more noble purpose or symbol like the American flag.[7]

The bosses stayed in office, or at least kept their supporters in elective office, by providing for their constituency. Under the leadership of boss rule the cities built new streets, collected the garbage, provided public transportation, laid out parks and playgrounds, added public buildings, and so forth. These were the types of activities one would expect from government under ordinary conditions; however, the cities functioned poorly before the bosses and city services continued to lag behind the growth of the urban population. It was uncommon, for example, to have effective, orderly garbage collection. It was uncommon for the cities to have paved streets, particularly where working-class immigrants lived. It was uncommon for cities to build parks and playgrounds. The bosses made up for deficiencies such as these. Even the infamous Boss Tweed added such services and it was under Boss Tweed's administration that New York City's Central Park was planned.

In addition to the official services the cities provided, the urban political leadership helped the ethnic working class in other ways. At a time when public assistance was virtually nonexistent, a family in need could often expect a basket of food or a turkey on Christmas, thanks to the political organization. A job might be found for an unemployed constituent, whether in the public sector or in the local building trades. Bail, lessening of sentences, an understanding word to a judge, a shortcut to citizenship, the ability to get a license for a pushcart or a small business, and the remission of some minor fine might be procured from the local political organization. The bosses advanced a de facto system of primitive public welfare at a time when the body politic would not approve such aid to the immigrant working class.[8]

To provide for so many persons in such a detailed fashion required not only a personal representative from the ward hierarchy, but also the development of an information network capable of reporting on the wards' daily requirements. Providing services often meant getting to a family before they were visited by representatives from the opposing party. Plunkitt told of trying to outguess the opposition in determining what kind of expensive or appropriate present to provide for the wedding of an important constituent.[9]

People did not often state their needs and, therefore, the bosses had to have a feel for actual community needs, acquired through a communications network of trusted captains. The information networks were based on foundations of trust between the boss, the captains, and the people in the wards. People would not unburden themselves to untrustworthy individuals. Without that trust there was no foundation and the power of the party and the boss quickly disintegrated. With trust in place, economic and social conditions could go bad while the people would still trust the party leadership. Trust was based on history of service and faithfulness on the part of the party and the boss. Such a history of personal favors in the form of licenses granted and food baskets delivered was recounted as loyal party workers escorted the voter to the polls on election day.

The political leadership also had an understanding, an empathy, a consideration of the mores of the immigrant groups within their constituency. In contrast, institutions and practices considered acceptable within the norms of the ethnic group were often considered immoral by society at large and indeed sometimes violated criminal laws. Gambling, for example, was a standard recreation for many of the immigrants from southern and southeastern Europe and for some of the east European groups. The society as a whole saw gambling in a much more negative way and laws made gambling illegal. Under the bosses the local police would ignore those rules. Of course, the officer on the beat would receive payment for his lack of observation and a portion of this payment would rise in the system through various levels of the police force and eventually reach the coffers of the party itself. The saloons that were open on Sunday in cities that had laws making the Sabbath sale of alcohol illegal followed the same procedure. The evasion of such laws held considerable importance to the ethnic groups. The German family, for example, expected to go on Sunday after church to the local German tavern where the family would drink some beer and socialize. Even the children would have a little beer, usually mixed with sugar, and then nap while the family had a pleasant Sunday singing songs from the old country. This was considered wholesome, family activity—at least by the German Americans. It was considered highly immoral by the white Protestant elite of the city and state. The bosses ignored the Sunday tavern closing laws and saw to it that their police force did as well. The political leadership from the top all the way down to the officer on the beat received their payments for this understanding.

Prostitution had a similar role. Many of the ethnic groups came from countries with legalized prostitution. Moreover, in every case, immigrant males arrived before their wives and sweethearts. Depending on the pattern of the ethnic group, it sometimes took five or six years for a family to be reunited. Many of the men deserted their families from the old country and started families anew in the United States. Prostitution, some argued, played a positive role by making desertion less common and thus keeping families together. This argument had little support among the existing American public. The bosses accepted the permissive point of view, and in doing so accepted as well the gratuities that came with overlooking prostitution.

In addition to providing the normal city services, the de facto help of an unofficial public welfare system, and the acceptance of particular mores of individual ethnic groups, the bosses provided jobs in a very direct sense. Their patronage eventually reached down to each major ethnic group. The political leadership consciously divided the spoils. It is true that generally one ethnic group, the Irish Catholics, was much more dominant than the others in the political process. But the system that the Irish political leadership put together resulted in all of the major ethnic groups receiving some of the attention and support over the years. The most obvious example of that was the "balanced ticket" in which the various ethnic groups were regularly represented among the candidates for major political office. If a German Jew appeared on the ticket, an Irish Catholic needed to be represented as well. Often bosses placed ethnic leaders in official positions according to the proportionate number of their ethnic constituency in the district. Leaders were valued in terms of how many people were loyal to them or how many votes could be garnered by a particular person's name on the ballot. It was a simple matter of counting heads.

The party also functioned as an engine of social mobility. Hard work for the party was recognized, respected, and rewarded. Persons without education or social standing were often thrust into leadership roles if they showed the proper loyalty and energetic commitment. Attention to rewards and mobility within the political organization was important. Political organizers recognized the importance of a reward system as well as consideration of promotional opportunities within their organizations. Even the most loyal of persons lost heart when their efforts went unrecognized.

While patronage provided some jobs, far more were provided through the general development and building of the cities of industrial America, for the bosses not only aided the immigrants but they worked very closely with business interests, particularly those concerned with urban development. On the whole business leaders opposed boss control. The exceptions were the builders of new homes, public buildings, sewer systems, the developers of public and private transportation, all of whom benefited from urban expansion.

The system worked very simply. The favored business interests received contracts from the public body and a proportion, often up to 80 percent, of the payment for the particular work involved was turned over to the party. It was in this area that the political bosses produced their largest incomes. It was from this source that the Christmas turkey or the fuel during a cold winter could be provided. Again, it should be noted that the bosses were not Robin Hoods robbing from the rich to give to the poor. They were pragmatic individuals who took what seemed to be a reasonable amount in order to provide services not usually rendered by the body politic. The bosses did not go unrewarded themselves, of course, but on the whole they were not extravagant nouveau riche parading their conspicuous consumption. They usually remained in the neighborhoods where they were born, living a moderately comfortable life style.

These bosses began their careers in the streets of local neighborhoods; they spoke directly to the people they knew personally from the backs of wagons and trucks. They themselves lived and worked there and had worked their way up through the ranks of the party. They were local products. They had gone to the local schools, sold newspapers on the corners, and grown up among relatives and friends who lived and worked in the neighborhood. They campaigned on street corners, at barbecues, and at picnics. They developed legions of followers, who in turn also spoke on their behalf in the electoral campaigns. They identified the city's needs with the party's needs.[10]

They also felt it was important to keep close to the people in the wards in terms of personal life style, display of property, and use of language. Even if they could afford it, they did not ride around in luxury cars or dress flamboyantly. Since many of their constituents could not even read, they did not use language that displayed sophisticated vocabularies. Being simple and clear in speaking to people and using the dialect were developed and practiced political skills. "Now nobody ever saw me puttin' on any style. I'm the same Plunkitt I was when I entered politics forty years ago. That is why the people in the district have confidence in me. If I went into the stylish business, even I, Plunkitt, might be thrown out of the district—another thing that people won't stand for is showin' off your learnin', that's just putting on style in another way. If you're

makin' speeches in a campaign, talk the language the people talk."
The bosses advertised their past and sought not to divorce themselves from their roots. This display of naturalness and identification with the neighborhood was an effective political tool. Many opponents were destroyed by the tactic of a boss reporting to the voters on having been born "just down the street," having gone to high school in "that particular neighborhood," married in "old St. Stephen's Church," going to the wedding of his son in another parish, in effect saying "You see, I grew up as you did; I have lived here too; you and I are the same. A vote for me is a vote for yourself."[11]

The obvious cost of this system was the corruption. There were the kickbacks on development, the patronage system itself, which was a form of kickback to the party for employment, and the various payoffs for vice and other kinds of illegal activities. But to most of the immigrant working class the costs were worth it. The evidence is simply that the bosses were elected and reelected over and over again. On the rare occasion following an extreme scandal when the bosses found themselves defeated the party remained out of office rarely more than one election. The working class and other allies of the bosses were soon to rally and bring them back to office. This is not surprising. The reformers who came into office and replaced the bosses were interested in enforcing the law, not overlooking its lack of empathy; they were interested in cutting taxes, not providing aid to those who needed it; they were interested in providing some patronage and perhaps civil service reform to some degree, but not jobs to the immigrant communities that would have to decide on their reelection. Thus the political system of the cities associated with political bossism remained a viable vehicle from the 1870s well into the late 1930s, and in some cities such as Chicago well beyond that. Ultimately it rested on organizational skill—the human contact on a day-to-day basis, street by street, tenement house to tenement house.

In summary, the organizing strategies of ward politics suggest some lessons from the past for contemporary community organizers: (1) the utility of a tightly structured organization, with a system of representation from top to bottom and delegated responsibility at each level of the organization, (2) the importance of a clear organizational purpose, (3) the value of centralized administrative control of the organization blended with considerable effort to delegate, (4) the importance given to the lowest units in close touch with the needs of the people to be organized, (5) the active use of a system of clear rewards and opportunities for promotion within the organization, (6) the importance of linking organizing goals to broader societal values, and (7) active efforts to provide for the social needs of the organization's members as well as accomplishing the political tasks.

Political organizing involves developing a variety of power bases, establishing geographical units of various sizes and responsibility, developing systems of discipline and control, paying attention to personal and social needs of members, and maintaining a highly visible leadership style among the constituency. Leadership skills relevant to effective organizing include the development of an organizing "style," a capacity for making correct and timely choices, knowing how and when to use power, and paying attention to the ethnic composition of the community in which the organizer is working. There are no substitutes for hard work, energetic leadership, and attention to details. The effective bosses had the necessary leadership skills to manage their political machines and maintain the loyalty of workers. Community organizers can learn from the lessons of the past. Acquiring such knowledge and skill is one of the primary lessons of ward politics.

10

The Conflict Approach to Community Organizing: Saul Alinsky and the CIO

Neil Betten and Michael J. Austin

SAUL ALINSKY'S style of organizing received considerable academic and public attention after the publication of Charles Silberman's *Crisis in Black and White* (1956), which depicted Alinsky's methods as an effective and innovative way to fight poverty. Alinsky's techniques were rooted in the labor movement, particularly the Congress of Industrial Organizations (CIO) of the 1930s; both used controlled conflict as their chief organizational tool. Alinsky's techniques were, in fact, dependent on traditional labor organizing methods. Although he had often been considered an innovator, Alinsky freely acknowledged borrowing many of his ideas from organized labor. He did, however, have a greater debt than he realized. In his last book, *Rules for Radicals*, Alinsky argued that professional labor organizers and Alinsky-trained community organizers had different perspectives, although he praised the CIO organizers of the 1930s. Occasionally, students of Alinsky have also suggested—rather uncertainly—that he was methodologically dependent on organized labor. Unfortunately neither labor historians nor other contemporary scholars knowledgeable about the emergence of the CIO have fully explored its organizing techniques in the 1930s. Thus, the method-ological relationship between Alinsky and the CIO has not been fully understood.[1]

Before emerging as a community organizer in 1939, Alinsky ex-isted on the fringe of the great CIO organizing drive of the 1930s. The CIO, first as a dissident group within the American Federation of Labor (AFL) and later as a rival federation, began organizing industrial workers in 1935. CIO organizers from the socialist-oriented Amalgamated Clothing Workers Union, from the more conserva-tive United Mine Workers, and from the disbanded Trade Union Unity League—a creation of the Communist party—utilized both traditional organizing techniques and innovative methods. Alinsky helped in organizing the CIO Newspaper Guild and aided dissident factions within the United Mine Workers. From his early experiences as an organizer, Alinsky reminisced about "the moonlighting I'd done as an organizer for the CIO." Although the miners he sup-ported opposed the United Mine Workers' president, John L. Lewis, Alinsky considered "many of John L. Lewis's tactics . . . brilliant in conception and execution." He added, "There are important lessons here for today's battles." Alinsky learned these lessons well, for he simply took labor's approach in organizing communities of indus-trial workers and applied it to geographically based communities of mostly working-class and low-income people.[2]

Both Alinsky and organized labor in the 1930s, using conflict as an organizational vehicle, aimed to wrest power from elite groups and redistribute it to their constituency. Power to organized labor meant ending employers' control over hours, wages, and working conditions, and meeting with management as equals at the collective bargaining table. To Alinsky, gaining power for a community-based people's organization was, by necessity, more complicated. The op-position was not a single employer, but a loosely interrelated power elite. Nevertheless, power remained the goal. Alinsky explained, "Progress occurs only in response to threats, and reconciliation only results when one side gets reconciled to it. . . . The power of orga-nized people is required to defeat the power of the establishment and its money." Alinsky related his position on power to the CIO outlook in his biography of Lewis. "The people who had worked and suffered in the auto industry knew that the vast corporations would listen only to the voice of power."[3]

If significant elements of a community wanted the power balance changed through organization, and wanted Alinsky's help, they had to invite him into the community and make a serious financial commitment to achieve the desired results. This, to a degree, also mirrored the CIO approach. Labor organizers rarely entered the fray until local workers indicated a desire to be organized. Industrial workers, whom the AFL had long ignored, literally clamored to be organized during the depression of the 1930s. Thus the CIO did not organize where workers did not welcome them. But in later years—even today—when potential members seem more difficult to find, most unions follow a similar policy for they reject spending considerable time and money in wasted effort. The unions, not the community being organized (as in the Alinsky approach), bear the financial organizing costs.

Once a handful of CIO staff members entered a target area, they immediately set out to discover the workers' major complaints and condensed them in pamphlets. They established friendly relations with newspaper editors and pastors, who could aid in disseminating the union point of view or who could influence public opinion. In discussing the CIO Steel Workers Organizing Committee (SWOC), a contemporary analyst pointed out, "The first job, of course, was to create contacts with key men who would serve as radial centers for the dissemination of SWOC doctrine." Like the labor organizers, Alinsky people searched for local opinion shapers. Sometimes they were pastors, sometimes local union officials, or often just ordinary people who seemed to be the natural opinion leaders of the people; as Alinsky put it, "Any labor organizer knows of the Little Joes."[4]

Alinsky organizers searched for the key issues as well. Like the American labor movement, Alinsky appealed primarily to the economic interests of his clientele and to the similar interests of potential community converts. Both Alinsky and the CIO sought out other salient issues as well. Labor organizers delivered a whole list of demands to management, and subsequent collective bargaining contracts often reached thirty or forty pages. Likewise, Alinsky advised community organizers to use "multiple issues," not only because one-issue organizations die when the one problem is resolved, but also because every person or interest block has "a hierarchy of issues." The organization that focuses on many concerns can appeal, Alinsky argued, to a larger number of supporters.[5]

Although many complex nuances were often involved, Alinsky told potential organizers that once they determined their stand it should be presented as completely correct, honest, and righteous. The opposition's position should be presented as wrong, corrupt, and evil. Alinsky's tactics permitted no "middle ground"; the opposition was clearly the enemy.[6] His tactic of polarizing issues and personalizing the enemy has been controversial, particularly in church circles—where Alinsky, nevertheless, had considerable support. Alinsky heightened the issues, threatened and attacked those immediately responsible for perpetuation of problems or those who could resolve them. His clientele, Alinsky believed, had to be sensitized—even enraged—to take strong action. "They must feel so frustrated, so defeated, so lost . . . that they are willing to let go of the past." In illustrating the polarization tactic, Alinsky used an example from the CIO that—unlike the official AFL posture—also polarized issues and personalized the opposition when practical. He quoted Lewis speaking to yet unorganized rubber workers, "Go to Goodyear and tell them you want some of those stock dividends. Say, so we're supposed to be partners, are we? Well, we're not, we're enemies."[7]

CIO spokespersons interpreted almost all the workers' problems as resulting from unjust management policies, and if possible they personalized the enemy. As Carey E. Haigler, a United Steel Workers official put it in discussing the 1930s, "There was no real necessity of local organizers to focus on the corporation as the enemy. It was the enemy." Haigler pointed out that occasionally a local corporate head had a favorable image and could not be used "as the villain." In most cases, as in the larger CIO industrial targets such as steel, labor used "the man in Pittsburgh or Chicago as the big bad wolf type."[8]

If enemies were militantly challenged, friends were courted as well. Alinsky pointed out that to build a people-based community organization effectively the organizer had to understand and relate to the client community and refrain from "rhetoric foreign to the local culture." Moreover, he added, "since people understand only in terms of their own experience, an organizer must have at least a cursory familiarity with their experience." Once the organizer understood the culture and made the right contacts, he could take advantage of additional community support. Alinsky organizers have been particularly adept at gaining support of clerics and using their church facilities.[9]

Although the old AFL often neglected this approach, the CIO unions in the 1930s found it important to understand the community and utilize its resources in dealing with the often hostile labor-relations environment in the company-dominated towns of the 1930s. CIO organizers made special efforts to understand local mores in attempting to relate to industrial workers. This posed a formidable task in immigrant communities having diverse traditions and sometimes conflicting values. Organizers participated at immigrant picnics and dances and "regularly attended mass at the working class churches," Steel Workers Organizing Committee member Brandan Sexton observed. He also pointed out that when organizers arrived in town they immediately went to visit the halls and newspaper offices of the ethnic societies. Moreover, union organizers insisted that major ethnic groups "were represented on the staff of the union and . . . put forward to speak for the union. Most of us tried to learn a few words of each language."[10]

Such special efforts paid off. Irwin L. DeShelter, CIO organizer and later staff member, reported that "CIO organizers used all local facilities that were available such as the Polish Clubs, Slovak Halls, Italian Clubs, and many others." Nicholas A. Zonarich, Organizational Director of the Industrial Union Department of the AFL-CIO recalled that in the 1930s the CIO capitalized on the immigrant clubs and fraternal organizations. "They were very effective in the early days of CIO organizing campaigns especially in those communities where the population was quite prominent among the foreign and ethnic groups." Likewise, Sexton related that "Polish, Croatian, Hungarian, Italian, etc., societies were almost always actively supporting the union organizing drives." In addition, in advancing pro-union propaganda such groups served numerous functions: "In many cases, the nationality halls or parish houses were natural places to set up strike headquarters," Sexton pointed out. He added that in east Baltimore a strikers' medical clinic operated out of a Polish hall, and in Bethlehem, Pennsylvania, an immigrant society expelled members that worked during a strike. The CIO organizing committees sometimes brought mutually hostile ethnic associations together in loose alliances and combined them with church groups and local clubs. In the steel industry the labor organizers fostered an inter-ethnic convention representing all racial, religious, and national elements of the community. Convention delegates discussed CIO strategy and coordinated the immigrant and ethnic role in the organizing drive.[11]

In order to recruit union members, indigenous leaders—whether unskilled laborers or local priests—were often sought out and CIO organizers secured their support. In Roman Catholic immigrant communities, where workers through religious and social commitments had strong ties to their church, the CIO made special efforts to influence the clergy. UAW organizer Brandan Sexton found that "the priests of the ethnic church and, in some cases, ministers of middle-class Protestant churches supported the union's efforts." Although he considered some pastors anti-union, "most were quite close to their congregations and friendly to the union." The CIO went to considerable effort to illustrate its virtues to reluctant clergy. Industrial unions often called on CIO allies, such as the Association of Catholic Trade Unionists (ACTU), for support during the depression. The ACTU had branches in the major industrial cities. Among other activities, it operated a speakers' bureau manned by "labor priests," who traveled to heavily Catholic CIO organizing cities where the clerics argued the case for unionization and denied accusations that Communists controlled the CIO. Likewise, CIO unions called upon the Catholic Worker Movement and the Catholic Radical Alliance for similar aid. Well-known prolabor priests such as Charles Owen Rice of Pittsburgh and theologian John A. Ryan helped the CIO legitimize itself to many suspicious communities.[12]

Supporters, whether from inside or outside the community, provided crucial help, but the organizer depended on members to achieve significant gains. In trying to correct abuses, Alinsky used a panorama of tactics, "everything at our disposal" as he put it, in discussing his famous Back of the Yards campaign of 1939; boycotts of stores, strikes against meat packers, rent strikes against slumlords, picketing of businesses, and sit-downs in city hall and in the offices of corrupt local machine bosses. Although later utilizing such militant tactics became more common in community organizing, they were seldom used in neighborhood organizing activities in the late 1930s and early 1940s. With this style Alinsky proposed to outflank his opposition—to hit them outside the usual realm of experience. In later years he added variations to these techniques, but the approach remained the same.[13]

These tactics borrowed much from the politically left labor movement of the 1930s. Boycotts of stores and products were ancient labor tools. Strikes and picketing were, of course, common. Rent strikes were often led by Communist tenants' leagues in the 1930s and the sit-down strike was made famous by the CIO auto and rubber workers. Alinsky refined and personalized these tactics. Ghetto Blacks picketing suburban homes of white slumlords, for example, became a well-publicized Alinsky nuance to traditional picketing.

Effective techniques alone did not immediately resolve complicated long-standing problems. Because Alinsky believed that "action comes from keeping the heat on," community action organizations needed to be permanent. When the Alinsky staff left an area they ideally left behind a stable, but militant, organization. Alinsky's people's organizations were structured to be democratic as well as long lasting. The internal structure of Alinsky organizations closely resembled the trade union structure, although there were some necessary differences as well.[14]

Alinsky organizations were made up of locally based formal associations such as church groups, local unions, block clubs, businesses, and parent-teacher associations. The typical Alinsky community organization, which might have two hundred such subgroups, was governed by an annual convention (called a congress), which elected officers, passed resolutions, and indicated the next year's thrust. Between conventions an executive board of officers supplemented by delegates from member organizations governed the body through monthly meetings. Similarly, a national union, made up of local unions, is governed by its annual convention, which elects officers (not necessarily annually), passes resolutions to establish policies, and determines the next year's program. Between conventions an executive board consisting of elected officers and a large number of vice-presidents—in effect delegates of the large locals—governs the organization. In addition other locally based groups or regional bodies meet. In some unions the locals were more autonomous than in others; some locals had sublocals or chapters or other minor variations.[15] Although the union and the Alinsky organizational structures were quite similar, Alinsky organizations had a greater dependence on paid professional staff than did unions. Other differences existed as well. Local union members usually had similar occupations and economic interests, while associations that came together to utilize Alinsky often had conflicting interests and totally different kinds of members. The structural similarities between Alinsky organizations and the national trade union, however, were so striking, it is impossible to conclude that it came about by accident or coincidence.

After Alinsky established an organization and it functioned effectively, his staff left to battle elsewhere. The fully independent community organizations hired their own staff. Local leaders who emerged during their organizational periods (or were helped to emerge because they had the necessary qualities) and those who had leadership roles before the organizing programs would govern the new independent organization.

Although Alinsky-assisted community organizations of low-income people emerged as local independent entities, newly organized CIO union locals did not sever their ties to the national union. Nevertheless, each union-organizing effort meant training new leaders to run the local union just as Alinsky organizers prepared local activists to direct their own community organization fully.

Even while organizing a strike, CIO officials prepared a new local for self-government by finding and training indigenous leaders. In other organizations, such as the Textile Workers, the United Auto Workers, the Hosiery Workers, and Rubber Workers, local and regional schools were established to train new leaders further. On the other hand, the Steel Workers, like their parent, the United Mine

Workers, depended on an informal recruitment of new talent. No matter what the techniques of individual unions, "the very success of the CIO was in its ability to develop local leadership," DeShelter persuasively argued, for the national staff "had to move on to other fields." Oliver W. Singleton, who organized in West Virginia, Kentucky, and Virginia, agreed that the CIO was rooted in "its ability to attract and develop indigenous leadership."[16]

Through their organization, strikes, political victories, and training of new leaders, labor unions achieved considerable gains for their members. Yet they face continued attack from the left as well as the right. Many of the recent criticisms of the Alinsky approach are analogous to the criticism that organized labor continues to face.

Unions have been attacked in recent years as too conservative. Yet labor leaders generally reflect their members' concerns and when a democratic union has a conservative membership, the leadership cannot move too far ahead of its constituency and remain in power. The oldest Alinsky organization, the Back of the Yards Neighborhood Council established in 1939, was later criticized for its conservative attitudes.

Some radicals accuse both Alinsky organizations and organized labor of having bourgeois tendencies. The labor movement bureaucrats are accused of being more concerned with a stable membership than with ideology or even organizing. Moreover, traditional unions serve management by policing members with regard to collective bargaining contracts so that labor does not violate a contractual relationship. Likewise Alinsky critics on the left argue that his organizations basically defend middle-class interests (e.g., they fight deterioration of housing so that adjacent middle-class homes do not depreciate in value), are run by white middle-class organizers from outside the community, are led by the better-off of the community and the most educated (such as clerics), and have middle-class goals. In the words of a sympathetic Alinsky analyst, Alinsky's organizations are based on "middle-class persons [who] are trying to combat lower-class problems."[17]

It is not surprising that labor and Alinsky faced similar criticism. Once the CIO could be considered "radical," so Alinsky also considered himself a "pragmatic radical." CIO leaders and Alinsky both had visions of a better society. Like the CIO, however, Alinsky moved, perhaps unconsciously, in a reformist direction. Both patched up the system rather than attempting to change it radically. Since Alinsky was a preserver of the system, it is not surprising that much of his financial support has come from such individuals as millionaire Marshall Field and through foundation grants from corporations such as Midas Muffler. Liberal corporate interests prefer the system to continue—in order to benefit them, at perhaps a more efficient rate of growth and without unnecessary hardships.

Whether ultimately protecting the system or not, Alinsky made a formidable contribution to the field of community organizing. He established controlled conflict as an important approach to be used on a neighborhood basis. Specialists in community organizing have recognized Alinsky's preeminence in using conflict strategies. A standard text in the field refers to Alinsky as "perhaps the best known practitioner in the field of community organizing."[18] Moreover, Alinsky successfully negated the traditional view held in the community organizing field before his rise to national prominence, that problems can be viewed as separate from the power structure of the community.

But this is not to say that Alinsky was a creative innovator, as some analysts have assumed. Alinsky clearly adopted his general power-building approach and specific tactics from the CIO (and from those organizations from which the CIO borrowed ideas). Thus, controlled conflict illustrates the intertwining of two aspects of community organizing: the building of the activist CIO unions of the 1930s and the creation of Alinsky's militant people's organizations, whose techniques grew out of the CIO experience.

11

Religious Organizations as a Base for Community Organizing: The Catholic Worker Movement during the Great Depression

Neil Betten and William E. Hershey

SINCE the earliest days of organized religion, religious-based groups have emerged in the form of loosely organized, locally based fellowships as well as tightly structured, international institutions. A common designation, "church," has been used by Christians to refer either to the "whole people of God" or to a particular local institution such as "University Congregational Church." Just as the "church" cannot be captured in any one organizational model, neither can there be one definition for religious activists and organizers. Leaders of religious groups have led movements that functioned both as societies serving the needy and as community institutions for worship and socializing. At various points in their history, churches have served as bases for social action. During the Great Depression, labor unrest and heavy unemployment caused a number of key religious organizers to respond to these societal concerns.

The Great Depression was an American, and international, catastrophe. The depression's massive poverty resulted primarily from unemployment. In 1933, thirteen million were unemployed in the United States while in 1934, 1935, and 1936 the total fluctuated between ten and eleven million. At the end of the decade, nearly ten million still remained without jobs. *Fortune* magazine, a voice of the American business elite, estimated that eleven million unemployed workers meant one out of every four of those employable, or 25,500,000 people, found their livelihood cut off. The percentage of those unemployed rose from 3 percent in 1929 to 25 percent in 1933. It never fell below 14 percent during the decade. These U.S. government figures actually underestimate the depth of the problem. Many groups were not counted as unemployed. Those entering the labor market for the first time, people returning to family farms after they could not find work, those employed part-time (and therefore unemployed part-time), those being supported by various government programs, and others were omitted from the unemployment statistics. Unemployment was also unequal. In some parts of the country, particularly areas based on a single hard-hit industry, almost an entire population suffered unemployment. Blacks faced particular problems. In the North, they were among the last groups to benefit from industrial employment and were one of the first groups laid off during the depression. In the South, the depression years ushered in an increased, highly volatile, and belligerent racism.

Unemployment often resulted in homelessness. Hoovervilles, shacks usually constructed of cardboard, tarpaper, and scraps, sprouted up in city dumps, abandoned factory areas, public parks, and any place else those evicted from their homes found space. The Hooverville became a symbol of the breakdown of the American economy. Poverty, hunger, inadequate public assistance, exhausted private charities, hundreds of bankrupt cities, three bankrupt states, closed schools, and teachers and other public employees occasionally paid in promissory notes (when paid at all) became part of the common lot in America, particularly during the early years of the depression.

Religious institutions responded to these circumstances in numerous ways. In some cases the churches became a base for community organizing. This was reflected in a variety of forms.

In the 1930s, an idealistic Roman Catholic's attempt to organize Catholic workers emerged as one example of this type of organizing effort. This utopian communal organization, known as the Catholic Worker Movement, was founded by Peter Maurin and

Dorothy Day. Maurin, a French itinerant philosopher, borrowed from thinkers such as Hillaire Belloc, Eric Gill, and Peter Kropotkin, in order to work out the Catholic Worker Movement's anticapitalist utopian ideology. Dorothy Day, the Movement's actual leader, kept Maurin's ideology relevant to contemporary America by continually introducing her practical point of view. The result was a dualism consisting of Maurin's agrarian communitarianism and Day's more pragmatic ideas oriented to the urban industrial worker. Although equally committed to an alternative economic order, her willingness to work within the capitalist system sowed the intellectual seeds of social reformism; Maurin's philosophy, on the other hand, was more uncompromising.

Maurin considered capitalism a completely corrupting way of life, a system that trained humans to prey on their fellows through economic competition.[1] The personal destruction resulting from individuals competing with one another and the impersonal nature of machines were seen as destroying the potential creativity in life and work. We thus faced, in Maurin's view, continuous assault by economic competition and psychological assault by the inhuman machine.[2]

Maurin argued that a compromise must not be made with the immoral system; a new way of life had to replace the old. He considered the 1930s a propitious time to construct a new way of life since capitalism was in disfavor and the social mood favored change. The New Deal, Maurin argued, did not go far enough in its attempts to reform the system, and merely reinforced the rotten beams of a corrupt structure. A complete change, Maurin felt, was needed; he called for a peaceful revolution through the establishment of agrarian communes across the country.[3] This utopia was the center of Maurin's ideological program: a decentralized back-to-the-land movement based on independent, primarily agricultural, communes, in which neither agriculture nor industry would be mechanized.

Maurin, however, did not set policy in Catholic Worker communes. He felt that the members of each commune should be truly independent to establish policy and respond to the needs of its own community. When asked for a specific communal plan, he responded, "I don't give blueprints."[4] Each commune was owned, administered, and financed independently. Local communal leadership often solicited advice from Maurin and Day, but the founders gave only philosophical direction and extended no controls.

By the end of the 1930s, several Catholic Worker communes were functioning, and approximately a dozen more arose independently but worked closely with the Movement.[5] Martin Paul, the director of the Catholic Worker group in Minneapolis, helped start the Holy Family Farm at Rhineland, Missouri.[6] The founders of the Philadelphia Catholic Worker house rented a large farm in Oxford, Pennsylvania, and used it for many years. The urban Catholic Worker house in Burlington operated in conjunction with a rural commune in Colchester, Vermont.[7] The Boston groups established St. Benedict's farm in Upton, Massachusetts.[8] In Cape May, New Jersey, Akron, Ohio, and South Lyon, Michigan, small independent communes sprang up trying to restore the idea of community.[9]

The New Yorkers' commune set the institutional pattern—even to the point where the others also seemed to emulate its uncertain beginnings. Its first attempt at agriculture began as a vegetable garden on Staten Island. This venture was superseded by a twenty-eight-acre farm situated about seventy miles from New York City near Easton, Pennsylvania.[10] In its first year, 1936, the farm of less than five acres was plowed mostly by a neighbor, who was paid to do the work. Catholic Worker settlers worked the remainder with a two-horse plow pulled by an old truck. While the settlement had some cows, chickens, and pigs, the main produce consisted of vegetables. Expanding in the following summer, the commune rented an adjoining forty-four-acre farm.

James Montague and Joseph Karella managed the New York commune during its early years, and much of the agricultural work was directed by Paul Toner, a Catholic Worker from Philadelphia.[11] Actual legal title of the property rested in the hands of what Dorothy Day called "the leaders of the Movement," the trustees of the Movement's newspaper, the *Catholic Worker*.[12] The original capital as well as operating expenses came mainly from donations.

The settlers worked the farm both communally and privately. Each member of the commune cultivated land that was held by all as well as a plot granted for his "exclusive and permanent use." The

Community, however, had final control over all sales of property and title reverted back to it if a member left permanently.[13]

Staff members, permanent residents, and people who came for short visits—from a weekend to several weeks—did the actual daily labor. Each contributed according to his or her own conscience. Slackers were officially accepted along with the others. The group's extreme toleration may be seen in the case of an asocial resident who lived alone on the commune but still caused continuous friction. Besides being an alcoholic who seldom worked, he periodically stole the meager tools of the commune to finance his drinking. Nothing in the way of personal, legal, or communal action was undertaken to exclude him from the commune. He lived there, taking what he felt he needed from the common storehouse of goods, until he died as an old man.[14]

While the New York commune was permissive, it still had problems distributing work equitably. Some of the permanent residents claimed that others did not do their shares, and they disapproved of the policy of providing hospitality to the many visitors, often students, who stopped at the farm. These guests often consumed communal produce and did only token work. The commune, nevertheless, continued its open policy. Maurin encouraged young intellectuals to visit the commune, hoping such visits would serve as an avenue for ultimate involvement. He stressed the role of the scholar through physical and craft labor. Like Kropotkin, he emphasized the regenerative power of the land; on it the scholar would be manually educated and the worker would become a scholar.[15] Scholars did not prove to be productive agricultural laborers, and it was predictable that the commune would not flourish economically.

Given the sources available, it is difficult to measure the prosperity of Catholic Worker communal life. Compounding this difficulty, the commune was also used as a recuperative center for the sick who sought help at the New York Catholic Worker center. Certainly, the commune operated efficiently enough so that residents ate well, at least by depression standards. It also gave unconsumed produce to the New York house, which distributed it to the unemployed. Consequently, unlike most communal movements, the Catholic Worker settlement did not attempt to reach any grand material heights. Idealizing the voluntary poverty of St. Francis, Maurin himself had few material possessions. He believed that in being poor, though not destitute, one could be truly free. Following his point of view, the commune never stressed material ends; still, it had adequate food and living space.

Visitors and workers alike lived in communal buildings and ate together in a large dining room. Maurin did not plan it this way. He preferred each family to own its individual private house. But a single family did not long occupy any new separate structure built by the commune. Lack of capital and, perhaps, the very experience of joint living at the New York settlement house resulted in primarily shared housing at the commune. Evidently, there was little dissatisfaction with the arrangement, since the commune survived. Other communes emerged and died. Yet the members recall them with fondness. William Gauchat, for example, one of the founders of the Cleveland commune, typically felt that life there was "never uncomfortable. . . . We felt poor and we were very happy there."[16]

Given the objectives of the Movement, however, the communal system failed. The New York commune never attracted many people. Nor did a large back-to-the-land movement that came along to emulate it. The communes became, as Joseph Zarella of the New York commune said, "Second house of hospitality,"[17] second to the urban settlement houses. Those attracted to the Movement liked the idea of a return to the land, but the communes remained, as Zarella had pointed out, "mostly theoretical propositions, since the great majority were more concerned with the immediate problems of daily living than with such grandiose philosophical schemes."[18]

The Movement's goal, nevertheless, remained a society based on a communal way of life. Maurin and Day began a propaganda drive to spread news about the Movement and its objectives. Their followers also organized urban settlement houses, both to deal with the problem of the unemployed and to win converts to the Movement. While they organized these activities in order to foster the primary goal of agricultural communitarianism, the urban organizing, in time, came to dominate the history of the Movement.

Dorothy Day, administrator and journalist, lived at the New York house. She helped direct its work and inspired most of it.

Maurin, to be sure, was respected by the staff, as the ideological leader of the Movement, but Day's personality was the more formidable. Nina Poleyn, one of the founders of the Milwaukee commune, and with the New Yorkers for a time, described Maurin as "an intellectual with a non-stop mind" who was "harder to be with" than the warmer Dorothy Day.[19] Zarella felt that her vibrant personality helped explain the movement: "There was nothing I wouldn't do for her,"[20] he stated. Since Maurin failed to emphasize the labor movement, which was seen as the panacea by many intellectuals in the 1930s, Day's concern for the unemployed heightened her influence and resulted in many Catholic Workers looking to her for direction. Also Day's experience as a journalist led to her editorship of the Movement's newspaper, the *Catholic Worker*. The administrative leverage it provided, combined with her personality, leadership qualities, and urban-labor orientation, led to an emphasis upon a more pragmatic approach to social problems as described in the *Catholic Worker*. The newspaper regularly published Maurin's "Easy Essays," which consisted of melodic free verse, but he had little else to do with the publication.

The *Catholic Worker* covered all aspects of what Day considered the workers' main concerns: the labor movement, racial problems, politics, the church and encyclicals, war, and general Catholic labor activities. It had a homespun quality that attempted to achieve an intimacy with its readers. Articles on the commune tended to be personal and gossipy. Day's columns often discussed her family and her friends within the Movement, and seemed to be directed toward an ingroup of readers.

Circulation nonetheless increased considerably during the 1930s. By the end of 1933, readers of the *Worker* numbered about 20,000. There were only about 700 subscribers, though many of these, local priests particularly, placed large orders and distributed the paper themselves. The balance were sold on the streets.[21] By 1938, circulation had risen from the previous year's 115,000 to 125,000.[22]

In addition to its newspaper, the Movement had other propaganda techniques. One was organizing street-corner meetings. Soon after the Movement began, two Catholic college students spoke on a Manhattan street corner for the Movement and distributed its newspaper.[23] Eventually, street meetings of the New York group were held on a regular basis three times a week.[24] Sometimes Maurin spoke on a corner or in Union Square, New York's popular gathering place for radicals. Frequently, he made arrangements for hecklers to attack his opinions, thereby giving him the attention needed to draw a crowd.[25]

Maurin's statements often drew heated responses, but Catholic Worker outdoor activities seldom led to physical violence. Conflicts with the followers of Father Charles Coughlin, the radio priest of the 1930s, were the only exceptions. William Gauchat reported that Coughlin's supporters harassed and threatened Catholic Worker activists in Cleveland. Comparing Coughlin's followers with another opposition group, the Communists, Gauchat depicted the Communists as "much more polite," almost sympathetic. "They would say here's a dollar; I'll take a half a dozen of the *Catholic Worker*."[26] While the Coughlinites harassed Gauchat's group, violence did not erupt in Cleveland; it did in New York and Pittsburgh, however. Father Charles Owen Rice, head of the Pittsburgh group explained (to Catholic theologian John A. Ryan) that Coughlinites disrupted local meetings by heckling and violence. Joseph Zarella reported similar confrontations as Coughlinites occasionally disrupted New York Catholic Worker picketing and outdoor demonstrations.[27]

Another aspect of Maurin's propaganda program, organized public discussions, caused fewer problems. The Manhattan Lyceum, at that time primarily a Communist and Socialist meeting place, hosted Catholic Worker meetings on a regular monthly basis.[28] In conjunction with these gatherings, the Movement attempted to establish a labor school, a common adjunct of worker-oriented organizations in the 1930s. At first, classes were held almost daily. They consisted of a talk or two generally preceded and followed by a discussion. Professors at local universities lectured and sometimes writers or clerics spoke.[29] By the middle of the decade, the labor school held more formal sessions, but only on one evening a month.[30] Maurin found that the popularity and spontaneity that he desired for the schools could not be sustained. His idea, however, did not die in the 1930s, since other units of the Movement had their own schools, and some ran summer schools for college students.

Maurin also advocated for urban refuges for the poor. These Houses of Hospitality, or hospices, as he called them, would serve as an immediate response to the depression. At these urban settlements, the unemployed could live along with Catholic Worker staff and everyone, ideally, would take what they needed from the common storehouse of goods while giving what they could of their time and abilities to society.[31] The establishment of hospices would, Maurin believed, lessen the need for impersonal bureaucratic unemployment measures. The destitute could be fed and housed with the expenses coming from charity. Once organized by the Catholic Worker community, however, the houses went beyond being urban refuges and avenues for rural communalization. They became centers for Catholic dissidents, intellectuals, and radicals, gathering places where they could read, argue, and test their views in informal debate. Major American Catholic social thinkers of the period— Virgil Michel, John A. Ryan, and Paul Hanley Furfey, among others—visited frequently, and thereby made contact with the resident radicals of these houses.[32] These youthful residents eventually stimulated considerable activity of their own; and Day guided a number of programs, many alien to Maurin's main thrust.

At the same time, Day and her followers were able to create the Hospitality House image Maurin desired and carried out many functions among the poor that he had visualized. The Catholic Worker followers procured food by making requests at neighboring markets. The farming communes provided all its excesses over subsistence.[33] The unemployed were fed and housed at autonomous Catholic Worker hospices in numerous cities.

Each local unit operated and financed itself independently, for Day did not extend her administration beyond the New York group. Nina Poleyn described the communes as autonomous, but "similar in spirit."[34] William Gauchat also could so testify. When his group wrote to the New York center for help in solving a problem, he was consistently told, "We can't give you any advice—you will have to work it out yourself."[35]

Thus, each hospice concentrated on a program particularly needed in its area or suited to its staff. The Boston group ran a bread line for men, feeding over two hundred daily.[36] In St. Louis, Timothy Dempsey, a priest, established a house where thousands were aided over the years.[37] The average daily meals for the month of April 1935, the only figures that appear in *Catholic Worker* for this hospice, indicate that the St. Louis hospice fed over twenty-seven hundred daily and distributed seven hundred baskets of food a week.[38]

In Washington, D.C., there were several houses. One was established to aid the Black unemployed and included among its founders Father Paul Hanley Furfey, the personalist theologian.[39] Another Washington house, St. Christopher's Inn, served as sleeping quarters for transients and, although closed for most of the day, provided meals to the destitute.[40] The Blessed Martin Home in Washington was virtually a one-man operation. Day described it as dilapidated with paper hanging from the wall, plaster falling off, and slats protruding. The floor sloped and the house was unheated; yet Llewellyn Scott, its manager, housed forty-five men a night during the winter of 1938–1939.[41]

In Harrisburg, Pennsylvania, the House of Hospitality sheltered evicted women until the Catholic Worker staff could find them new homes.[42] In Akron and Chicago, the main efforts went into feeding hungry children. The Detroit group, in addition to feeding six hundred daily and participating in demonstrations, established a workers' school.[43]

The degree of autonomy that existed for Catholic Worker units can be seen at the hospice established in Pittsburgh. Considering itself a Catholic Worker unit, as its correspondence to the *Catholic Worker* indicated, the hospice also visualized its role as an umbrella for various other Catholic radical causes.[44] In addition to organizing the largest hospice in the movement, the Pittsburgh unit held lectures and classes, distributed the *Catholic Worker,* and even sponsored a radio program. "Your Pittsburgh branch," its founder, Father Charles Owen Rice, reported, "has been prospering." Housed in a three-story building that belonged to the diocese, it completely supported forty staff members, fed eight hundred on its food lines, slept three hundred nightly, and was the only Catholic Worker branch at the time to have a clinic.[45] In the spring of 1938, the Pittsburgh group began working a farming commune.[46]

Significant differences, however, arose between the Catholic Worker community and its Pittsburgh affiliate as the latter enlarged the scope of its activities. Some of the Pittsburgh unit's subsidiary objectors, and a local branch of the Association of Catholic Trade Unionists, severed their institutional ties with the New York Catholic Worker Movement. In addition, the Pittsburgh unit's anti-Communist position combined with a strong trade-union orientation led eventually to a merger with the national Association of Catholic Trade Unionists. It finally dissolved its relations with the Catholic Worker Movement altogether.[47]

Each Catholic Worker group thus went its own direction without being hampered, controlled, or administered by the parent group in New York. Lists of Catholic Worker institutions appeared in the *Catholic Worker* for 1938 and 1939. In 1939, twenty-two houses existed in the United States, which included nineteen cells or families providing room for the overflow from local hospices and three communes. In 1939, three houses were added, increasing the total to twenty-five; the number of cells fluctuated between thirteen and sixteen; and there were four farms.[48]

The New York group was the most important, modeling informal programs and organizational structures that were adopted by other houses. Day stated that they did not want the house to have the aspect of a mission: No one preached to men who had to listen on empty stomachs.[49] She also emphasized the necessity of smallness so that bureaucratic machinery would not create impersonal relations within the hospices.[50]

The first House of Hospitality in New York City began as a cooperative apartment in a condemned tenement. It housed three men of the Catholic Worker group.[51] A cooperative apartment for unemployed women followed a short time later.[52] A store, office, dining room, and kitchen housed several more; Day's own apartment, which she and her daughter shared with several women, became another Movement residence.[53] Donations from laymen, revenue from canvassing, and contributions either from individual priests or from their collections were used to pay the rent.[54] Since these resources were unable to keep so many places running at one time, the Movement replaced the various apartments with one small house, the Charles Street house. Residents and staff lived on the upper floors while the newspaper and pamphlets were published on the first floor as well as in the basement.[55]

In the spring of 1936, the Catholic Worker Movement was permitted to use a building, the Mott Street house, one block from New York's Chinatown. It had twenty rooms plus several other apartments in an adjoining building. Two stores on the ground floor served as a dining room for the unemployed, a reading room, editorial offices, a print shop, and a kitchen. The main building provided one floor for men and two for women. Sometimes the stores and offices also served as bedrooms. In addition, several Catholic Worker staff members had their own apartments or rooms elsewhere and spent their days working at Mott Street.[56]

The Catholic Worker community remained at Mott Street through the 1930s. This busy headquarters, full of neighborhood children, lines strung with laundry, radios blasting, and countless discussions going on, managed to feed breakfast to one thousand a day in addition to its regular residents and staff members.[57]

The New York house, in serving as a center for various types of Catholic dissidents, provided an atmosphere that encouraged the emergence of other Catholic social action groups. It also acted as a catalyst for bringing together various aspects of the Catholic Worker Movement, a process that disturbed Maurin but was supported by Day.

In contrast with Maurin, Day visualized the labor movement and the strike as a temporary means for dealing with immediate community problems. "When we were invited to help during a strike," she felt "we went to perform works of mercy, which include not only feeding the hungry, . . . but enlightening the ignorant and rebuking the unjust."[58] She also believed that when the Movement participated in strikes, "workers should be reached when they are massed together for action. We are taking advantage of a situation."[59] Day argued that when men are striking, "they are fighting for a share in management, for the right to be considered partners. . . . They are fighting against the idea of their labor as a commodity, to be bought and sold."[60]

The *Catholic Worker* served as an instrument to advance Day's point of view by strongly supporting organized labor and regularly reporting labor news. The readers were told not to buy specific products or patronize particular concerns.[61] Catholics were urged to organize within the union, to fight for social justice.[62] A 1936 editorial clearly illustrated the Movement's point of view: "The *Catholic Worker* does not believe that unions, as they exist today in the United States, are an ideal solution for social problems. . . . We do believe that they are the only efficient weapon which workers have to defend their rights as individuals."[63]

In 1934 and 1935, the Catholic Worker group participated in its first major strike as Manhattan department store employees walked off the job. The strike affected only two large establishments, S. Klein and Ohrbach's. The Catholic Worker Movement picketed with the workers and carried signs quoting papal support of unions. Police regularly arrested the picketers who did not belong to the Catholic Worker group.[64] Enjoined by the courts from picketing, the Catholic Workers engaged in civil disobedience by violating the injunction. In addition, the Movement's staff attended strike meetings and informed the workers of Catholic thought regarding strikes, picketing, and nonviolent techniques.[65] Meanwhile, the *Catholic Worker* told its readers not to patronize the department stores. "You are not upholding social justice if you disregard the plea of these workers."[66] Catholic Workers, during this strike, worked closely with local Communists, a repeated situation that inevitably led to criticism within the church. Day, however, defended these arrangements. She found that the issues raised by the Communists were often just: "'The truth is the truth,' writes St. Thomas, 'and proceeds from the Holy Ghost, no matter from whose lips it comes.'"[67]

The Catholic Workers' greatest involvement with strike action emerged out of their support of Joseph Curran's leftist leadership in the organization of the National Maritime Union, at the time of the maritime strike of May 1936. The young union leader appealed to the *Catholic Worker* to help in housing and feeding some of the strikers; about fifty men were immediately accepted into the Mott Street house.[68] Before the strike was over the Catholic Workers had rented a store in the strike area, using it as a reading room and kitchen.[69] They also performed the usual service of picketing with Catholic-oriented signs.[70]

During the New York seamen's strike of 1937, the Catholic Worker Movement again participated on the docks. Once more, a waterfront branch office became a resting place for idle seamen. Conveniently located around the corner from strike headquarters, it attracted many strikers. The seamen filled the storefront office to capacity from early morning until midnight. Picketers could relax and read Catholic newspapers and magazines.[71] More important, the Movement fed thousands of strikers, which resulted in a three-thousand-dollar debt; yet the storefront remained open, even after the strike had ended, feeding over one thousand a day until the men again went back to their ships.[72]

In a similar fashion, the Catholic Worker group in Pittsburgh aided the labor movement, especially the CIO's Steel Workers Organizing Committee (SWOC). Father Charles Owen Rice, the local Catholic Worker leader, spoke to overflow crowds at the immigrant meeting houses where large numbers of Catholic laborers gathered. Concurrently, his supporters distributed the *Catholic Worker* at ethnic social halls.[73] Father Rice and his associate, Father Carl Hensler, led their staff members on steel worker picket lines, and encouraged workers over SWOC loudspeakers.[74]

Sometimes the Catholic Worker Movement negotiated with management over a labor dispute. A major New York City department store chain, for example, laid off a number of nonunionized saleswomen without severance pay. They had been employed there from twelve to twenty years. The Catholic Worker community offered to join the women in picketing company stores, and then met with company officials, threatening them with public attacks both in the *Catholic Worker* and from the lecture platform. The firm then agreed to provide severance pay for some and to take back the rest.[75]

These instances were typical of the labor activities of the Catholic Worker Movement. The Movement harassed numerous companies it considered unjust: The National Biscuit Company, Borden Milk, Heinz Corporation, Loose-Wiler, and American Stores of Philadelphia were some of the more well known.[76] Vermont marble workers, Boston fishermen, Arkansas sharecroppers, Michigan autoworkers, Massachusetts textile workers, New York brewery workers, printers, librarians, meat packers were just some of the striking workers who sought and received moral support, publicity in *Worker* columns, and countless thousands of meals from Catholic Worker groups throughout the country.[77] At least one company placed paid advertisements in the *Catholic News* and *Brooklyn Tablet*, major Catholic newspapers, attacking the Movement.[78]

To judge by the space accorded organized labor on the *Worker's* front page, nearly equal attention was given to labor issues as to the hospice programs during the 1930s. Yet Day's effort did not end here. Catholic Workers also founded a Catholic Union of unemployed headed by Timothy O'Brien,[79] an ex-Communist. They also spent considerable effort in moving evicted families. They transported furniture, found new apartments and, when a family was settled, provided it with clothing and additional furniture.[80] To coordinate these kinds of activities, they organized neighborhood councils, patterning them after the Communist party's unemployed councils.[81]

The Catholic Worker Movement, in this manner, attempted to influence the lives of the workers and the effectiveness of the labor movement. It is difficult to measure its success, especially when such activities as art classes for culturally deprived slum children or resettlement of the homeless and the evicted were involved. Considering the magnitude of the problems in depression America, the Movement's contribution was small but significant. It did, through its organizing, feed thousands, provided shelter and clothing for a significant number, aided in many strikes, and at times contributed to labor settlements favorable to the workers. The Movement also supported the CIO by aiding in organization, and providing it with propaganda in its conflict with the AFL. But CIO growth was unrelated to the Movement itself.

Catholic Workers made no concentrated attempt to effect Catholic social reform; yet, ironically, they had their greatest influence in this area. By stressing the disparity between the practices of American life and the social ideals of the church, the Movement attracted young Catholic radicals, who otherwise might have filtered into the secular left. The Catholic Worker Movement, therefore, provided a source of direction for social Catholicism and an early avenue of involvement for Catholic radicals who later moved in other, though still liberal, directions. Numerous Catholic social institutions were directly stimulated by the Catholic Worker Movement. William Callahan organized the first American branch of Pax at Mott Street. It eventually became the Association of Catholic Conscientious Objectors, and ran forestry as well as hospital camps in New Hampshire, Illinois, and Maryland during World War II.[82] Sitting around the kitchen table of the Mott Street house, John Cort and other Movement members organized the Association of Catholic Trade Unionists.[83] Moreover, many independent labor schools and Interreligious Friendship Houses were outgrowths of the Movement.[84]

A number of liberal Catholic journalists and publishers received their first impetus from the Catholic Worker Movement during the thirties. In addition to the New York City newspaper, Movement newspapers were published in Chicago, England, and Australia. The Canadian *Social Forum*, the first *Christian Front*, and *The Source* also emerged out of the Movement.[85] Individuals such as John Cogley, editor of *Commonweal*, began their activities in social action causes by leading Catholic Worker units. Cogley ran the Movement's hospice in Chicago and edited the Chicago *Catholic Worker*.[86] Edward Willock, cofounder of *Integrity*, and Edward Marcinak, founder of *Work*, came out of the Movement. John Cort, a prolific writer on social Catholicism, and social critic Michael Harrington were members of the New York group. The *Catholic Student's Digest* was specifically launched by the New York house.[87]

The Catholic Worker Movement may have done little to affect the labor movement directly, but its contribution to the development of social Catholicism in America supported a climate of opinion favorable to organized labor. More important, it rekindled Catholic social reform activities, relatively dormant for over a decade, and began a tradition of antiestablishment American Catholic activism. These results of the Catholic Worker Movement are to a degree ironic, for neither the labor movement nor the social reformism of groups and individuals that grew out of the Catholic Worker Movement represented Peter Maurin's goal of organizing communitarian society.

The Catholic Worker organizing style during the 1930s depended upon two elements, street meetings and the *Catholic Worker*, the movement's newspaper. Street meetings had a secondary role. The Catholic Worker speaker would draw a crowd stimulating discussion and hecklers while making points that appealed to those with a similar point of view in the audience. After the talk, interested stragglers would be invited to the Catholic Worker house, where discussion would continue and perhaps a new volunteer would be recruited.

Although street meetings remained a useful technique, the Catholic Worker newspaper reached far greater numbers. The paper was sold at nominal cost and given away at labor meetings, demonstrations, picketing sites, political gatherings, and perhaps most effectively at church functions including Sunday mass. The positions, actions, and goals presented in this dramatic, well-written, and amply illustrated propaganda vehicle drew the unemployed. Some of the unemployed found a place to stay at the Catholic Worker houses of hospitality; some even went to the Catholic Worker communes and hence into the movement from those directions. Catholic Worker volunteers who served on picket lines, helped evicted families find new housing, and worked within labor unions also recruited others with whom they came into contact. But on the whole, the newspaper was the key to the Catholic Worker organizing. *Catholic Worker* stories ignited a spark. People simply turned up at Catholic Worker headquarters to help with some aspect of the program. Thus, active organizing took second place to passive recruitment, but the benign style that brought together Catholic radical activists resulted in Catholic Worker communes, houses of hospitality, and a significant long-term impact on Catholic social action.

The Role of Religious Organizations in Organizing for Social Change

The characteristics of religious organizations like the Catholic Worker Movement appear to include several features regardless of denomination: (1) a ready-made constituency, (2) a mission, (3) organizational networks, (4) leadership resources and training capacities, (5) financial resources, and (6) social action models of community organization. These organizational characteristics offered both a base for community organizing and a force for change.

A ready-made constituency. There are millions of Americans who belong to churches or synagogues. Practically every urban neighborhood has a religious institution located within walking distance. Although all the members do not necessarily attend services regularly, they tend to consider themselves part of an organization. Each of these religious organizations has some form of educational program that initiates its membership into full rites of passage. Membership specifically carries with it the expectation of action as one response to the organization's message. This response has often come from a minority of the membership.[88] The Catholic Worker Movement saw action beginning with the individual Christian who makes a commitment: "Thus a change in the world began with man, he must put on the Christ and action which began his own salvation and that of the universe too."[89] The Catholic Worker supporters constituted a small committed minority community within American Catholicism, but were able to have influence in Catholic circles, in great part, by taking advantage of a ready-made constituency: working-class Catholics, idealistic clerics, and lay intellectuals.

A mission. Religious organizations have theologies, which serve as a base for their ethical action. These may be as complex as St. Thomas Aquinas's *Summa Theologica* or as simple as a restatement of the golden rule "of doing unto others what we would have others do unto us." Usually the purpose of religious organizations is described for all its members in terms of a God who cares for humanity and expects His followers to do likewise.[90] This mission or model for action is used as a reference point by organizers within the church; it is the higher purpose to which one is committed and the daily strategies are related to the higher purpose.

From its origins in 1933, the Catholic Worker Movement has repeatedly pleaded the cause of the lonely, the poor, the persecuted, and in addition has acted in their behalf. It has not chosen to separate itself from the Catholic faith, but rather tried to build a new age from within the bosom of that faith. Its overall mission, philosophy and vision, direct personal action, and simplicity of organization, were all marks of a movement as old as the church itself.

Organizational networks. Most religious organizations have structures that link them with regional, national, and international units. Those networks can be excellent tools for organizers. Although religious organizations are usually rooted in a local setting, their national and international character exceed local boundaries. A

Catholic worker was both a New York and an international phe-
nomenon; the Catholic international and national print media, in
particular, provided a dynamic organizational tool. The Catholic
Worker Movement utilized the existing Roman Catholic organizational network.

Leadership pool and training capacity.   Vast potential for training
and education is found in the systems of education of religious organizations that begin at the elementary level and proceed through
professional training. Many religious organizations have social action committees established to sensitize their congregations to the
local and national needs for justice and action.[91] The Catholic
Worker Movement used retreats, educational forums, and conferences to spread the word concerning the importance of their movement and to teach the Catholic Worker philosophy.[92] Religious organizations provided the community organizers of the 1930s with a
large pool of trained professionals and lay leaders who were ready
and willing to respond to the call for action. Although laymen provided significant leadership for the Catholic Worker Movement,
clerical activists, such as Father Charles Owen Rice, also assumed
major roles.

Financial resources.   Important for any organizational effort is
the availability of money. Religious organizations often provided a
financial resource for organizing. Dorothy Day used the voice of the
Catholic Worker to appeal for financial support from its essentially
Catholic readership. A pool of sympathy, which in turn evoked a
pool of money, was accepted by organizers as means to achieve their
goals.

Social action model of community organization.   Although religious organizations and individuals engage in institutional or individual charity, the social action model of community organizing requires a recognition of the disadvantaged segment of the society that
needs to be brought into an alliance with others in order to make
demands for increased resources and social justice. Making basic
changes in major institutions or community practices involves the
redistribution of power, resources, or decision making in the community as well as changing basic policies of formal organizations.
Religious social action groups in the 1930s were organized to meet

such goals. The Catholic Worker Movement sought, among other goals, to serve the poor directly and personally through food distribution and lodging at hospitality houses.

The strategy for implementing these goals was simple: Point to the gap between the Christian ideal and what, in fact, was the social situation and call for action to meet the injustice. The expected response was usually individualistic. For the Catholic Worker Movement, it meant each individual "beginning where you are with what you have."[93] For Catholic immigrants, the promise of American freedom and justice for all was equated with the morality of Catholic teachings. To point out injustice in the social fabric meant reminding them of these expectations of justice in a new country. Wherever injustice was found, the *Catholic Worker* reminded the workers of the Christian ideal and called for righting the wrong, be it poverty or racism.[94]

The specific social action tactics of community organizers based in religious organizations during the Great Depression included nonviolent direct action, educational activities including moral persuasion, public demonstrations, economic boycotts, and civil disobedience. The Catholic Worker Movement used all these approaches in attempting to create a society where a Christian sense of love and community would prevail. Its prophets projected a vision that generated a committed following, remarkably similar to the original church that helped inspire its birth.

PART V

Epilogue

12

The Legacy of Community Organizing at the Close of the Great Depression

Michael J. Austin and Neil Betten

 AT THE 1939 National Conference of Social Work, Robert P. Lane, writing for community organizing specialists, prepared a report that included the evaluation of the processes and objectives of community organization. The report, recognizing that community organization takes place "outside, as well as inside, the general area of social work," summarized the state of the art as it had developed by 1939.

The report noted that some social welfare institutions mainly engaged in community organizing while other agencies primarily performed additional services, and secondarily utilized community organizing. It reported on community organizing at the neighborhood level, as well as on the statewide and national levels. This report saw community organizing primarily as a force to mobilize resources, initiate social services, coordinate institutional efforts, and build welfare programs.

In discussing community organizing characteristics, the Lane report suggested that community organizing is "perhaps always concerned with inter-group relationships," linking social welfare resources with social welfare needs. To reach that goal, community organizing objectives included developing a factual foundation for planning and action, initiating and orchestrating services to coordinate resources and needs, improving individual agencies' performance, and establishing better public relations.

The report also suggested methods for achieving community organizing goals. These included the collection and publication of social work agency financial and service data, interagency planning, the initiation of studies and surveys, joint budgeting by various agencies, the use of public relations, joint financial campaigns, interagency consultation, group discussions and conferences, and political activity including lobbying for legislation.

The Lane report reflected those roots of community organizing emanating from professional social work–based community organization and did not deal with organizing outside the social work field. In our case studies, we selected some additional areas of community organizing that generally fall outside of the traditional social agency arena. For example, the Cincinnati Unit Experiment, the Catholic Worker Movement, the various political machine politicians, and to some degree the Saul Alinksy phenomena have certain features in common. They were all political in orientation. The Cincinnati Unit Experiment presented itself as politically benign. The socialists behind the Experiment used the rhetoric of the Progressive Movement, which by 1917 seemed so embedded in the political ideology of Americans that it appeared to be uncontroversial, and perhaps in the minds of many people not political—at least until the Red Scare rekindled American fears of political change and immigrant involvement in American life. The Unit was led by "closet" socialists, who wanted to give a greater degree of power (although they did not use this word) to segments of the working class that they hoped to organize through the Experiment. They were certainly not revolutionary in the Bolshevik sense, and they were astounded when they were attacked as such. They were engaged in politics, even though they may not have acknowledged it. Moreover, they were engaged in a radical type of politics trying to camouflage it as Progressivism at a time when the Communist revolution in Russia and left-wing activity in the United States made even the progressive wings of the major parties suspect.

The Catholic Worker Movement in the 1930s had radical political objectives. Its members described themselves as radicals, and Dorothy Day and Peter Maurin understood the political implications of their ideology. The Catholic Worker Movement involved itself in traditional politics by endorsing the New Deal of Franklin Roosevelt and the activities as well as political objectives of much of the labor movement, particularly the CIO. Saul Alinsky, although influenced by the CIO, was less involved with labor activities once he became an established community organizer. Although Alinsky's thrust was not in political organizing as such (i.e., organizing for candidates), the very nature of his organizing style was political. He organized a community to confront the economic or political establishment or both. This consciously confrontational style differed considerably from the attempt at accommodationist politics of the Cincinnati Unit Experiment, or the pacifist approach of the Catholic Worker Movement, or the pragmatic patronage politics of the political machines. The highly political content of community organizing was reflected primarily in groups outside the traditional domain of social service organizations. Future historical research would do well to explore further the roots of political action as an element of effective community organizing.

Pre–World War II community organizing in the social service arena primarily stressed pragmatic short-term goals. This was far less true for the more politically oriented organizations that we have observed. The Catholic Worker Movement was ultimately utopian in its goals. Its members wanted to make vast changes in society and replace the capitalist system with a more humane communalist environment. They had short-term goals as well and various tactics, but ultimately they remained utopian idealists seeking a vastly changed society. The socialists behind the Cincinnati Unit Experiment were more pragmatic, but their inclinations also led toward a utopian conclusion. The Phillipses originally saw Cincinnati as the first step in establishing similar social units throughout the country. The cooperative nature of the social units was designed to move beyond mere health-care programs to support consumer cooperatives of various kinds. If the formation of consumer cooperatives was followed by the formation of producer cooperatives, then the image of the Cincinnati Unit being a "state within a state" with its own politics and socialist-oriented economic system was not farfetched.

The political machines of the late nineteenth and early twentieth centuries clearly were not utopian. Although there were exceptions, the goals of the urban political bosses were primarily to stay in office and keep political power. We would not characterize Saul Alinsky as a utopian either. Although he described himself as a radical, the community organizations he put in place were left to formulate their own objectives. In the long run, they generally sought a bigger piece of the capitalist pie and were not oriented toward changing the nature of the political and economic system.

A major difference between community organizations inside the social service arena and community organizations in the wider community was that the latter were led by high-profile individuals, often with charismatic personalities. The political bosses were of considerable variety, but they were all clearly designated as individual leaders. They served as a locus of power and spoke for the local party and its constituents. Wilber Phillips, the central figure in the Cincinnati Unit Experiment; Dorothy Day, the effective leader of the Catholic Worker Movement; and Saul Alinsky all were highly respected leaders, in the forefront of the hierarchy, bureaucracy, or following of their organizations. They had far more active political postures and community leadership roles than did the heads of social service organizations in local communities.

Undoubtedly, there are profound differences between the goals, purposes, and roles of social work–based community organizations and those of the community organizations unconnected to the social work field that arose from the needs of changing economic and political conditions. We have attempted in this book to identify some of the taproots of community organizing. Community organizing at the neighborhood level reflected a concern for the social and economic well-being of the residents. The organizing at the agency level focused primarily on the planning, coordinating, and financing of social services. And the organizing at the community level responded to the political and economic conditions through the taking of social action to promote change.

Early community organizing produced a vast array of approaches and practitioners. We have dealt with some but have omitted others, such as A. J. Muste, a pacifist labor leader, socialist, agitator, and founder of the Fellowship of Reconciliation, who engaged in community organizing through passive resistance. His techniques, as well as individuals he trained, emerged in later years in the Civil Rights Movement. The Black churches then and now have organized their constituencies in support of legal reforms such as a federal anti-lynching law, civil rights, and economic and social improvement. The utopian socialists of the 1820s and 1840s—both secular and religious—established primarily agricultural communities in reaction to early industrial development, which they considered inhumane and destructive of a sense of community. The American Communist party carried out numerous organizing ventures including tenants, leagues, civil rights and civil liberties groups, labor organizations, and immigrant associations.

Our case studies focus on groups and individuals, from the fiery Saul Alinsky, who directed carefully planned but highly disruptive confrontations, to Edith Bremmer, who taught immigrant groups to organize themselves to preserve their culture and conversely to better adapt to American society. These case studies represent part of the rich history and varied roots of community organizing.

Notes and Index

Notes

CHAPTER 1

1. Ralph M. Kramer and Harry Specht, eds., *Readings in Community Organization Practice* (Englewood Cliffs, N.J.: Prentice-Hall, Inc., 1969), 13.

2. Anatole Shaffer, "The Cincinnati Social Unit Experiment, 1917–1919," *Social Service Review* 45, no. 2 (June 1971): 164.

3. Roy Lubove, *The Professional Altruist: The Emergence of Social Work as a Career, 1880–1930* (New York: Atheneum Publishers, 1969), 183.

4. Fred M. Cox and Charles Garvin, "The Relation of Social Forces to the Emergence of Community Organization Practice, 1865–1968," in *Strategies of Community Organization: A Book of Readings*, ed. Fred M. Cox et al. (Itasca, Ill.: F. E. Peacock, 1970), 46.

5. William J. Norton, "Social Work Grows Up," *The Survey* 59 (1927): 36.

6. Lubove, *Professional Altruist*, 180.

7. Robert Perlman and Arnold Gurin, *Community Organization and Social Planning* (New York: John Wiley and Sons, 1972), 15.

8. Clarke A. Chambers, *Seedtime of Reform: American Social Services and Social Action, 1918–1933* (Ann Arbor: University of Michigan Press, 1963), 82.

9. John T. Howard, "City Planning as a Social Movement, a Governmental Function, and a Technical Profession," in *Planning and the Urban Community*, ed. Harvey S. Perloff (Pittsburgh: University of Pittsburgh Press, 1961), 164.

10. Meyer Schwartz, "Community Organization," in *Encyclopedia of Social Work*, ed. Harry L. Lucie (New York: National Association of Social Workers, 1965), 177.

11. Robert P. Lane, "The Field of Community Organization," *Proceedings of the National Conference of Social Work*, vol. 66, ed. Howard R. Knight (New York: Columbia University Press, 1939), 27.

12. Jack Rothman with John E. Tropman, "Models of Community Organization and Macro Practice Perspectives: Their Mixing and Phasing," in *Strategies of Community Organization, Fourth Edition*, ed. Fred M. Cox et al. (Itasca, Ill.: F. E. Peacock, 1987), 20–36.

CHAPTER 2

1. Jesse Frederick Steiner, *Community Organization: A Study of Its Theory and Current Practice* (New York: D. Appleton-Century Co., 1930), 231; see also Roy Lubove, *The Professional Altruist: The Emergence of Social Work as a Career, 1880–1930* (New York: Atheneum Publishers, 1969), 183–84, 215.

2. Lubove, *Professional Altruist*, 202; Steiner, *Community Organization*, 218–19.

3. Clarke A. Chambers, *Seedtime of Reform: American Social Services and Social Action, 1918–1933* (Ann Arbor: University of Michigan Press, 1963); Fred M. Cox and Charles Garvin, "The Relation of Social Forces to the Emergence of Community Organization Practice, 1865–1968," in *Strategies of Community Organization: A Book of Readings*, ed. Fred M. Cox et al. (Itasca, Ill.: F. E. Peacock, 1970), 37–53.

4. Robert P. Lane, "The Field of Community Organization," *Proceedings of the National Conference of Social Work* (hereafter cited as *Proceedings*), vol. 66, ed. Howard R. Knight (New York: Columbia University Press, 1939), 496–511.

5. Meyer Schwartz, "Community Organization," in *Encyclopedia of Social Work*, ed. Harry L. Lucie (New York: National Association of Social Workers, 1965), 177.

6. Walter W. Pettit, *Case Studies in Community Organization* (New York: Century Co., 1928).

7. Eduard C. Lindeman, *The Community: An Introduction to the Study of Community Leadership and Organization* (New York: Association Press, 1921), 129.

8. B. A. McClenahan, *Organizing the Community* (New York: Century Co., 1922), 36.

9. R. J. Haynes, "The Contribution of the Community Chest to Welfare Planning," *Proceedings*, vol. 55, ed. Sherman C. Kingsley (Chicago: University of Chicago Press, 1928), 405–7. Community chests predominated in such community planning until about 1931. Meanwhile, however, councils of social agencies began to exercise more community planning responsibility including formulation of techniques integrating areawide social welfare plans. It was recognized that a different plan had to be formulated for each community in answer to its specific needs. Councils recognized the need for "joint planning" between community chests and agencies. Acknowledging the contributions of chests to community planning, they considered community chest action alone to be insufficient. To acquaint the public with the various social agency services and opportunities offered by a council, welfare

councils launched an intensive educational campaign. See Eduard C. Linde-man, "Agency Autonomy and Community Organization: Summary of Dis-cussion," *Proceedings*, vol. 58, ed. Howard R. Knight (Chicago: University of Chicago Press, 1931), 400–404; A. W. McMillen, "The Council of Social Agencies and Community Planning," *Proceedings*, vol. 59, ed. Howard R. Knight (Chicago: University of Chicago Press, 1933), 404, 411.

10. Steiner, *Community Organization*, 164.

11. Ibid., 168.

12. McClenahan, *Organizing the Community*, 143–45. This plan at-tempted to centralize private and public welfare resources into a cooperative agency in Grinnell, Iowa. Public and private funds were expanded through what came to be called the Social Service League. Operating like a voluntary bureau of community service, it promoted "clean-up days, playgrounds, a garden club, a health survey, school nursing, the organization of Boy Scouts, Camp Fire Girls, and mothers' clubs or parent-teacher associations, the pro-tection and care of dependent, neglected, and delinquent children (largely assuming their responsibility), cooperation of all charitable agencies during the year and at Christmas, and a cooperative plan of the League and the City for the care of homeless men." The Iowa Plan necessitated a community organizer that engaged in both social planning and implementing services. The power structure of a community (e.g., county commissioners and agency boards of directors) hired an organizer to serve the total community by coordinating existing groups and organizations with generally common goals. Satisfying the public interest was seen as the goal of community or-ganizing. Throughout the 1920s and 1930s there was a considerable amount of cooperation between public and private welfare agencies and between welfare councils and the state and federal governments. See A. M. Tunstall, "State and Community Organization for Child Welfare: Alabama's Program of State and Local Cooperation," *Proceedings*, vol. 58: 97–104; C. M. Book-man, "The Social Consequences and Treatment of Unemployment," *Pro-ceedings*, vol. 59: 23; A. M. Johnson, "The County as a Unit for Coordinate Planning and Service in Public and Private Social Work: Point of View of Public Officials," *Proceedings*, vol. 64, ed. Howard R. Knight (Chicago: Uni-versity of Chicago Press, 1937), 360–68.

13. Steiner, *Community Organization*, 173.

14. McClenahan, *Organizing the Community*, 203–5.

15. Ibid., 109–211.

16. Lindeman, *Community*, 14–15.

17. Gisela Konopka, *Eduard C. Lindeman and Social Work Philosophy* (Minneapolis: University of Minnesota Press, 1958), 120–27.

18. Lindeman, *Community*, 123–24.

19. Konopka, *Lindeman*, 117, 127.

20. Reinhold Niebuhr, *The Contribution of Religion to Social Work* (New York: Columbia University Press, 1932).

21. Joseph K. Hart, *Community Organization* (New York: Macmillan Co., 1927), 149.

22. Ibid., 149

23. Ibid., 3–9, 91.

24. Ibid., 50.

25. Ibid., 139.

26. McClenahan, *Organizing the Community*, 39.

27. Konopka, *Lindeman*, 103.

28. Eduard C. Lindeman, "New Trends in Community Control," *Proceedings*, vol. 59: 301–9.

29. Hart, *Community Organization*, 101.

30. Steiner, *Community Organization*, 56.

31. Konopka, *Lindeman*, 104.

32. Ibid., 105.

33. McClenahan, *Organizing the Community*, 208.

34. Hart, *Community Organization*, 102.

35. Steiner, *Community Organization*, 383, 416–17.

36. Pettit, *Case Studies*.

37. McClenahan, *Organizing the Community*, 119.

38. Hart, *Community Organization*, 84–85.

39. K. L. Pray, "Where in Social Work Can the Concept of Democracy Be Applied?" *Proceedings*, vol. 58: 630.

40. Jesse Frederick Steiner, "Interrelation between City and Rural Life," *Proceedings*, vol. 54, ed. John A. Lapp (Chicago: University of Chicago Press, 1927), 345–51.

41. McClenahan, *Organizing the Community*, 134. An example of rural community organizing, the Commonwealth Fund child-health demonstrations attempted to unify health services. The fund placed a high value on promoting participation in and understanding of the health program by citizens of the community. They were encouraged to participate in developing programs through countywide and district committees. Demonstration programs led to closer teamwork and coordination between physicians, dentists, teachers, nurses, health officers, and citizens. Other examples of organizing on a countywide basis during the twenties were the State Charities Aid Associations, Boy Scouts, YMCA, Farm Bureau, and Red Cross. "Small villages cannot develop these facilities for themselves, and wherever they exist

at all, they are inevitably called upon to render service throughout the county."

42. Arthur Dunham, *The New Community Organization* (New York: T. Y. Crowell Co., 1972), 45.

43. Steiner, *Community Organization*, 162–63.

44. Lane, "Field of Community Organization," 496–97.

45. Schwartz in *Encyclopedia of Social Work*, 177.

46. William J. Norton, "Community Organization," *Proceedings*, vol. 46, ed. Howard R. Knight (Chicago: Rogers and Hall, 1919), 665–70.

47. Chambers, *Seedtime*.

48. Eduard C. Lindeman, "New Patterns of Community Organization," *Proceedings*, vol. 64: 317–23.

CHAPTER 3

1. Samuel P. Hays, "The Politics of Reform in Municipal Government in the Progressive Era," *Pacific Northwest Quarterly*, October 1954, pp. 157–69; Bruce M. Steve, "Urban Bosses and the Reform," in *The Urban Experience: Themes in American History*, ed. Raymond A. Mohl and James F. Richardson (Belmont, Calif.: Wadsworth Publishing, 1973), 188–89.

2. The Mohawk-Brighton area's population of twelve thousand was about half Protestant and half Catholic, fourteen hundred of whom were foreign born but a much larger proportion of whom were second- and third-generation German Americans. Zoe LaForge and Haven Emerson, *The Social Collection*, Social Welfare History Archives, University of Minnesota.

3. Edward T. Devine, "The Social Unit in Cincinnati: An Experiment in Organization," *The Survey*, November 15, 1919, p. 121; *Christian Herald* (undated clippings); *Trenton Times*, December 21, 1918; *Detroit News*, quoted in *Pittsburgh Dispatch*, November 29, 1919; *Dayton Journal*, November 23, 1919.

4. Seba Eldridge, "Community Organization and Citizenship," *Journal of Social Forces*, September 1928, p. 139; Gertrude Mathews Shelby, "Extending Democracy: What the Cincinnati Social Unit Has Accomplished," *Harper's Magazine*, April 1920, p. 692; S. Gale Lowrie, "The Social Unit—An Experiment in Politics," *National Municipal Review*, September 1920, p. 560.

5. For an excellent chronological review of the Cincinnati Social Unit's development and an elaboration of the ideological and institutional origins of the Social Unit, see Anatole Shaffer, "The Cincinnati Social Unit Experiment, 1917–1919," *Social Service Review*, 45, no. 2 (June 1971): 159–72. The organization's funds for the first year came from the National Social Unit's

philanthropic sources, from well-known wealthy progressives (about thirty-four thousand dollars), and from local Cincinnati sources (about fifteen thousand dollars). (We were unable to locate the full names of some of the women involved in the National Social Unit.)

6. *Outline of the Unit Plan*, Bulletin No. 2, Cincinnati, 1957, Cincinnati Social Unit, Collection Social Welfare History Archives, 9; Wilber C. Phillips, *Adventuring for Democracy* (New York: Social Unit Press, 1940), 343; "Social Work by Blocks," *Literary Digest*, December 6, 1919, p. 34.

7. Jesse Frederick Steiner, *Community Organization: A Study of Its Thought and Current Practice* (New York: D. Appleton-Century Co., 1930), 351.

8. Lowrie, "Social Unit," 560.

9. Mary L. Hicks and Roe S. Eastman, "Block Workers, As Developed under the Social Unit Experiment in Cincinnati," *The Survey*, September 1, 1920, p. 672.

10. Shelby, "Extending Democracy," 651–52; Phillips, *Adventuring for Democracy*, 277.

11. Shelby, "Extending Democracy," 692; Phillips, *Adventuring for Democracy*, 220.

12. Courtenay Dinwiddie, "Community Responsibility: A Review of the Cincinnati Social Unit Experiment," *Studies in Social Work*, 1921, pp. 6–103.

13. *The Social Unit Bulletin* (hereafter cited as *Bulletin*), October 23, 1920, p. 1, in printed materials, Cincinnati Social Unit, Collection Social Welfare History Archives, University of Minnesota (hereafter cited as Unit Papers); "Social Work by Blocks"; Shelby, "Extending Democracy," 690–92.

14. Devine, "Social Unit," 121–22.

15. *Bulletin*, December 8, 1917, p. 1.

16. Courtenay Dinwiddie, "Comment on the Report of the Council of Social Agencies on the Social Unit Organization," *Bulletin*, July 7, 1919, p. 140; Eldridge, "Organization and Citizenship," *Bulletin*, December 22, 1917, p. 138.

17. Phillips, *Adventuring for Democracy*, 243–44.

18. *Bulletin*, April 4, 1919, pp. 3–4; Shelby, "Extending Democracy," 693; Lowrie, "Social Unit," 566; *New Republic*, April 19, 1919, p. 366; *New York Times*, March 16, 1919, pp. 5–6.

19. Eldridge, "Organization and Citizenship," 129; Lowrie, "Social Unit," 560; Steiner, *Community Organization*, 352; Haven Emerson, "The Social Unit and Public Health," *Proceedings of National Social Unit Conference*, quoted in Steiner, *Community Organization*, 253; *Bulletin*, April 4, 1919,

p. 2. Courtenay Dinwiddie, "The Work Accomplished by the Social Unit Organization" (Paper presented at the National Conference of Social Work, May 1918). For further information on health services, see Pennet L. Mead, "Statistics of Health Services in the Unit District," *Studies in Social Work*, 1921.

20. *Bulletin*, November 24, 1917, p. 4; February 16, 1918, p. 1; and February 8, 1919, p. 1; Phillips, *Adventuring for Democracy*, 197; Shelby, "Extending Democracy," 694.

21. Phillips, *Adventuring for Democracy*, 255.

22. A school medical inspector described immigrant parents and guardians as "an obstreperous quantity . . . who resent the interference of a medical officer, do not respond to his advice, and refuse to go to a clinic or district physicians," while an Associated Charities visitor complained of those "who utterly refuse to enter a hospital. . . . A horror takes possession of them at the mention of such a place." Zane L. Miller, *Boss Cox's Cincinnati: Urban Politics in the Progressive Era* (New York: Oxford University Press, 1968), 19, 23, 39, 66.

23. "Social Work by Blocks"; *New Republic*, April 19, 1919, 365; *Bulletin*, March 26, 1919, pp. 1, 4; *Cincinnati Times-Star*, March 11, 1919 (Clipping in Unit Papers); J. H. Landis to Wilber Phillips, June 24, 1918; Wilber Phillips to J. H. Landis, June 26, 1918; Wilber Phillips to John Galvin, March 11, 1919, in Unit Papers, Box 3; Phillips, *Adventuring for Democracy*, 183; Devine, "Social Unit," 115.

24. *New Republic*, April 19, 1919, p. 367; *Bulletin*, November 1920, p. 1; William J. Norton, "The Social Unit Organization of Cincinnati," *Studies for the Helen S. Trounstine Foundation*, February 1919, p. 183; *Bulletin*, April 4, 1919, p. 2.

25. *Bulletin*, June 7, 1919.

26. Shelby, "Extending Democracy," 689–90; Phillips, *Adventuring for Democracy*, 127.

27. "National Social Unit Organization, Estimated Expenditures for 1919–1920," report in Unit Papers, Box 4; "Answers by W. C. Phillips and Elsie L. G. Phillips to the Committee Appointed by the Council of Social Agencies" (Mimeographed), Unit Papers, p. 13.

28. Phillips, *Adventuring for Democracy*, 348.

29. *Bulletin*, April 18, 1919, p. 2. Phillips, *Adventuring for Democracy*, 349; "Answers by W. C. Phillips," Unit Papers, 14–15; John H. Walker, in *Illinois State Federation of Labor Weekly Newsletter*, January 10, 1920, and in *Boilermakers and Iron Ship Builders Journal*, December 1919, pp. 989–90; Wilber C. Phillips, "Unity, a Philosophy of Democracy," Unit Papers, p. F2.

30. *Bulletin*, June 7, 1919, p. 1; July 3, 1920, p. 1; and November 3, 1919, p. 1; Cincinnati *Tribune*, December 4, 1919, in Unit Papers, Scrapbook Box 3; Phillips, *Adventuring for Democracy*, 363.

31. Minute Books of "The Conference Relative to the Future Work in the Mohawk-Brighton District," unpaginated, Unit Papers.

32. Miller, *Boss Cox's Cincinnati*, 36.

33. Black Warwick, "The Social Unit Ended in Cincinnati," *National Municipal Review*, February 1921, p. 72.

CHAPTER 4

1. For initial YWCA interest in the immigrant problem, see YWCA, *Some Urgent Phases of Immigrant Life* (New York, 1910). For Bremer's early reports on International Institute work, see YWCA, Department of Immigration and Foreign Communities, Reports, 1910–1921, Archives of the National Board of the YWCA, Social Welfare History Archives, University of Minnesota. See also Edith Terry Bremer, "The International Institute for Young Women" (master's thesis, Yale University, 1932); Raymond A. Mohl, "The American Federation of International Institutes," in *Greenwood Encyclopedia of American Institutions: Social Service Organizations*, ed. Peter Romanofsky et al., 2 vols. (Westport, Conn.: Greenwood, 1978), 1: 59–63; Raymond A. Mohl, "Edith Terry Bremer," in *Notable American Women: The Modern Period*, ed. Barbara Sicherman and Carol Hurd Green (Cambridge, Mass.: Harvard University Press, 1980), 105–7.

2. Edith Terry Bremer, "Development of Private Social Work with the Foreign Born," American Academy of Political and Social Science, Annals, 262 (March 1949), 147; Edith Terry Bremer, "The International Institutes in Foreign Community Work: Their Program and Philosophy," ca. 1923 (Mimeographed), American Council for Nationalities Service Papers, Immigration History Research Center, University of Minnesota, Box 3, p. 9 (hereafter cited as ACNS Papers).

3. On the Institute withdrawal from the YWCA see Irma Wagner, "A Message from a Past Executive Secretary," Fiftieth Anniversary, *The International Institute of Gary*, 1969, p. 4, and Box 1 Shipment 3, ACNS Papers.

4. Edith Terry Bremer, "The National Institute Faces 1936: First Annual Report, September 1, 1934–December 1, 1935," ACNS Papers, 2–3; Mohl, "American Federation of International Institutes," 59–63.

5. Bremer, "Development of Private Social Work with the Foreign Born," 139; "A Summary of the Program of the International Institutes and

the National Social Work behind Them," ca. 1933–1934, ACNS Papers, p. 2; Bremer, "International Institutes in Foreign Community Work," 6–10. Horace M. Kallen introduced the specific use of the term "cultural pluralism" through a series of articles beginning in 1915. He is also usually credited with first introducing the concept at the same time; Nathan Glazer, "Ethnic Groups in America: From National Culture to Ideology," in *Freedom and Control in Modern Society*, ed. Morroe Berger, Theodore Abel, and Charles Page (New York: Van Nostrand, 1954), 158.

6. Bremer, "The National Institute Faces 1936," 6.

7. Alice L. Sickels, *Around the World in St. Paul* (Minneapolis: University of Minnesota Press, 1945), 115.

8. In 1942 an incident occurred that illustrated this. At the outbreak of World War II, the Italian-American community chose to withdraw from the festival rather than embarrass the program. At a major meeting the other nationality groups strongly urged the Italians to take part. One of the major speakers at that meeting, the representative of the Greek community, urged the Italians to remain, although at that very time Italy was invading Greece. A resolution was unanimously passed that "a place can be left open for the participation of Americans of Italian background: that if no committee from the Italian community desires to participate, then the general festival committee shall arrange some way of giving recognition to the contribution of Italians to American Life." The Italian young people's dance group eventually participated in the program; ibid., 164–66, 178, 183.

9. There was a significant satisfaction in wearing the native costumes, usually designed centuries ago and especially important to those immigrants whose homeland suffered foreign domination. Often when their language was under attack, their religion forbidden, and their flag declared illegal, the traditional costume became for the immigrant group the symbol of nationality. A pride in their costume was duplicated by a pride in the homeland and its achievements—the latter could be portrayed at the festivals, and few people wanted their ethnic group left out. Ibid., 26, 91, 93, 129, 186, 193–96.

10. Ibid. 72, 82–88, 100, 109, 123, 178.

11. Edith Terry Bremer, "The Field of International Institutes and Its Place in Social Work" (Speech delivered 1925), ACNS Papers, Box 3, p. 7.

12. *Hairenik* (Boston), July 15, 1938 (Clipping), Boston International Institute Papers, Immigration History Research Center, University of Minnesota (hereafter cited as BII Papers); *Nippon Times* (Tokyo), n.d. (Clipping), Annie Clo Watson Papers, Immigration History Research Center, University of Minnesota.

13. *International Beacon* (Boston), January 1933, November 14, 1934, Sep-

tember 15, 1935; Boston International Institute, Monthly Reports, March 1931, December 1931, December 1932, September 1935, December 1935, January 1936, November 1937, BII Papers; Annual Reports, 1937, 1940, 1941, BII Papers; International Institute Board of Directors, Minutes, June 5, June 26, November 12, 1935, BII Papers.

14. Philadelphia International Institute, Annual Report, 1940, Philadelphia Nationalities Service Center Papers, Urban Archives, Temple University, Series 1, Box 1, folder 16 (hereafter cited as PNSC Papers); International Institute Committee of Management, Minutes, March 14, April 3, 1928, October 24, 1935, January 13, 1941, PNSC Papers, Series 1, Box 1; "Field Work of the International Institute of the Philadelphia YWCA," 1932 (Typescript), PNSC Papers, Box 1, folder 14; *YWCA News* (Philadelphia) 9 (February 1933), PNSC Papers, Box 1, folder 9; Catherine Shimkus, "Report of the Russian Worker in the International Institute," ca. early 1930s, PNSC Papers, Box 4, folder 117; Philadelphia International Institute, *For a United America* (Unpaginated pamphlet), PNSC Papers, Box 1, folder 10.

15. San Francisco International Institute, Annual Reports, 1927–1934, San Francisco International Institute Papers located in the offices of the San Francisco International Institute (hereafter cited as SFII Papers).

16. Dorothy G. Spicer, *Folk Festivals and the Foreign Community* (New York: The Womans Press, 1923); Allen H. Eaton, *Immigrant Gifts to American Life* (New York: Russell Sage Foundation, 1932), 92–94; Philadelphia International Institute, *News Notes*, February 25, 1940, PNSC Papers, Box 11; Philadelphia International Institute, Scrapbooks, 1940–1942, PNSC Papers, Box 11; San Francisco International Institute, Annual Report, 1930, SFII Papers.

17. Bremer, "The National Institute Faces 1936," 2; Bremer, "International Institutes in Foreign Community Work," 7.

18. Bremer, "The National Institute Faces 1936," 5–6.

19. Ibid., 7.

20. Bremer, "Development of Private Social Work with the Foreign Born," 139.

21. Bremer, "International Institutes in Foreign Community Work," 4.

22. Bremer, "Field of International Institutes," 2.

23. "A Summary of the Program of the International Institutes and the National Social Work behind Them," 1–3.

24. Bremer, "International Institutes in Foreign Community Work," 9.

25. Bremer, "Development of Private Social Work with the Foreign Born," 147; Bremer, "Field of International Institutes," 12–13.

26. Bremer, "International Institutes in Foreign Community Work," 9; Bremer, "Field of International Institutes," 9–10, 14.

27. Bremer, "Field of International Institutes," 14–15.

28. Bremer, "International Institutes in Foreign Community Work," 8.

29. Bremer, "Field of International Institutes," 9–15.

30. "Notes on the Early History of the International Institute of Gary, 1919–1937," Gary International Institute Papers, Columet Regional Archives, Indiana University, Northwest, Gary (hereafter cited as GII Papers); Annual Report, 1921, GII Papers.

31. George Cary White, "Social Settlements and Immigrant Neighbors, 1886–1914," *Social Service Review* 33 (March 1959): 55–66; Allen F. Davis, *Spearheads for Reform: The Social Settlements and the Progressive Movement, 1890–1914* (New York: Oxford University Press, 1967), 86–90. The best example of a successful immigrant-oriented settlement program—the Hull-House Labor Museum—is described in Jane Addams, *Twenty Years at Hull-House* (New York: Signet Ed., 1961), 169–85. Monthly Report, September 1919, GII Papers.

32. Monthly Reports, September 1920, March 1921, GII Papers.

33. Monthly Reports, September 1919, March 1921, October 1921, May 1923, February 1924, GII Papers; Annual Report, 1922, GII Papers; "Notes on Early History," GII Papers; *Gary Post-Tribune*, April 9, September 27, 1923.

34. The Monthly Reports of the International Institute nationality workers (GII Papers) are full of references to work among the various ethnic groups of Gary. See also "Notes on Early History," GII Papers.

35. Monthly Reports, September 1919, October 1919, GII Papers.

36. National Board of YWCA, "A Year's Plan for Community Programs," n.d. (mimeographed), GII Papers.

37. "Notes on Early History," GII Papers; Monthly Reports, November 1920, April 1925, September 1931, GII Papers; Annual Report, 1931, GII Papers; *Gary Evening Post*, November 13, 1920.

38. See, for example, YWCA, *Handbook on Racial and Nationality Backgrounds* (New York, 1922); YWCA, *A Brief Reading List on Immigration, Immigrant Backgrounds and Attitudes toward the Foreign-Born* (New York, 1932); YWCA, *National Costumes of the Slavic Peoples* (New York, 1920); Marion Peabody, *Music Suggestions for the Christmas Season* YWCA (New York, 1934); and the following mimeographs in GII Papers: YWCA, "The Value and Technique of Foreign Handicraft Exhibits," 1927; YWCA, "Organization Hints for a Play, Pageant or Festival," 1927; YWCA, "Czechoslo-

vakia—Holidays for 1927," 1927; YWCA, "Some Helpful Books on Folk Dances, Games, and Songs," 1927; YWCA, "Holidays and Festivals of Ancient Mexico and Modern Mexicans," 1928.

39. Monthly Reports, February 1921, October 1921, November 1924, December 1925, GII Papers.

40. Annual Report, 1921, GII Papers; "Report to Department of Immigration and Foreign Communities of the National Board of the YWCA," 1931, GII Papers.

41. Taylor, "At Gary: Some Impressions and Interviews," 65, GII Papers; Monthly Reports, July–September 1920, GII Papers.

42. Monthly Reports, February 1921, April 1923, January 1925, January 1926, February 1929, October 1929, GII Papers; Annual Report, 1929, GII Papers; Maude Cooley to Minnie M. Newman, August 18, 1920, GII Papers; "Study of the Foreign-Born in Gary," 1929, GII Papers; "*Good Daily Health Practices*," n.d. (Poster), GII Papers.

43. Monthly Reports, October 1930, December 1932, GII Papers.

44. Monthly Reports, November 1930, February 1931, May 1931, October 1932, November 1932, April 1933, December 1933, GII Papers. Annual Report, 1931, GII Papers.

45. Carroll, "Alien of Relief," 16–17, 100–101, GII Papers; Carroll, "Alien Workers in America," 23, 82, 84–86, 89, GII Papers; Monthly Reports, October 1931, December 1932, December 1933, February 1934, March 1934, March 1936, June 1936, GII Papers; Radio Scripts, 1936, GII Papers.

46. Walter J. Riley, *The Story of Unemployment Relief in Lake County, Indiana* (1932), 2, 9–11; Monthly Reports, December 1930, May 1931, September 1931, May 1932, September 1932, January 1933, May 1933, GII Papers; *Gary Post-Tribune*, January 14, February 27, March 16, April 20, May 11, 16, 1932.

CHAPTER 5

1. For example, see Mary Parker Follett, *The New State: Group Organization, the Solution of Popular Government* (New York: Longmans, Green, 1918). Follett served as vice-president of the National Community Center Association in 1917.

2. On the development of the recreation movement in public schools, see Clarence Rainwater, *The Play Movement in the United States: A Study of Community Recreation* (Chicago: University of Chicago Press, 1921).

3. On the work of the People's Institute, see Robert Fisher, "The

People's Institute of New York City, 1897–1934: Culture, Progressive Democracy, and the People" (doctoral dissertation, New York University, 1974).

4. Edward Ward, *The Social Center* (New York: Appleton, 1913); Eleanor T. Glueck, *The Community Use of Schools* (Baltimore: Williams and Wilkins, 1927), 20. For a similar analysis, see City of New York, Superintendent of Schools, *Fourteenth Annual Report*, 1911–1912: 9.

5. Fisher, "People's Institute," chapters 9 and 10. Woodrow Wilson speaking in 1911 before a conference on social-center development, noted that, while "the study of the civic center is the study of the spontaneous life of communities," the goal was to solve the problem of modern "disconnected" society, which lacked communication mechanisms between "portions of the community" and democratic problem-solving capacities to eliminate "misunderstanding," "hostilities," and "deadly rivalries." Arthur Link, ed., *The Papers of Woodrow Wilson*, vol. 23, 1911–1912 (Princeton, N.J.: Princeton University Press, 1977), 481–82.

6. See Jack Rothman, "Three Models of Community Organization Practice," in *Strategies of Community Organization: A Book of Readings*, ed. Fred M. Cox et al. (Itasca, Ill.: F. E. Peacock, 1970); Martin Rein and Robert Morris, "Goals, Structures and Strategies for Community Change," in *Social Welfare Forum, 1962: Proceedings of the National Conference on Social Welfare* (New York: Columbia University Press, 1962); Irving Spergel, *Community Problem Solving* (Chicago: University of Chicago Press, 1968).

7. Clinton S. Childs, *A Year's Experiment in Social Center Organization: An Account of the Activities Conducted in Public School 63, Manhattan* (Pamphlet printed by the New York Social Center Committee for the Wider Use of School Properties, 1912). See also Jean Quandt, *From the Small Town to the Great Community: The Social Thought of Progressive Intellectuals* (New Brunswick, N.J.: Rutgers University Press, 1970), 49.

8. For a discussion of the role of legitimation and "informal cooperation" in a community organization, see Phillip Selznick, *TVA and the Grass Roots: A Study in the Sociology of Formal Organizations* (Berkeley: University of California Press, 1949).

9. Clarence A. Perry and Marguerita Williams, *New York School Centers and Their Community Policy* (New York: Russell Sage Foundation, 1931). Childs and Ward were community secretaries in their respective centers. Childs was elected; Ward was appointed by the Board of Education.

10. Jesse Frederick Steiner, *Community Organization: A Study of Its Theory and Current Practice* (New York: D. Appleton-Century Co., 1930), 183.

11. People's Institute of New York City, *Annual Reports*, 1913–1915.

12. Ward, *Social Center*, 199–200; Blake McKelvey, *Rochester: The Quest for Quality, 1890–1925* (Cambridge, Mass.: Harvard University Press, 1956), 102–7. Within three years after the inception of social centers in Rochester, public appropriation for centers had increased to twenty thousand dollars, and centers had been established in eighteen public schools. The cuts in appropriations by the "boss" faction were so severe that, in March 1911, centers were closed in Rochester because of a lack of funds. Steiner, *Community Organization*, 184.

13. Steiner, *Community Organization*, 187. This was especially true after the election in 1913 of the fiscal conservative John P. Mitchell as mayor of New York City.

14. Sherry R. Arnstein, "A Ladder of Citizen Participation," *Journal of the American Institute of Planners* 35 (July 1969): 216–24.

15. For a discussion of varieties of decentralization, see Howard W. Hallman, *Small and Large Together: Governing the Metropolis* (Beverly Hills: Sage Publications, 1977), especially 113–14.

16. Harvey W. Zorbaugh, *The Gold Coast and the Slum* (Chicago: University of Chicago Press, 1948), 202; Allen F. Davis, *Spearheads for Reform: The Social Settlements and the Progressive Movement, 1890–1914* (New York: Oxford University Press, 1967), 81.

17. The "Gramercy district," according to the People's Institute, included School District 10, extending from Ninth Street to Twenty-ninth Street on the east side of Manhattan. Clinton Childs said the area had a population of some eighty-five thousand. PS 40, the Institute's community center in this district, was located in the northern part of the area, on East Twentieth Street.

18. From the first use of the term "community organization" in the early 1910s, community organizers sought the correlation of organizations and activities as one of their major goals. Initially, in the community-center movement, this goal was played down in favor of process objectives. See Monna Heath and Arthur Dunham, *Trends in Community Organization: A Study of Papers on Community Organization Published by the National Conference on Social Welfare, 1874–1960*, University of Chicago Social Service Monographs (Chicago: University of Chicago Press, 1963), especially 33.

19. People's Institute of New York City, *Annual Report*, 1918: 40.

20. Fisher, "People's Institute," 322–23 as well as chaps. 9 and 10. In addition, the Institute conducted a large-scale survey in the Gramercy district into the causes of juvenile delinquency in order to convince the NYC Board of Estimate of the need for play streets and community centers. This

demonstrates, again, the planning and service orientation of the organizers during this period. Surveys were conducted by the Institute before 1913 as a method of supporting planning objectives; thus, even in the period of community development, community recreational planning was a major facet of the Institute's neighborhood work. It was, however, more pronounced after 1915 and especially so in the Gramercy "model" neighborhood.

21. See Robert Fisher, "Community Organizing and Citizen Participation: The Efforts of the People's Institute of New York City, 1910–1920," *Social Service Review* 51 (September 1977), for more information on the founding of the NCCA.

22. John Collier, "The Dynamics of the Community Movement," *The Community Center*, February 1917: 12. *The Community Center* can be found in the New York Public Library.

23. Fisher, "Community Organizing," 480; *Proceedings of the National Community Center Association*, 1917, Leroy Bowman MSS, Columbia University.

24. While most organizers saw the neighborhood as the ideal local unit, they were not "parochial localists." This interpretation runs counter to Quandt, *From Small Town*. Quandt details the limitation of the "neighborhood vision" held by such intellectuals and activists as Mary Parker Follett, Charles Horton Cooley, Jane Addams, and John Dewey.

25. *New York Times*, April 21, 1916, p. 118. For a more complete statement of the goals of conference organizers, see *National Conference on Community Centers and Related Problems: Summary of the Tentative Findings of Special Committees* (Pamphlet printed by the New York Training School for Community Workers), available at the Columbia University School of Social Work.

26. By 1918 there were eighty or so community centers in New York City. People's Institute of New York City, *Annual Report*, 1918: 19; Perry and Williams, *New York School Centers*, 26.

27. It is difficult to determine the number of community centers nationally because the best source of statistics for this period includes all school center activities held in public schools after hours. See Clarence A. Perry, *School Extension Statistics* (Washington, D.C.: Government Printing Office, 1917).

28. Initially, the Institute funded the PS 63 effort. By 1915, the center was paying for half its costs and the other half was picked up by the Board of Education. Mayer N. Zald and Patricia Denton, "From Evangelism to General Service: The Transformation of the YMCA," *Administrative Science Quarterly* 8 (September 1963): 214–34.

29. Jack Rothman, *Planning and Organizing for Social Change: Action Principles from Social Science Research* (New York: Columbia University Press, 1974), 438–39.

30. There is no evidence to suggest that organizers turned to professional planning out of frustration with trying and failing to get resident participation in these working-class neighborhoods. Regarding the nature of the neighborhoods in which the Institute organized community centers, the area around PS 40 on East Twentieth Street had a much higher percentage of natives and middle-class professionals than did the PS 63 neighborhood on East Fourth Street. Both neighborhoods, however, had sizable foreign-born, working-class populations. While many centers in urban areas may have been based in middle-class neighborhoods, the large majority were situated in poorer areas where organized activities and associations were less common or less accessible and where organizers felt they could have a greater impact.

31. Fisher, "Community Organizing," 482.

32. See John Collier, "Community Councils: Democracy Every Day," *The Survey* 40 (August 31, September 21, and September 28, 1918): 604–6, 689–91, 709–11, 725; Heath and Dunham, *Trends in Community Organization*, 31. As Clarence Perry noted, Collier had a tendency to credit centers with abilities not demonstrated in actual practice. Clarence A. Perry to Mr. Glenn, May 8, 1916, Perry MSS, Russell Sage Foundation.

33. Wingate Community Center, *Annual Report*, 1917–1918: 1–2; Fisher, "Community Organizing," 482–83.

34. Heath and Dunham, *Trends in Community Organization*, 31. Also, see Mildred V. Bennett, "Community Council Study for New York City," *Proceedings of the National Community Center Association*, March 1919, Leroy Bowman MSS, Columbia University.

35. The New York City Council of National Defense had a general director based in the Municipal Building, a director for each borough, boroughs divided into zones, and zones divided into local councils. In addition, close public supervision of center activities was exercised. See Bennett, "Community Council"; Fisher, "Community Organizing."

36. Glueck, *Community Use*, 32. The states included Minnesota, New Hampshire, Massachusetts, New York, Delaware, Alabama, West Virginia, Ohio, Michigan, North Dakota, Iowa, Utah, and California.

37. People's Institute, *Annual Report*, 1918: 25; Sidney Dillick, *Community Organization for Neighborhood Development: Past and Present* (New York: William Morrow, 1953), 74.

38. Glueck, *Community Use*, 133; Quandt, *From Small Town*, 141–44; Zorbaugh, *Gold Coast*, 204–6.

39. Jesse Frederick Steiner, "Community Organization: A Study of Its Rise and Tendencies," *Journal of Social Forces* 1 (November 1922): 15.

40. Glueck, *Community Use*, 36–40.

41. Jesse Frederick Steiner, "An Appraisal of the Community Movement," *Journal of Social Forces* 7 (March 1929): 336.

42. Fisher, "Community Organizing," 483–84.

43. Arthur Hillman, *Community Organization and Planning* (New York: Macmillan, 1950), 137; Quandt, *From Small Town*, 152–53.

44. Leroy Bowman, "Population Mobility and Community Organization: Sources and Methods," in *The Urban Community*, ed. Ernest W. Burgess (Chicago: University of Chicago Press, 1926); Zorbaugh, *Gold Coast*, especially 16; Steiner, "Appraisal of the Community Movement," 338–41; Glueck, *Community Use*, especially 2; Jesse Frederick Steiner, "Community Organization and the Crowd Spirit," *Journal of Social Forces* 1 (March 1923): 221–26.

45. Glueck, *Community Use*, 2, 124.

46. "One Difference between the Community Center and the Other Community Organizations," *Journal of Social Forces* 7 (September 1928): 97.

47. Steiner, *Community Organization*, 170.

48. Glueck, *Community Use*, 113–14, 134. For example, in 1919–1920, the center at PS 40 in Manhattan was sponsoring five types of activities on six evenings per week. By 1930, the center had only two types of activities—athletics and club-meetings—and was open only two evenings per week. Clarence A. Perry, *School Center Gazette, 1919–1920* (Pamphlet published by Russell Sage Recreation Department); Perry and Williams, *New York School Centers*, 56. Also, Glueck's survey recorded that in cities of over five thousand people, recreational activities occurred in 72 percent of the centers, civic activities in 15 percent, and educational and cultural activities in approximately 12 percent.

49. Perry and Williams, *New York School Centers*, 44–48; Clarence A. Perry, *Ten Years of the Community Center Movement* (Pamphlet printed by Russell Sage Foundation, 1921), 4–5; Steiner, *Community Organization*, 393–94.

50. Rothman, *Planning and Organizing*, 165; Quandt, *From Small Town*, 146–49; Steiner, *Community Organization*, 199.

51. Glueck, *Community Use*, 82–83, 100–101; Perry and Williams, *New York School Centers*, 44–49.

52. Glueck, *Community Use*, 83; Perry and Williams, *New York School Centers*, 28.

53. "Policy of New York City Board of Education in Reference to Forums," *NCCA Members Bulletin*, February 1926, p. 7, Leroy Bowman MSS, Columbia University.

54. Glueck, *Community Use*, 35–38; Roy Lubove, *The Professional Altruist: The Emergence of Social Work as a Career, 1880–1930* (New York: Atheneum Publishers, 1969); Leroy Bowman, "The 1929 Content of the Community Concept," *Journal of Social Forces* 7 (March 1929): 407–9; Leroy Bowman, "Community Progress: Developments in Community Organization," *Journal of Social Forces* 5 (September 1926): 91–94; Zorbaugh, *Gold Coast*, 211–18.

55. *The Community Center*, January–February 1921: 6; Leroy Bowman, "Community Organization," *American Journal of Sociology* 35 (May 1930): 1008.

56. Glueck, *Community Use*, 84; Steiner, *Community Organization*, 384; John Daniels, *America via the Neighborhood* (New York: Harper and Brothers, 1920).

57. Leroy Bowman, "Community Centers," *Social Work Yearbook*, 1933, ed. Fred Hall (New York: Russell Sage Foundation, 1933), 91–93; Jesse Frederick Steiner, "Community Centers," in *Encyclopedia of the Social Sciences*, vol. 4, ed. Edwin R. A. Seligman (New York: Macmillan, 1931), 105–6.

58. Lubove, *Professional Altruist*, 220–21; Glueck, *Community Use*, 145–46. Other sources point to efforts of local officials, businessmen, and religious leaders to dilute or abolish political orientation of centers. Zorbaugh, *Gold Coast*, 215–20; Steiner, *Community Organization*, 67–72, 345.

CHAPTER 6

1. Russell Lord, *The Agrarian Revival*, American Association for Adult Education (New York: George Grady Press, 1939), 123.

2. Ibid., 140.

3. J. H. Kolb and Edmund de S. Brunner, *Recent Social Trends in the United States* (New York: McGraw-Hill, Inc., 1934), 507.

4. Lord, *Agrarian Revival*, 140.

5. Jesse Frederick Steiner, *Community Organization: A Study of Its Theory and Current Practice* (New York: D. Appleton-Century Co., 1930), 309–10.

6. R. K. Bliss, ed., *The Spirit and Philosophy of Extension Work* (Washington, D.C.: Graduate School, U.S. Department of Agriculture; Epsilon Sigma Phi, National Honorary Extension Fraternity, 1952), 255.

7. C. E. Lively, "Changes and Trends in Rural Neighborhood Life," *Proceedings of the National Conference of Social Work* (hereafter cited as *Proceedings*), vol. 58, ed. Howard R. Knight (Chicago: University of Chicago Press, 1931), 296–98.

8. Kolb and Brunner, *Recent Social Trends*, 505.

9. Lord, *Agrarian Revival*, 111–15.

10. Ibid., 117.

11. Ibid., 119.

12. Ibid., 122.

13. Edmund de S. Brunner and E. Hsin Pao Yang, *Rural America and the Extension Service* (New York: Bureau of Publications, Teachers' College, Columbia University, 1949), 31.

14. Brunner and Yang, *Rural America*, 79.

15. Edmund de S. Brunner, Irwin T. Sanders, and Douglas Ensminger, *Farmers of the World* (New York: Columbia University Press, 1945), 191–92.

16. Kolb and Brunner, *Recent Social Trends*, 507.

17. Walter A. Terpenning, "Requisites to Rural Social Organization," *American Journal of Sociology* 33, no. 5 (March 1928): 737.

18. Kolb and Brunner, *Recent Social Trends*, 507.

19. Ibid., 509.

20. Ibid., 510.

21. Edmund de S. Brunner and J. H. Kolb, *Rural Social Trends* (New York: McGraw-Hill, Inc., 1933), 175.

22. Kolb and Brunner, *Recent Social Trends*, 535.

23. Terpenning, "Rural Social Organization," 741–53.

24. Steiner, *Community Organization*, 309–10.

25. Ibid.

26. Ibid., p. 53.

27. Ibid., 55–56.

28. R. K. Bliss, ed., *The Spirit and Philosophy of Extension Work*, 230–31.

29. Ibid., 231.

30. Lord, *Agrarian Revival*, 107.

31. Ibid., 107.

32. Brunner and Yang, *Rural America*, 116.

33. Brunner, Sanders, and Ensminger, *Farmers of the World*, 191–92.

34. William C. Smith, "The Rural Mind: A Study in Occupation Attitude," *American Journal of Sociology* 32, no. 5 (March 1927): 771–75.

35. Ibid., 781–82.

36. Gisela Konopka, *Eduard C. Lindeman and Social Work Philosophy* (Minneapolis: University of Minnesota Press, 1958), 102.

37. Ibid., 120.

38. Brunner and Yang, *Rural America*, 78.

39. Dwight Sanderson, *Research Memorandum on Rural Life in the Depression*, Social Science Research Council, N.Y., Bulletin 34 (1937), 115.

40. Brunner and Kolb, *Rural Social Trends*, 273–74.

41. Ibid., 274.

42. Alexander Macleran, "Some Specific Accomplishments in Social Welfare in Rural Communities," *Proceedings*, vol. 51, ed. William H. Parker (Chicago: University of Chicago Press, 1924), 432–37.

43. Elizabeth A. Cooley, "West Palm Beach County, Florida: A Unit for Social Work," *Proceedings*, vol. 53, ed. Howard R. Knight (Chicago: University of Chicago Press, 1926), 268.

44. Ibid., 470.

45. E. L. Morgan, "The Challenge of the Rural Community—Social and Economic," *Proceedings*, vol. 54, ed. Howard R. Knight (Chicago: University of Chicago Press, 1927), 329.

46. R. D. McKenzie, review of *Organization of Public Health Nursing*, *American Journal of Sociology* 26 (July 1920–May 1921): 660.

47. Brunner and Yang, *Rural America*, 93–115.

48. Lincoln David Kelsey and Cannon Chiles Hearne, *Cooperative Extension Work* (Ithaca, N.Y.: Comstock Publishing Associates, 1963), 190.

49. George E. Haynes, "The Church and the Negro Spirit," *Survey Graphic*, 1925.

50. Brunner and Yang, *Rural America*, 93–115.

CHAPTER 7

1. Robert E. L. Faris, *Chicago Sociology, 1920–1932* (Chicago: University of Chicago Press, 1967).

2. Gertrude Springer, "Block Aid," *The Survey* 68 (May 1932): 182–83.

3. Perle Graham, "The Cleveland Study of Community Centers from the Standpoint of the Schools and Private Effort," *Proceedings of the National Conference of Social Work*, ed. Howard R. Knight (Chicago: University of Chicago Press, 1931).

4. Clifford R. Shaw et al., *Delinquency Areas* (Chicago: University of Chicago Press, 1929); Clifford R. Shaw, *The Natural History of a Delinquent Career* (Chicago: University of Chicago Press, 1931); and Frederic M. Thrasher, *The Gang* (Chicago: University of Chicago Press, 1936).

5. Ernest W. Burgess, Joseph D. Lohrman, and Clifford R. Shaw, "The

Chicago Area Project," *Yearbook of the National Probation Association*, 1937 (New York: National Probation Association, 1937).

6. Richard Cleveland and Lloyd Ohlin, *Delinquency and Opportunity* (Glencoe: Free Press, 1961).

7. Solomon Kobrin, "The Chicago Area Project—A 25-year Assessment," *The Annals of the American Academy of Social and Political Science*, 1959: 25.

8. Steiner, *Community Organization*, 37.

9. Allen F. Davis, *Spearheads for Reform: The Social Settlements and the Progresive Movement, 1890–1914* (New York: Oxford University Press, 1967), 65.

10. Robert Perlman, "Social Welfare Planning and Physical Planning: A Case Study of Their Relationship in Urban Renewal" (doctoral dissertation, Brandeis University, 1961), 47.

11. Herbert J. Gans, "Social and Physical Planning for the Elimination of Urban Poverty," in *Readings in Community Organization Practice*, ed. Ralph M. Kramer and Harry Specht (Englewood Cliffs, N.J.: Prentice-Hall Inc., 1969), 425. Howard's Garden City called for a new pattern of city growth. He proposed that "a city [be] limited from the beginning in numbers and in density of habitation, limited in area, organized to carry on all the essential functions of an urban community [including] business, industry, administration, education; equipped too with a sufficient number of public parks and private gardens." Lewis Mumford, *The City in History: Its Origins, Its Transformations, and Its Prospects* (New York: Harcourt, Brace and World, Inc., 1961), 515.

12. Mumford, *The City in History*, 515.

13. See Christopher Tunnard and Henry Hope Reed, *American Skyline* (Boston: Houghton Mifflin Company, 1956), 136–53.

14. William I. Goodman and Eric C. Freund, *Principles and Practice of Urban Planning* (Washington, D.C.: International City Managers Association, 1968), 20.

15. Ibid., 22.

16. Arthur B. Gallion, *The Urban Pattern: City Planning and Design* (New York: D. Van Nostrand Co., Inc., 1968), 119.

17. Goodman and Freund, *Urban Planning*, 22.

18. Gallion, *The Urban Pattern*, 119.

19. Goodman and Freund, *Urban Planning*, 23–24.

20. Harvey S. Perloff, ed., *Planning and the Urban Community* (Pittsburgh: University of Pittsburgh Press, 1961), 84.

21. Ibid.

22. Goodman and Freund, *Urban Planning*, 28.

23. Roy Lubove, *Community Planning in the 1920s* (Pittsburgh: University of Pittsburgh Press, 1963), 1.

24. Ibid., 31.

25. Ibid., 89.

26. Ibid., 71.

27. Ibid., 61.

28. Goodman and Freund, *Urban Planning*, 25.

29. Lubove, *Community Planning*, 107.

30. Perloff, *Planning*, 153.

31. Goodman and Freund, *Urban Planning*, 26. See also U.S. National Resources Committee, Urbanism Committee, *Our Cities: Their Role in the National Economy* (Washington, D.C.: U.S. Government Printing Office, 1937), 63–64.

32. U.S. National Resources Committee, *Our Cities*, 25.

33. Gallion, *The Urban Pattern*, 26.

34. Goodman and Freund, *Urban Planning*, 26.

35. Gallion, *The Urban Pattern*, 147.

36. Ibid., 141.

37. Ibid., 147.

38. For a thorough discussion of the efforts to unite physical and social planning, see Harvey S. Perloff, "Common Goals and the Linking of Physical and Social Planning," in *Urban Planning and Social Policy*, ed. Bernard Frieden and Robert Morris (New York: Basic Books, Inc., 1968), 346–59.

39. Mel Scott, *American City Planning since 1890* (Berkeley: University of California Press, 1969), 333.

40. F. Stuart Chapin, *Urban Land Use Planning* (Urbana: University of Illinois Press, 1965).

41. Ibid., 107.

42. Ibid., 150.

43. Ibid., 181.

44. Ibid., 224.

45. Ibid., 254.

46. Harvey S. Perloff, *Education for Planning: City, State, and Regional* (Baltimore: Johns Hopkins Press, 1957), 12.

47. The authors are indebted to the work of Sidney E. Zimbalist, especially his chapter on "The Rise and Fall of the Social Survey Movement" in "Major Trends in Social Work Research, 1900–1950," (doctoral dissertation, Washington University, 1955).

48. Ibid., 168.

49. Clarke A. Chambers, *Paul U. Kellogg and the Survey* (Minneapolis: University of Minnesota Press, 1971).

50. A. L. Mandel, "How Much Use Can or Should Be Made of the Survey Method?" in *Proceedings of the National Conference of Social Work*, vol. 51, ed. William H. Parker (Chicago: University of Chicago Press, 1924).

51. Paul U. Kellogg, "The Story of the Survey," *The Survey* 43 (March 1920): 792.

52. B. A. McClenahan, *Organizing the Community* (New York: Century Co., 1922), 42.

53. Ibid., 45–46.

54. Rowland Haynes, "The Statistical Side of Social Work," in *Proceedings of National Conference of Social Work*, vol. 54, ed. Howard R. Knight (Chicago: University of Chicago Press, 1927).

55. Ruth Hill, "Some Community Values in a Social Survey," in *Proceedings of National Conference of Social Work*, vol. 55, ed. Howard R. Knight (Chicago: University of Chicago Press, 1930), 428.

56. "Make No Little Plans," *The Survey* 64 (1929): 196.

57. F. F. Stephan, "Basic Research in Planning Social Work Programs," *Proceedings of National Conference of Social Work* (1934), vol. 61, ed. Howard R. Knight; and Madeline Berry and Bradley Buell, "Statistical Base for Community Planning," in *Proceedings of National Conference of Social Work* (1935), vol. 62, ed. Howard R. Knight.

58. Robert Perlman, "Social Welfare Planning and Physical Planning," *American Institute of Planners Journal*, July, 1966.

CHAPTER 8

1. For an introduction to the abundant literature engaged in commenting critically upon the role of the Jewish federations in America, see Eli Ginsberg, "The Agenda Reconsidered," *Journal of Jewish Communal Service* (hereafter cited as *JJCS*), Fall 1966, pp. 275–82; Jacob Neusner, "Jewish Education and Culture and the Jewish Welfare Fund," *The Synagogue School*, Winter 1967, pp. 9–40; Judah Shapiro, "The Philistine Philanthropists: The Power and Shame of Jewish Federations," *Jewish Liberation Journal*, October 1969, pp. 1–4; Martin Greenberg, "Planning for the Jewish Community—The Process of Establishing Priorities and Goals," *JJCS*, Winter 1971, pp. 151–58; Charles Zibbell, "Federations, Synagogues, and Jewish Educa-

tion in the 70s," *Jewish Education*, Fall 1974, pp. 40–45; David Polish, "Rabbis and the Federations," *Jewish Spectator*, Fall 1975, pp. 220–22; Gerald Bubis, "Brokha Brokers and Power Brokers," *Jewish Spectator*, Spring 1975, pp. 58–61; Samuel Dresner, "The Dais and the Pulpit: The Tension between Federation and Synagogue," *Moment*, December 1975, pp. 24–28.

2. *American Jewish Year Book* 5668 (1907–1908): 359 (hereafter cited as *AJYB*); Associated Charities of Columbus, Ohio, *Sixth Annual Report. November 1904–November 1905*, 21; *Ninth Annual Report*, 27; *Fifteenth Annual Report, May 1, 1914–May 1, 1915*, in *The Social Servant*, December 1915, pp. 6–12; *Sixteenth Annual Report, May 1, 1915–May 1, 1916*, in *The Social Servant*, December 1916, pp. 25–32.

3. Barbara M. Solomon, *Pioneers in Service* (Boston: Associated Jewish Philanthropies of Boston, 1956), 1–69; Jacob Neusner, "The Impact of Immigration and Philanthropy upon the Boston Jewish Community (1880–1914)," *American Jewish Historical Quarterly* 46, no. 2, pp. 71–85; Boris D. Bogen, *Jewish Philanthropy* (New York: Macmillan, 1917); Joseph Jacobs, "The Federation Movement in American Jewish Philanthropy," *AJYB* 5676 (1915–1916): 159–98.

4. Associated Charities of Columbus, Ohio. *Report of the Committee on Charities and Corrections of the Chamber of Commerce* (Columbus, 1910), 37–38; *Third Annual Report, November 1, 1901–November 1, 1902*, 22. The Sheltering House, relatively unused during the 1920s, became a busy way-station once again during the depression. An eight-room house was dedicated in 1931 at 485½ Livingston, and replaced by a new home at 525 Livingston in 1934. See *Ohio Jewish Chronicle* (hereafter cited as *OJC*), May 1, June 5, July 10 and 24, 1931, August 17, 1934, and November 1, 1935; *Council of Social Agencies of Columbus and Franklin County, Handbook of Social Resources of Columbus and Franklin County* (1936), 38.

5. Dora Abrams, interview by Lynda E. Kalette, May 16, 1974, Ohio Historical Society, Columbus, Ohio.

6. *Ohio State Journal* (hereafter cited as *OSJ*), November 20 and 21, 1902.

7. *Eighth Annual Report of the Federated Jewish Charities and Affiliated Societies of Columbus, Ohio, November 1, 1916*.

8. *Ninth Annual Report, 1917*.

9. *OSJ*, November 2, 1910.

10. *OJC*, December 17, 1926, September 15, 1922, April 15, 1927, December 20, 1929, October 17 and April 25, 1924, August 11, 1922, December 17, 1929; *Columbus Dispatch*, December 16 and December 19, 1929; *Columbus Citizen*, December 16, 1929; *American Israelite*, June 10, 1909. For a description of suits filed against the executors of the will for more than a quarter of

a million dollars, see Columbus daily newspapers on July 24 and November 19, 1931, June 8, 1932, and February 10, 1933.

11. *Associated Charities of Columbus, Ohio. Fifteenth Annual Report*, in *The Social Servant*, December 1915, pp. 6–12; *Associated Charities. Sixteenth Annual Report*, in *The Social Servant*, December 1916, pp. 25–32; *Eighth Annual Report of the Federated Jewish Charities and Affiliated Societies of Columbus, Ohio, November 1, 1916*; *Ninth Annual Report, 1917*; *Eleventh Annual Report, 1919*; *Chamber of Commerce. Handbook of Social Resources* (Columbus, 1922), 73. The HFLA was incorporated in February 1912: *Annual Statistical Report of the Secretary of State to the Governor, November 15, 1912* (Springfield, Ohio, 1913), 38.

12. *Annual Statistical Report of the Secretary of State to the Governor, November 15, 1912* (Springield, Ohio, 1913), 38.

13. Joseph Hyman's close relationship with Schonthal continued for some years. In 1920–1921 he worked in Poland for the Joint Distribution Committee, and from 1921 to 1924 he was Director of Reconstruction, Medical Work, Child Care, and Care of Refugees for the JDC in the Baltic States. In the latter capacity he organized the Schonthal Children's Summer Home in Riga during 1923; see *OJC*, April 13, 1923, and January 18, 1924. For a more complete biography, see *OJC*, August 17, 1928, and *Who's Who in American Jewry*, 1928.

14. Founded in 1868, the Cleveland Orphan Asylum housed three Columbus Jewish children among the initial group of "inmates"; between 1868 and 1927, thirty-one out of four thousand children admitted were from Columbus. See *First Annual Report of the Board of Trustees of the Orphan Asylum, District No. 2, I.O.B.B. at Cleveland, Ohio, For Year Ending October 1, 1869* (Cincinnati, 1869), 13, and *OSJ*, July 10, 1927.

15. *OJC*, March 3, 1922, October 12 and August 17, 1923, January 25, 1931.

16. Various dates are given for its inception; it celebrated its thirtieth anniversary in 1930 and its thirty-fifth anniversary in 1932, while as early as 1907 its beginnings were listed as 1899; see *OJC*, January 10, 1930, December 2, 1932; *AJYB* 5668 (1907–1908): 359.

17. *OJC*, May 27, 1932, April 21, 1933, April 12 and December 6, 1935, April 24, 1936, May 6, 1938, April 21, 1939; Sylvia Schecter, interview by Marc Lee Raphael, September 22, 1974.

18. *OJC*, February 9, 1923.

19. *OJC*, March 24, 1923, April 14 and April 7, 1922. Valuable experience in fund raising was also gained during World War I, when leading Columbus Jews participated in the United War Work Campaign and the Liberty Loan Drive. One ad, in the local Jewish newspaper, accused Jews who had not

purchased Liberty Bonds of being "a discredit to your country . . . a blot on the fair name of Judaism . . . and an aid to the Kaiser!" See *Columbus Jewish Chronicle*, April 26, September 27, November 1, November 22, 1918.

20. *OJC*, March 31 and April 7, 1922.

21. "Articles II and IV," Constitution of the United Jewish Fund, June 24, 1926, Ohio Historical Society. The first treasurer of the UJF, Simon Lazarus (1882–1947), was to serve in that capacity through 1944 and then as president from 1945 to 1947.

22. Board of Directors meeting, June 29, 1926, and September 21, 1926; Finance and Budget Committee, October 22, 1926, Ohio Historical Society.

23. Regular meeting, Board of Directors of the United Jewish Fund, March 27, 1927, Ohio Historical Society. Everywhere federations emerged there was a self-denying ordinance on the part of the constituent bodies whereby the latter declared that they would not collect money themselves; see Jacobs, "Federation Movement."

24. Grouping analysis, September 29, 1926; Edwin J. Schanfarber to Board of Directors, December 20, 1929, Ohio Historical Society.

25. *OJC*, April 16, April 23, and April 2, 1926.

26. Edwin J. Schanfarber to Board of Directors, March 28, 1929; Special meeting of the Board of Directors of the United Jewish Fund, December 20, 1929, Ohio Historical Society.

27. *OJC*, November 20, 1931.

28. *Annual Report*, 1932, Jewish Welfare Federation, Ohio Historical Society.

29. *Jewish Social Work*, 1930, Statistical Report of Volume and Trends in Four Functional Fields and Comparisons with Previous Years (New York: Bureau of Jewish Social Research, July 1931); *Jewish Social Work*, 1932, Statistics of Service: Relief and Family Welfare, Child Care, Care of Aged, Hospitals and Out-Patient Service; *Jewish Social Work*, 1933. Council of Jewish Federations and Welfare Funds Papers, American Jewish Historical Society (Waltham, Massachusetts) (hereafter cited as CJFWF Papers).

30. *Yearbook of Jewish Social Work*, 1935, CJFWF Papers, American Jewish Historical Society (Waltham, Massachusetts).

31. The nine men were Allen Gundersheimer, Alfred J. Kobacker, Simon Lazarus, Sol M. Levy, Morris Resler, E. J. Schanfarber, Robert W. Schiff, J. W. Steinhauser, and Samuel N. Summer. That there was a direct relationship between "Big Gifts" and inclusion on the Board of Directors was affirmed by E. J. Schanfarber and is confirmed by the records. All nine made "Big Gifts" (the top fifteen or twenty contributions in the community), while every member of Bryden Road Temple serving on the Board of

Directors in 1943 (nineteen out of twenty-five) made a "Big Gift" (one thousand dollars or more).

32. General subscribers' meeting, United Jewish Fund, Report of the President, April 2, 1940, Ohio Historical Society; *OJC*, October 28 and December 16, 1938.

33. General subscribers' meeting, United Jewish Fund, Report of the President, April 2, 1940, Ohio Historical Society. The Junior Division, first organized in 1936 under the direction of Jane Schanfarber and Regina Kobacker, was reorganized periodically; see *OJC*, July 10, 1936, June 16 and 30, 1939. Ida Kobacker (1891–1972) headed the Women's Division launched in 1940; see *OJC*, May 24, 1940.

34. General subscribers' meeting, United Jewish Fund, April 2, 1940, Ohio Historical Society.

35. 1940 United Jewish Fund of Columbus budget, March 15, 1941, Ohio Historical Society.

CHAPTER 9

1. The single best, brief review of the issues involving the bosses in America is found in Raymond A. Mohl, *The New City: Urban America in the Industrial Age, 1860–1920*, (Arlington Heights, Ill.: H. Davidson, 1985), 83–107.

2. For the various points of view among historians concerning the role of machine politics, see Scott Greer, ed., *Ethnics, Machines, and the American Urban Future* (Cambridge, Mass.: Harvard University Press, 1981).

3. Mike Royko, *Boss Richard J. Daley of Chicago* (New York: E. P. Dutton & Co., 1971), 115.

4. William J. Riordon, *Plunkitt of Tammany Hall* (New York: E. P. Dutton & Co., 1963), 92–93.

5. Riordon, *Plunkitt*, 10.

6. Edward J. Flynn, *You're the Boss: The Practice of American Politics* (New York: Collier Books, 1962), 235–51.

7. Riordon, *Plunkitt*, 17.

8. For the most influential study of the "latest functions" of the political machine, see Robert K. Merton, *Social Theory and Social Structure*, 2d ed. (New York: Basic Books, 1957).

9. Riordon, *Plunkitt*, xix.

10. Royko, *Daley*, 180.

11. Riordon, *Plunkitt*, 50.

CHAPTER 10

1. Saul D. Alinsky, *Rules for Radicals: A Practical Primer for Realistic Radicals* (New York: Random House, Inc., 1971), 66–67.

2. "Saul D. Alinsky, A Candid Conversation with the Feisty Radical Organizer," *Playboy*, March 1972, 72; Saul D. Alinsky, *John L. Lewis: An Unauthorized Biography* (New York: Random House Inc., 1970), xiv.

3. Alinsky, *John L. Lewis*, ix, 104.

4. Herbert Harris, "How the CIO Works," *Current History and Forum* 46 (1937): 63; Saul D. Alinsky, *Reveille for Radicals* (Chicago: University of Chicago Press, 1946), 177.

5. Alinsky, *Rules*, 76.

6. Alinsky, *Reveille*, 154–55.

7. Ibid., xix, 136.

8. Carey E. Haigler to Neil Betten, July 29, 1971, in possession of the authors.

9. Alinsky, *Rules*, 8.

10. Brandan Sexton to Neil Betten, June 15, 1971, in possession of the authors.

11. Irwin L. DeShelter to Neil Betten, September 5, 1971; Nicholas A. Zonarich to Neil Betten, June 9, 1971; Sexton to Betten, June 15, 1971; Harris, "How the CIO Works," 65.

12. Sexton to Betten, June 15, 1971.

13. *Playboy*, 74.

14. Alinsky, *Rules*, p. xxiii.

15. Robert Bailey, Jr., *Radicals in Urban Politics: The Alinsky Approach* (Chicago: University of Chicago Press, 1974).

16. DeShelter to Betten, September 5, 1971; Oliver W. Singleton to Neil Betten, August 20, 1971.

17. Bailey, *Radicals in Urban Politics*, 136.

18. Ibid., 58.

CHAPTER 11

1. Peter Maurin, *The Green Revolution: Easy Essays on Catholic Radicalism* (Fresno, Calif.: Academy Guild Press, 2d ed., 1961), 57, 102. This work is a compilation of Maurin's essays over the years and goes back prior to the establishment of the Catholic Worker Movement.

2. Ibid., 98; Dorothy Day, *The Long Loneliness: The Autobiography of Dorothy Day* (New York: Harper and Brothers, 1952), 184, 202, 280; Ade De Bethune, *Work* (Newport: B. J. Stevens, 1939), 4, 7, 30.

3. Maurin, *Green Revolution*, 7, 60, 62, 70; Day, *The Long Loneliness*, 222; Dorothy Day, *House of Hospitality* (New York: Sheed & Ward, 1932), 71.

4. Quoted in Arthur Sheehan, *Peter Maurin: Gay Believer* (Garden City, N.Y: Hanover House, 1959), 186.

5. Day, *The Long Loneliness*, 228; *Catholic Worker*, June 1939, p. 3.

6. Sheehan, *Peter Maurin*, 174.

7. Ibid., 187.

8. Ibid., 186.

9. Day, *The Long Loneliness*, 228.

10. Dorothy Day, *Loaves and Fishes* (New York: Harper & Row, 1963), 43; Sheehan, *Peter Maurin*, 131.

11. *Catholic Worker*, May 1939, p. 2; Sheehan, *Peter Maurin*, 133.

12. *Catholic Worker*, February 1936, p. 2; Day, *The Long Loneliness*, 234.

13. *Catholic Worker*, February 1936, p. 8.

14. Day, *Loaves and Fishes*, 53–57.

15. Maurin, *Green Revolution*, 93.

16. William Gauchat, interview, December 13, 1968.

17. Joseph Zarella, interview, December 13, 1968.

18. Ibid.

19. Nina Poleyn, interview, December 13, 1968.

20. Joseph Zarella, interview, December 13, 1968.

21. John Gillard Bruni, "Catholic Paper versus Communism," *Commonweal*, November 24, 1933, p. 97.

22. "For Christ the Worker," *Time*, April 18, 1938, p. 46. Following the depression, circulation decreased considerably: see "Dorothy Day's Diary," *Newsweek*, January 21, 1952, p. 85; "Fools for Christ," *Time*, May 24, 1948, p. 56.

23. *Catholic Worker*, July–August 1933, p. 2.

24. Sheehan, *Peter Maurin*, 111.

25. Maurin would then put down the heckler with a cogent argument that was meant to appear spontaneous.

26. William Gauchat, interview, December 13, 1968.

27. Joseph Zarella, interview, December 13, 1968. Letter from Rev. Charles Owen Rice and John Ryan, February 10, 1938, Catholic University Archives, Ryan Correspondence, 1938 E–R.

28. Bruni, "Catholic Paper versus Communism," 97.

29. John Sheery, "The Catholic Worker School," *Commonweal*, August 3, 1934, p. 349; *Catholic Worker*, February 1, 1934, pp. 1, 4; *Catholic Worker*, March 1, 1934, p. 1; Joseph Brieg, "Apostle on the Bum," *Commonweal*, April 1938, p. 12.

30. Eleanor Carroll, "The Catholic Worker" (Master's thesis, Catholic University, 1935), 20.

31. Carroll, "Catholic Worker," 92, 93, 125.

32. David O'Brien, "American Catholic Thought in the 1930s" (doctoral dissertation, Rochester University, 1965), 99.

33. Maurin, *Green Revolution*, 1, 11.

34. Nina Poleyn, interview, December 13, 1968.

35. William Gauchat, interview, December 13, 1968.

36. *Catholic Worker*, April 1938, p. 2.

37. Sheehan, *Peter Maurin*, 144.

38. *Catholic Worker*, June 1935, p. 1.

39. Sheehan, *Peter Maurin*, 145.

40. *Catholic Worker*, February 1, 1934, p. 1.

41. Dorothy Day, "Tale of Two Capitals," *Commonweal*, July 14, 1939, pp. 280–83.

42. Day, *House of Hospitality*, 271.

43. *Catholic Worker*, May 1938, p. 1.

44. Father Charles Owen Rice, *Catholic Worker*, February 1938, p. 6.

45. Ibid.

46. *Catholic Worker*, April 1938, p. 6.

47. Ibid., May 1931, p. 7.

48. Ibid., September 1938, p. 7; March 1939, p. 4; June 1939, p. 3. To the list of houses established in June, the New York house added two more founded after the list was compiled.

49. Day, *The Long Loneliness*, 249.

50. Day, *House of Hospitality*, 236.

51. *Catholic Worker*, May 1939, p. 1.

52. Ibid., December 15, 1933, p. 1.

53. Ibid., May 1939, p. 1.

54. Ibid., December 15, 1933, p. 5.

55. Ibid., May 1939, p. 1.

56. Ibid., May 1939, p. 1.

57. "House of Hospitality," *Commonweal*, April 15, 1939, p. 683; "For Christ the Worker," *Time*, April 18, 1936, p. 46; Marieli G. Benzinger, "Caitas Christ," *Catholic World*, February 1938, p. 6.

58. Day, *The Long Loneliness*, 181.

59. Day, *House of Hospitality*, 148.

60. Ibid., 142.

61. *Catholic Worker*, July–August 1933, p. 1.

62. Ibid., 5.

63. Editorial, *Catholic Worker*, February 1936, p. 4. For differences between Day, who supported the New Deal, and Maurin, who did not, see Day, *The Long Loneliness*, 174; *House of Hospitality*, 71; Maurin, *Green Revolution*, 57, 70. The *Catholic Worker* followed her point of view; see *Catholic Worker*, September 1933, p. 6; October 1933, p. 3; November 1933, p. 2; February 1934, p. 71.

64. Day, *The Long Loneliness*, 206.

65. *Catholic Worker*, March 1935, p. 1.

66. Ibid., February 1935, p. 1.

67. Day, *The Long Loneliness*, 206.

68. Ibid., 208.

69. Ibid., 208–9.

70. *Catholic Worker*, June 1937, pp. 1, 7.

71. Day, *House of Hospitality*, 180–81.

72. Ibid., 188.

73. *Catholic Worker*, May 1937, p. 7; June 1937, p. 1.

74. Day, *House of Hospitality*, 263.

75. *Catholic Worker*, February 1935, p. 3.

76. Ibid., July 1937, p. 6; June 1936, p. 1; April 1935, p. 1; May 1935, p. 1; March 1935, p. 1; Day, *The Long Loneliness*, 207–8; *Catholic Worker*, April 1938, p. 1.

77. *Catholic Worker*, June 1936, p. 1; March 1935, p. 1; April 1935, p. 1; May 1935, p. 1; April 1936, p. 1; February 1936, p. 1; Day, *The Long Loneliness*, 207–9.

78. *Catholic Worker*, April 1936, p. 1; Day, *The Long Loneliness*, 208.

79. "For Christ the Worker," 47.

80. Day, *The Long Loneliness*, 183, 203; *Catholic Worker*, November 1933, p. 3.

81. *Catholic Worker*, September 1933, p. 4.

82. Ibid., 127–28.

83. *Labor Leader*, March 28, 1947, p. 1.

84. "Peter Maurin," *Commonweal*, August 27, 1949, p. 165.

85. Day, *House of Hospitality*, xxxi; *Catholic Worker*, October 1938, p. 4.

86. Day, *The Long Loneliness*, 226; Sheehan, *Peter Maurin*, 149.

87. Day, *The Long Loneliness*, 226; Sheehan, *Peter Maurin*, 149.

88. John Reumann, *Words and Witness II* (Philadelphia: Lutheran Church of America, 1980), 103.

89. William D. Miller, *A Harsh and Dreadful Love* (New York: Liveright, 1973), 181.

90. Reumann, *Words and Witness II*, 163.

91. Ibid., 161.

92. Miller, *Harsh and Dreadful Love*, 114, 185.

93. Ibid., 6.

94. Ibid., 221.

CHAPTER 12

Note: This chapter's summary of the Lane Report is taken from *The Proceedings of the National Conference of Social Work: Selected Papers from Sixty-sixth Annual Conference, Buffalo, New York, June 18–24, 1939*, vol. 66, ed. Howard R. Knight (New York: Columbia University Press, 1939), 495–511.

Index